ROBERT E. WALLACE

A
PRISM
of
SONG

*Seeing the Old Testament
through the Psalms*

Also by Robert E. Wallace

Preaching During Covid-tide
Sermons of Hope to Empty Pews

The Narrative Effect of Book IV of the Hebrew Psalter
Studies in Biblical Literature 112

Advance Praise for
A Prism of Song: Seeing the Old Testament through the Psalms

"*A Prism of Song: Seeing the Old Testament through the Psalms* thoughtfully ties various psalms to the many and varied narratives and writings in the Old Testament. It thereby expands the readers' understandings of and appreciation for both the book of Psalms and other texts in the Old Testament. This work will undoubtedly provide teachers and students with an innovative and refreshing path to the study of the Old Testament."

—*Nancy L. deClaissé-Walford*
Emerita Professor of Old Testament and Biblical Languages
Mercer University School of Theology

"Superbly written, masterfully arranged, brilliantly insightful! Bravo! Wallace's work is itself a Psalm of glory to God. Would I recommend this work as an introduction to Old Testament study? Yes! A thousand times, YES!"

J. Randall O'Brien
Former Professor of Religion and Provost, Baylor University
President Emeritus, Carson-Newman University

"Wallace has developed an approach to understanding the Old Testament through the lens of the book of Psalms. Israel's hymnbook is viewed as a collection of reflections about God at work in the communal life of His people through multiple generations. This is a creative, energetic, enjoyable deep dive that will be of benefit to those who want to grow in their engagement with the Old Testament."

—*Timothy, G. Crawford, PhD*
Dean of the College of Christian Studies
University of Mary Hardin-Baylor

"Weaving biblical poetry with biblical prose and ancient context with contemporary illustrations, Wallace guides students of the Old Testament to see the grand story of the Old Testament. By contextualizing their learning in the book of Psalms, Israel's book of praise and prayer, Wallace provides readers with a way to make meaning of the complexity and vastness of Israel's larger story of faith."

—*Reverend Dr. Christine Jones*
Associate Pastor, King's Cross Church

"Anyone who has taught, preached, or read the Old Testament has necessarily struggled with the vastness of the material: it's a big, diverse book. In *A Prism of Song*, Robert Wallace shows how the Psalms can serve as a guide through this complexity—not in ways that reduce the complexity but rather in ways that illuminate its beauty and theological power. Wallace's survey is an accessible, engaging introduction that will help new generations see the Old Testament more clearly in all its multifaceted splendor."

—*Rebecca Poe Hays*
Assistant Professor of Christian Scriptures
George W. Truett Theological Seminary
Baylor University

"Excelling as both a biblical scholar and pastoral theologian, Wallace provides the reader with a faceted lens through which to understand the diverse writings of the Old Testament. The beautiful poetic and musical compositions of the Psalter become a catalyst through which to achieve a renewed vision of the historical expanse of God's activity among God's people. Wallace provides a remarkable guide that allows the theological shorthand of the Psalms to come into full view as he links particular psalms or collections of psalms to primary faith claims. Humor and contemporary cultural references help the reader grasp the original meaning of the biblical text. Under Wallace's careful translation and interpretation, the book of Psalms becomes a cipher through which the reader can comprehend the complexity of the Old Testament witness, grow in faith comprehension, and celebrate the wonder that is God."

—*Mark A. Torgerson, PhD*
Professor of Theological Studies
Judson University

A PRISM OF SONG

Smyth & Helwys Publishing
6316 Peake Road
Macon, Georgia 31210-3960
1-800-747-3016
©2025 by Robert E. Wallace
All rights reserved.

Library of Congress Cataloging-in-Publication Data

Names: Wallace, Robert E., 1970- author.
Title: A prism of song : seeing the Old Testament through the Psalms / by Robert E. Wallace.
Description: Macon, GA : Smyth & Helwys Publishing, [2024] | Includes bibliographical references.
Identifiers: LCCN 2024038456 | ISBN 9781641735827 (paperback)
Subjects: LCSH: Bible. Psalms--Criticism, interpretation, etc. | Bible. Old Testament--Criticism, interpretation, etc. | Bible. Old Testament--History of Biblical events. | Allusions in the Bible.
Classification: LCC BS1430.52 .W3556 2024 | DDC 223/.206--dc23/eng/20240907
LC record available at https://lccn.loc.gov/2024038456

Disclaimer of Liability: With respect to statements of opinion or fact available in this work of nonfiction, Smyth & Helwys Publishing, nor any of its employees, makes any warranty, express or implied, or assumes any legal liability or responsibility for the accuracy or completeness of any information disclosed, or represents that its use would not infringe privately-owned rights.

Contents

Foreword	ix
Introduction	1
Chapter 1: What Are the Psalms?	7
Chapter 2: The Old Stories (Genesis 1–11)	27
Chapter 3: Ancestors	49
Chapter 4: The Exodus	71
Chapter 5: Torah	91
Chapter 6: Wilderness	111
Chapter 7: Settlement	133
Chapter 8: Kingship	155
Chapter 9: Prophets	177
Chapter 10: Wisdom	205
Chapter 11: Exile	237

Foreword

W. H. Bellinger Jr., Baylor University (Emeritus)

Robert Wallace has written a delightful and insightful book to help students, persons of faith, scholars, and pastors who are faced with reading and understanding the Old Testament. Students in an Old Testament religion class are often overwhelmed by the task of reading so many unfamiliar and old-fashioned pages. Likewise, pilgrims of faith who want to grow from reading the Old Testament hardly know how or where to begin. *A Prism of Song* is written with these readers in mind and with the goal of helping them enjoy and learn while reading the pages of the Old Testament. The "Song" in the book's title refers to the book of Psalms as a place to begin. In many ways, Psalms—as a collection of the prayers and praises of ancient Israel—is the center of the Old Testament and its faith. It offers a starting point of powerful depth and joy.

Dr. Wallace is an honest interpreter. He explores the issues covered in the Old Testament from a different context than readers experience in the twenty-first century. He also notes issues that are not covered. I suggest four reasons to take on the fun task of reading Dr. Wallace's book.

1. The book provides the basics for understanding Psalms as a lens to read the Old Testament meaningfully. It then moves to Genesis and creation and provides the background for a full, informative reading of these texts, emphasizing the context in which the Old Testament originated.

2. The book also includes appealing gems related to the context of readers today, such as the description of tribalism in relation to *The Godfather* (p. 50), the paraphrase of Jacob's name as "con artist" (p. 64), and the description of kingship as a shape that we can imagine, like a grand piano with a cloth covering "hiding" it (p. 155).

3. The book clearly articulates the broad vision of the Old Testament and its various parts as well as issues in specific texts. There is also variety in the book's formatting. Dr. Wallace includes lists, shaded blocks that explore certain issues, quotes from biblical texts, and review questions to conclude chapters. These visuals aid readers' interaction with the book.

4. The book insightfully attends to the various parts of the Old Testament such as history, prophecy, practical and skeptical wisdom, and texts related to the exile. The Psalms and these other parts of the Old Testament originated in an ancient setting yet also relate to life today. The book's title and approach suggest that the songs of the book of Psalms give readers a prism for understanding the Old Testament. A prism reflects light, revealing one's surroundings in unique, colorful ways. That is what Psalms does for the Old Testament.

Robert Wallace is an accomplished Old Testament teacher-scholar and pastor and an excellent guide for readers of the Old Testament. He was my student at Baylor University. It is my privilege to congratulate him on this perceptive and excellent resource for people reading the Old Testament. Studying the Old Testament requires a place to begin. I have suggested that a powerful place to begin in accounting for the theology of the Old Testament is the book of Psalms. In *A Prism of Song*, Dr. Wallace suggests the same starting place for a study of the Old Testament: "The book of Psalms walks alongside Israel on that journey" (p. 256). I invite you to be a part of that journey and hope you will find joy along the way.

Introduction

> *Each of these books, you see, is like a garden which grows one special kind of fruit; by contrast, the Psalter is a garden which,* besides *its special fruit, grows also some of those of all the rest.*
>
> —Athanasius's letter to Marcellinus

A Prism of Song

In 1704, Isaac Newton published *Opticks: Or, A Treatise of the Reflexions, Refractions, Inflexions and Colours*. The work is one of the most significant in the history of science. Among other discoveries, Newton's experiments revealed that what human beings see as a single beam of light is something far more complex. When passed through a prism, white light reveals its building blocks, and the individual colors of the rainbow, from red to violet, are visible. Something that looked simple was actually far more complex. His experiments provided the starting point for understanding the wondrous complexities of the electromagnetic spectrum.

Newton's experiments also can serve as a helpful parable when examining the biblical text. While it is easy to think of the Bible as a single book, the Bible is a library containing books that were composed by numerous authors over hundreds of years. Much like light, the Bible can have an appearance of unity obscuring remarkable complexities beneath the surface. Psalms can serve as a helpful literary (and musical) "prism" that can reveal the building blocks of the text. The psalms can be a starting point for understanding the wondrous complexities of the diverse library of the Old Testament.

Why the Book of Psalms?

The early church recognized the Psalms contributed something distinct to the biblical story. The book has its own material, but it also contains a sample of the themes found in the rest of the Hebrew Bible. Creation, covenant, patriarchs, exodus, prophetic correction, monarchy, exile—the reader can find all of these topics represented in the 150-piece, liturgical snapshot, called the "Psalms." When a new Bible translation is released, Bible publishers often, whether consciously or unconsciously, reinforce this point. Bibles are first published as a "New Testament & Psalms," as though if readers have the Psalms, they have a pretty good representation of the Old Testament.

In recent years, the scholarship of education has suggested that students learn best when theory is contextualized and discovery based.[1] Rather than learning abstract concepts in a vacuum, material that is contextualized leads to better comprehension and retention. Bringing this educational theory to the study of the Bible means that one needs a context in which to talk about the Old Testament.

In truth, any context could work for this survey. In fact, "reception history" has become an increasingly popular field of biblical studies. With reception history, scholars join the disciplines of church history and biblical studies to look at how a text has been read throughout its history. Scholars discuss, for example, Athanasius's use of Psalms or the church reformers' readings of the Torah. Contextualizing the Old Testament aids in understanding of both the historical period and the ancient texts.

This text will provide a survey of the Old Testament using the book of Psalms as the context for that survey. What better place to start surveying the Old Testament than with a text that is itself a miniature Old Testament survey? The Psalms as a starting point for an Old Testament survey provides unique benefits.

It is a comprehensive place

As the early church father Athanasius noted, the book of Psalms (or "Psalter") houses "some of the fruit of each tree in the rest of the garden."[2] One can discuss every significant issue in the Hebrew Bible through the lens of Psalms. Even its shape and shaping provide an opportunity to discuss canon and canonization.

Where Psalms does not explicitly include material from the rest of the Old Testament, it still has a sampling of the themes discussed. For example,

---

1. D. E. Rose, "Context-Based Learning," in N. M. Seel, ed., *Encyclopedia of the Sciences of Learning* (Boston: Springer, 2012).

2. *Athanasius: The Life of Antony and the Letter to Marcellinus*, trans. Robert C. Gregg (New York: Paulist Press, 1980), 102.

while Job's name does not occur explicitly within the psalms, the suffering of the righteous is a common theme throughout the text. Occasionally, the psalms may be songs that represent an understanding and appropriation of stories they do not specifically reference. Psalm 29 says God sits "enthroned above the floods" (v. 10), using the same word for "flood" that occurs in Genesis 9. Even the silence of the psalms on issues provides interesting opportunities for discussion.

It is a familiar place

The psalms are part of the language of the church. Selections from Psalms find their way into worship music, sermons, prayers, and blessings as well as onto church walls, pens, keychains, inspirational pictures, paperweights, plates, checkbook covers, etc. Beyond the church, the psalms have found their way into popular culture. Psalm 23 has been recited in movies like *Titanic* and *Saving Private Ryan* and television shows like the *Twilight Zone*. It has even been referenced by hip-hop artists like Coolio, Jay-Z, and Tupac. Woe unto the pastor who fails to read Psalm 23 by the graveside of the recently deceased. The grieving family will never forgive that egregious sin, even if their loved one was not particularly religious.

If one needs to contextualize the Old Testament with a familiar entry point, the ubiquitous book of Psalms is a natural fit.

It is an early place

Scholars do not have precise dates for the final composition of the texts of the Old Testament. Like most of the Old Testament, the collection of Psalms likely came together over an extended period. The psalms, however, represent Israel's earliest encounter with its traditions that contemporary scholars possess. The singers in the psalms were aware of their stories. The way they sang about them provides a glimpse into how they understood them. Since these songs were originally used in worship, the psalms represent an early and intentionally theological encounter with the texts.

It is difficult to know how widespread access to these biblical texts would have been. If the literacy levels in ancient Israel were relatively low and public worship was the primary means by which common people encountered theology, then the psalms' "reading" of Israel's traditions would represent the theological beliefs of many, if not most, worshipers in ancient Israel. When they thought about the themes of creation, kingship, and Torah, they were shaped by this early musical encounter with the tradition.

It is a liturgical place

Biblical scholar G. W. Anderson wrote an article in 1963 titled "Israel's Creed: Sung, Not Signed." In this text, Anderson states that the Old Testament is a "confessional document."[3] In composing the Old Testament, Israel was not attempting to write a systematic theology. These texts came from a community's shaping of their theological ideas and practices in worship. The psalms are not simply what Israel believed about creation or the exodus but how Israel believed those themes should be sung in worship. While not knowing much about the daily life of the common people of ancient Israel, it is not unreasonable to believe that the worship experience was the primary way in which the common person experienced the traditions of the larger biblical text.

Anderson noted that Israel was always better at glorifying God than at theological reflection. Perhaps this can in part be attributed to the power of music. It is rare to meet someone who has not been inspired by music. Music invokes passion. Music has the power to aid memory—children begin learning to read by singing the ABCs. Music provides communal connection and, at the same time, is intensely personal.

All texts have agendas and occasions. When part of that agenda is music and worship, the stories are deepened and given color they might otherwise lack.

It is a canonical place

Contemporary readers of the Old Testament have a rich, two-millennium history that could provide fascinating entry points to contextualize the Old Testament. Church reformer Martin Luther's use of the law could provide an interesting gateway into a discussion of the Torah. The use of Psalms in the monastic Rule of St. Benedict could be equally compelling. One could use the artistic depictions of biblical stories of the Italian Renaissance (or any other country or period) to provide an entry point to discussing the individual texts.

A "canon" is simply a list of books that a community has established as useful for faith and practice. The community affirms that something different is at work within certain texts—God's voice can be heard. In the case of the Christian canon, the community of faith recognized and affirmed Genesis to Revelation as authoritative for the Christian community. Using

---

3. G. W. Anderson, "Israel's Creed: Sung, Not Signed," *Scottish Journal of Theology* 16/3 (1963): 277–85.

Psalms as a canonical starting point—a gateway—into the rest of the Old Testament provides a special, and perhaps even sacred, place to begin.

It is a beautiful place

When NASA was trying to determine the landing site for Apollo 15, mission commander Dave Scott was given the final choice of two sites. One site was safer, but with less scientific interest. The other site was a mountainous and rocky area. It would be a more dangerous landing site, but the area provided more scientific promise. Scott opted for the dangerous site hoping to confirm some of the lunar origin theories, but Scott added that the mountainous site offered an additional benefit. It had "grandeur," and he believed it was good for the human spirit to explore beautiful places.

The psalms are an important theological encounter with Israel's traditions, but they also represent an intentional *artistic* encounter with those traditions. They have grandeur, and it is good for the human spirit to explore beautiful texts.

What Are the Psalms?

Israel knew how to come into the presence of the Lord, and she knew how to behave when she got there.

—W. H. Bellinger

The book of Psalms is the hymnbook of ancient Israel. Psalms are words the community directed to God in worship. While much of the Bible represents "Thus says Yahweh to Israel," the psalms represent "Thus says Israel to Yahweh." So, while the rest of the Bible is words *from* God, the psalms are words *to* God that—if one believes in divine direction through the canonical process—have now come back as words *from* God. In other words, through the process of these songs being understood as "Scripture," these words Israel spoke to God became words that God, through human action, directed Israel to preserve.

The 150 preserved songs do not represent all the songs Israel wrote in the millennium before Jesus. Other psalms have found their way into the narrative texts of the Old Testament, like the Song of Deborah in Judges 5 or the Song of Hannah in 1 Samuel 2. Some have been lost to history. Editors of the biblical text preserved and prioritized these 150 songs, however, as a separate and special book called "Psalms." Before using the psalms as a gateway to the rest of the Old Testament, it would be helpful to answer two questions: "What are the psalms?" and "Why these 150 songs?"

What Are the Psalms?

The Jewish organization of the Hebrew Bible is divided into three sections: Torah (Law), Nevi'im (Prophets), and Kethubim (Writings). The last of the three sections to be understood as Scripture was the Writings, only achieving final "official" status at the end of the first century CE. Within this collection of books, Psalms seems to have been the first to achieve canonical status. In the Gospel of Luke, traditionally dated to the middle of the first century, Psalms is singled out as special and in a list with Torah and Prophets: "[Jesus] said to them, 'This is what I said when I spoke to you while I was still with you—that it was necessary to fulfill everything that had been written about me in the law of Moses and in the prophets and in the Psalms'" (Luke 24:44).[1]

It is possible that at the time of the writing of the Gospel of Luke, only Psalms had achieved status as Scripture. When the Jewish council of Jamnia sanctioned the Hebrew Bible's canon in 90 CE, several books in the Writings did have their value debated (e.g., Ecclesiastes, Song of Songs, and Esther), but the book of Psalms was not one.[2] By the writing of the Gospel of Luke (likely predating Jamnia), Psalms was understood as special.

THE SHAPE AND SHAPING OF PSALMS

The 150 psalms had an interesting journey to the list readers find in the Bible today. Indeed, though it is called the "the book of Psalms," the text is divided into five smaller books. The origin of the five-book division is unknown, but these sections may provide a clue to the shaping of the book. These individual books within the Psalter may represent collections of songs that came together over time (see page 9). Historically, the book of Psalms has been read as an anthology. In other words, the overall book was viewed as a collection of songs assembled randomly over time. Interpretations of the psalms assumed that one could select a random psalm to read, analogous to the way one might select a random hymn to sing from a contemporary hymnbook.

The *Revised Common Lectionary* (1994), though it has consecutive readings of other books of the Bible, selects psalms seemingly at random with an occasional thematic connection to Sunday's other readings. The *Rule of St. Benedict* (6th century CE) insists its readers read the entire Psalter in one week; however, the psalms are listed in a shuffled order. The *Rule of Benedict* even concedes that the order it prescribes should not be restrictive, and if someone is displeased, they can arrange the psalms in any order they see fit, provided all 150 psalms are read in one week.[3] While the psalms themselves have been important throughout church history, reading them in their canonical order has not.

---

1. I am using my own translation of Bible passages in this book. For more, see the section "My Translation Philosophy" in chapter 1.

2. Albert C. Sundberg Jr., Thomas J. Sienkewicz, and James E. Betts, eds., "The Old Testament of the Early Church Revisited," *Festshchrift in Honor of Charles Speel* (Monmouth, IL: Monmouth College, 1997).

3. *Rule of St. Benedict*, ch. 18.

> ### Five "Books" and Other Collections in the Book of Psalms
>
> The five books of Psalms are divided as follows:
>
> Book I   Pss 1–41
> Book II   Pss 42–72
> Book III Pss 73–89
> Book IV   Pss 90–106
> Book V   Pss 107–150
>
> While the five-book division is the primary organizing principle of Psalms, other collections exist within the Psalter as well. Psalms 42 to 84 have been called the Elohistic Psalter because of their preference for the name "Elohim" for God rather than "Yahweh." Within and around the Elohistic Psalter are the Asaphite psalms (Pss 50, 73–83) and the Korahite collection (Pss 42–49, 84–89). The "Songs of Ascent" are in Book V (Pss 120–134). The Enthronement Psalms are Pss 93–99, and the Hallelujah collection is Pss 111–118. The psalms also end with a Hallelujah doxology (Pss 146–150).

Reading plans like these reinforce the historic belief that the order of the psalms is arbitrary and that although Books I through V might contain collections from different points in Israel's history, the book as a whole was assembled over time with little (or no) regard for thematic or lexical concerns. Indeed, psalms across books are occasionally duplicated (Ps 14 and Ps 53, Ps 40:13-17 and Ps 70, and Ps 60:5-12 and Ps 108), reinforcing the impression of a random assembly over time. Psalms as a randomly collected anthology has been the dominant interpretive approach for years, but recent interpretations have convincingly demonstrated that the psalms have a complex editorial history, revealed within the text itself.

More recently, scholars have begun to interpret the Psalms as a single, complex book. Several sections of the Psalter demonstrate clear editorial purpose. Some scholars have demonstrated intentional shaping in the order of the psalms by the later community.[4] Others have shown how the psalms at the beginnings of the individual books give shape to what follows.[5] Still

---

4. Gerald Wilson, *The Editing of the Hebrew Psalter*, SBL Dissertation Series, no. 76 (Chico, CA: Scholars Press, 1985).

5. Nancy deClaisse-Walford, *Reading from the Beginning* (Macon: Mercer University Press, 1997).

others read the entire book of Psalms from Ps 1 to Ps 150 as a microcosm of the journey of faith.[6] In each of these approaches, and a host of others, the psalms are not simply part of a loose anthology compiled over time. The book of Psalms literally becomes a "book" with editorial and even narrative purpose.

The Occasion of the Bible

The biblical text did not come together in a vacuum but was written to address the culture around it. The composition of texts was often motivated by a specific circumstance. No individual in the ancient world sat down in the local Jerusalem coffee shop and thought, "I think I'll put a creation story together." Stories were composed to address a need in the community. It is far likelier that someone thought, "Other people are saying this about creation, but Yahweh is king! Creation happened this way, 'In the beginning . . . .'" The needs the authors perceived in the culture surrounding them impacted the way the stories were told. This is self-evident when looking at the letters of Paul in the New Testament where specific issues facing early Christianity motivated his writings to the individual churches. For example, 1 Corinthians 7:1 makes the occasion of the text explicit with the words, "Now, on to the matters you wrote about . . . ."

While the occasional nature of letters is easy to see, it is more difficult to remember that the rest of the Bible was also composed to address the concerns facing the ancient authors. Sensitivity to the historical and cultural occasion of a text can be as important as sensitivity to its literary context. While it is easy to remember that the language of this ancient text must be translated, it is easy to forget that the culture of the text needs to be translated as well. In the same way that knowing the characteristics of the city of Corinth in the first century can help a reader better hear what Paul meant when he addressed them in 1 Corinthians, knowing the characteristics of the flood stories that the cultures surrounding Israel told can help a reader better hear what Genesis 6–9 is trying to say. Ultimately, understanding what an ancient author was trying to say to the ancient audience will help a faithful, contemporary reader better hear what God is saying to them.

By affirming these books are Scripture, a person of faith is claiming that the Bible's influence does not end in that original occasion. A scriptural text speaks to different historical settings for a faith community. Sensitivity

---

6. Walter Brueggemann, "Bounded by Obedience and Praise: The Psalms as Canon," in *The Psalms and the Life of Faith* (Minneapolis: Fortress, 1995).

to the original historical context of a biblical passage—to the degree that it can be known—can add depth to the interpretation of that text in new historical settings.

The occasional nature of the text means that authors assume their readers will understand language and associations that unfortunately a contemporary reader might miss. This is analogous to the way someone shares "inside jokes" or make references knowing that other friends or family members will get the point. One benefit of studying the ancient world surrounding the biblical text is that it allows the contemporary reader to better "hear" what the text is trying to say. A contemporary American writer might refer to "Gettysburg," "Normandy," "Selma," or "9/11" without telling the stories associated with those terms. Most American readers would hear a depth of meaning associated with them. In the same way, the authors of the biblical text could be assured that the audience would have certain knowledge and make certain associations. "Babylon," "Egypt," "Ur of the Chaldees," and "Nineveh" were locations steeped in significant social and political associations that are often lost on the contemporary reader.

Important Dates in Israel's Timeline

Since this book moves fluidly between the psalms and the rest of the Hebrew Bible, it might be helpful to note some important dates in the timeline of Israel.

20th–17th centuries BCE: Time of the Ancestors
17th–13th centuries BCE: Time of Egyptian Oppression
13th century BCE: The Exodus from Egypt
13th–11th centuries BCE: Settlement Period and Time of the Judges
1000–931 BCE: United Monarchy
931–722 BCE: Divided Monarchy
    Northern Kingdom of Israel (Capital: Samaria)
    Southern Kingdom of Judah (Capital: Jerusalem)
722–586 BCE: Last Years of Southern Kingdom of Judah
597 BCE: Exile Begins/First Deportation to Babylon
586 BCE: Destruction of Jerusalem and Temple
530s BCE: Persian defeat of Babylon/End of Babylonian Exile
5th century BCE: Ezra and Nehemiah Rebuild Jerusalem/Second Temple Period Begins

The Occasion of Psalms

As already mentioned, the book of Psalms has a long and complicated editorial history. One possible explanation for the five books of the Psalter is that these books represent stages of composition. Each book of the Psalms might represent in some way what the Israel's worship book looked like at some point in its history. This explanation seems likely. Psalm 72 may provide evidence for a staggered editorial history. At the end of Book II, Ps 72 is one of the two psalms of Solomon, but its last verse reads, "The prayers of David, son of Jesse, are finished" (v. 20).

It is true that most of the seventy-three total "psalms of David" are in the first two books of the Psalms. Despite the assurance of Ps 72:20, however, the prayers of David are not quite finished in Ps 72. David appears in the superscription of one psalm in Book III, two psalms in Book IV, and fourteen psalms in Book V. It seems that the last verse of Book II represents an editorial comment from what was at one time the ending of the book of Psalms. Sometime later, Book III was added, followed by Books IV and V.

While there is no way to know for certain, the themes found in the individual books give some indication to their occasions:
- Books I and II emphasize the Davidic monarchy
- Book III wrestles with the Babylonian exile
- Book IV looks for answers following the exile
- Book V comes together in the second temple period.

This is not to suggest that the individual psalms were necessarily composed during the occasion suggested for the book in which they appear but rather that the book itself was edited, possibly with new and old psalms, to speak to the people's need at that time. For example, it is possible that Ps 110, a psalm celebrating Davidic kingship, was an older psalm preserved for years by the community. It found canonical status in the second temple period as people began to look forward to a messiah to deliver Israel.

The Poetry of Psalms

Unlike its surrounding nations, Israel did not use poetry to tell its stories. Poetry was used for nearly every other genre of writing. A few psalms use poetry to tell Israel's history in a manner that resembles the epic histories of the nations around Israel (e.g., Ps 78, 105, 106), but by and large, Israel preferred prose to tell its stories.

The psalms are a unique genre in the biblical text since they represent not only poetry but also musical compositions. Unfortunately, the music for these texts and many of the definitions for the musical terms have been lost to history. What remains is complex and beautiful poetry, and understanding the features of that poetry is useful when reading the text. This has broader application than the psalms. Poetry was used for prophetic speech. In fact, most of the oracles of the "writing prophets" are preserved in poetry. Poetry was also used for teaching, as in Proverbs and Job.

Parallelism

The most common characteristic of Hebrew poetry is parallelism. Hebrew is an inflected language, and word endings often have the same form; therefore, rhyming is not difficult. As a result, Hebrew poetry focuses more often on the structure of a text. One common structural feature in a poetic text is the relationship between the lines. Some have said that instead of rhyming the sound of the words, Hebrew poetry "rhymes the meaning."

Often, the second line of a verse will paraphrase the first line. This is known as a synonymous parallelism. One example comes from Ps 1: "Because of this, the wicked cannot stand in the judgment, or sinners in the congregation of the righteous" (v. 5). Occasionally, the psalms will use contrasting ideas in the same verse. This is called antithetical parallelism. This is particularly useful when talking about the righteous and the wicked, as in the last verse of Ps 1: "For Yahweh knows the pathway of the righteous, but the pathway of the wicked goes to destruction" (v. 6).

One other important form of parallelism is the "synthetic" or "stairstep parallelism." This is when the second line does not directly paraphrase the first line but further develops the thought of the first line. On occasion, neither line expresses a complete thought. For example, see Ps 42:1: "As a deer longs for rivers of water, so my soul longs for you, God." Or Ps 29:1: "Give to Yahweh—divine beings—give to Yahweh glory and might!"

The Hebrew authors would demonstrate their creativity by using different parallelisms in sequence. In Ps 68:6, the author cleverly uses two different styles of parallelism in one verse:

> God gives a home to the one dwelling alone.
> God frees prisoners with prosperity.
> But the rebellious dwell in a parched place.

The first two lines affirm God's provision for the forgotten in a synonymous parallelism. The last two lines contrast God's favor on the prisoners and the judgment on the rebellion in an antithetic parallelism. These three lines contain both a synonymous and an antithetic parallelism that pivot on the second line.

Acrostic

One of the most impressive features of Hebrew poetry is the acrostic. In an acrostic poem, each line, or groups of lines, in a psalm begins with successive letters of the Hebrew alphabet. Nine psalms use an acrostic pattern.[7] Psalm 119 is perhaps the most famous and impressive. Psalm 119 has twenty-two stanzas of eight lines each, making it the longest chapter in the Bible at 176 verses. Each stanza has eight lines that begin with the same Hebrew letter, and each stanza uses successive letters of the Hebrew alphabet. The first four chapters of Lamentations are also acrostic poems.

Acrostics would likely aid in memorization and demonstrated an author's compositional skill. Acrostics also offer a metaphor for "wholeness" or comprehensiveness. An English speaker might say "From A to Z" to capture the same idea.

Why These 150 Songs?

Canon and Community

"Why these 150 songs?" is a question of "canon." The word canon has been used several times to this point. To better understand it, consider a moment from recent history. On April 25, 2014, the official Star Wars website officially made policy what fans had been speculating for months; the stories of the "Star Wars Expanded Universe" were no longer officially part of the Star Wars story. Disney purchased the rights to the Star Wars properties, planning to release new movies and shows, and wanted to give their writers and directors as much creative freedom as possible. They decided it would be too difficult to fit the new stories into the plotlines established by the existing books. The announcement made it official. The stories that committed Star Wars fans had enjoyed reading for years were no longer "canon." Many fans were furious. Following Disney's announcement, some fans speculated that Disney had been engaged in a secret war against the stories of the "Star Wars Expanded Universe." Some of them responded by

---

7. Pss 9, 10, 25, 34, 35, 111, 112, 119, and 145.

saying it was a cash grab by Disney and denied canonical status to any of the Disney Star Wars stories set after *Return of the Jedi*.

But what difference could this decision possibly make? Why did fans care? Why would fans write numerous emails and blogs protesting this decision? The Star Wars Expanded Universe books still existed and continued being sold in bookstores around the world. Disney was not going to confiscate fan libraries. Fans continued to own the books. Anyone could read these stories whenever they wanted. Why the uproar? Simply put, stories that the fans loved had now been demoted. These books were no longer "official." Their stories would be forgotten in the legacy of the Star Wars franchise, relegated to the role of "alternate universe" or "apocrypha." If an entertainment franchise could cause this kind of controversy by declaring an official list of fictional texts, one can imagine what is at stake when religion is involved!

Communities and Canonization

At its most basic, being "canon" makes a text "official." Different religious groups have different canons. For Islam, it is the Quran. For Judaism, the canon is the thirty-nine books that Christians label the "Old Testament." For Protestant Christians, it includes the thirty-nine books of the Old Testament and the twenty-seven books of the New Testament. For Catholic Christians, the canon includes the sixty-six books of the Protestant Bibles and additional Jewish texts written immediately prior to the New Testament. These additional books are known as "deuterocanonical" texts in Catholic tradition and "Apocrypha" for groups for whom they are not canon.

Unlike the Star Wars canon, the Bible had no unified, sanctioning body to make unquestionable and authoritative declarations about "official" texts. While Jewish and Christian councils did make pronouncements regarding texts, those councils convened hundreds of years after the texts were composed, and likely, their decisions reinforced the decisions that the religious communities already made through their practice. Part of the challenge is that the Jewish and Christian texts did not come from a single place or a single moment in time. They came together over a long period of time and from a variety of geographic locations.

Some religious groups tell dramatic stories for the origin of their sacred texts. For those groups, a text came together dramatically in a holy moment. The Christian and Jewish canons, however, have far more boring origin stories. The biblical texts came together over the course of centuries in unremarkable ways. A large part of the New Testament has the form it does because specific churches decided to save the correspondence they received from the Apostle Paul. Different churches saved, shared, and made copies of Paul's letters, and after generations people began to formally declare that these were no ordinary letters but "scripture." For a person of faith, God was working not only within the authors composing the texts but also within the communities who received those texts. The community played a role by recognizing that God was doing something extraordinary within these seemingly ordinary writings. They began sharing them and preserving them from generation to generation.

THE SHAPE OF THE PSALMS

As seen in the Luke 24 text, the Psalms were scripture. But how many psalms? Which order? The Septuagint (LXX)—the Greek translation of the Hebrew Scriptures—lists the 150 psalms found in the traditional Hebrew text. Although the LXX has the 150 psalms in the same order, the psalms are broken up in different ways.

Hebrew Numbering	Greek Numbering
1–8	1–8
9–10	9
11–113	10–112
114–115	113
116:1-9	114
116:10-19	115
117–146	116–145
147:1-11	146
147:12-20	147
148–150	148–150
	151

While there is a myth about the translation of the LXX,[8] the date of the text's completion is lost to history. While the Pentateuch was likely completed by the third century BCE, other parts of the Hebrew Bible came to the Greek text in the next century or so. Unfortunately, it is difficult to be more precise than that.

---

8. The story goes that seventy (seventy-two?) scholars translated the text during the reign of Ptolemy II Philadelphus in the third century BCE. This story gives the "LXX" abbreviation of the text, using the Roman numerals for "seventy."

To add to the confusion, the "Great Psalms Scroll" was discovered among the Dead Sea Scrolls in 1956.[9] The scroll dates to the early first century CE, and while it maintains canonical order for selections from the Psalms of Ascent (Pss 121–132), the scroll shuffles a number of psalms known from the traditional Hebrew psalm from Books IV and V. The scroll also contains several psalms previously unknown or unincluded in the book of Psalms (including a two-part, more developed "Ps 151").

Jesus claimed the Psalms as scripture in Luke 24; however, one must concede:

1. the similar witnesses of the traditional Hebrew text and the LXX might mean the community that produced the Great Psalm Scroll was an aberration with their own, unique ideas about canon; or

2. the differences in all three texts might represent different "text families" that existed in the first century, and the question of "what is settled scripture" might not be answered by the people until much later.

The answer to the question "What is the official text?" might bother contemporary readers more than ancient ones. The Dead Sea Scrolls also contained both Hebrew and Greek copies of the book of Jeremiah, and the Greek copy of Jeremiah is more than 12 percent shorter.[10] Both seemed to have been used and kept together, implying acceptance.

Community Shaping and Individual Psalms

In truth, the community's role was not limited to the text's preservation and transmission; they also played a role in the text's composition. For many, this kind of community involvement is troubling and contrasts with how they imagine texts are composed today. People visualize an author sitting in a coffee shop with a story burning in their mind while they furiously type on a laptop. It is easy to believe that an editor simply made edits, checked the grammar, and published the text. In reality, a single author may send a text to a publisher, but that publisher often involves editors, assistant editors, proof editors, and marketing and production departments. By the time a book is published, anywhere from ten to fifty individuals might have made a substantive contribution to its composition.

---

9. Gerald H. Wilson, "The Qumran 'Psalms Scroll' (11QPsa) and the Canonical Psalter: Comparison of Editorial Shaping," *CBQ* 59/3 (1997): 448–64.

10. Joseph Blenkinsopp, *A History of Prophecy in Israel* (Westminster John Knox Press, 1996), 130.

In the ancient world, texts were also shaped by communities, though often less officially and over much longer periods of time. Communities would first preserve texts orally. The oral period could be relatively short. In the case of the New Testament, less than a generation separates the life of Jesus and the written Gospels. This oral period could also take place over a significantly longer period. For example, the events of the book of Ruth are set in the Judges period, but the evidence suggests it was not written down until after the exile, possibly eight hundred years later![11]

The Septuagint (LXX)

Although the Septuagint was a translation of the Jewish Hebrew Bible, it remains the most important Bible translation in Christian history. When the first Christian missionaries began to spread the Christian faith, everyone in their world spoke Greek, thanks to the conquests of Alexander the Great in the fourth century BCE and the spread of Greek culture. The Septuagint became *the* Bible for the first Christians. In fact, most, if not all, quotations of the Old Testament by the New Testament come directly from the LXX.[†]

The Septuagint contains the thirty-nine texts that Protestants normally think of as the Old Testament. It also contains several additional books and additions to books (e.g., Esther and Daniel) that were written in the centuries before the New Testament period. These additions are often called "Apocrypha" and are the primary difference between the Catholic and Protestant "canons." Catholics recognize these additional Jewish texts as scripture (calling them "deuterocanonical"), and Protestants do not. Interestingly, the early Jewish council, when discussing which books should be considered scripture, omitted the Apocrypha from the approved lists.

[†] In an English Bible, these quotations have been translated from Hebrew to Greek and finally to English. Most English Old Testaments, like the translations in this book, are translated directly from Hebrew to English. For this reason, if one compares an NT quotation of an OT passage to the original OT passage, the "spirit" of the verse is likely the same, but the wording can be quite different.

---

11. If the authority of a text is connected to its authorship, then this long period of time and communal shaping can make people of faith nervous. If, however, one believes the ultimate authorship of this text is through the inspiration of God, then this long period of community shaping should not be a concern. God can be at work in both the composition of a texts and the shaping of the text over the centuries.

The psalms provide some examples that reveal the communal shaping that has taken place in the text. One is found in Psalm 51, a "Psalm of David." The superscription specifically sets the occasion of this psalm as David's prayer of forgiveness after the incident between David and Bathsheba. Near the end of the psalm, the psalmist focuses on what God requires from humanity:

> O Sovereign! Open my lips, and my mouth will declare your praise, because you do not delight in sacrifice. If I were to give a burnt offering, you would not accept it. Godly sacrifices are humble spirits. God will not despise a humble and repentant mind.... (Ps 51:15-17)

The psalm emphasizes that the external manifestations of worship are not what God finds acceptable. In fact, the psalm explicitly says that God does not want sacrifice. God desires only a broken spirit and a humble worshiper.

Immediately following this blanket statement regarding God's lack of interest in sacrifice, the psalm offers this curious statement:

> [O God] do good and show Zion your favor! Build the walls of Jerusalem. Then you will delight in right sacrifices and whole offerings. Then bulls will be offered on your altar. (Ps 51:18-19)

It does seem odd that these verses offer wholehearted support of sacrifices, even going as far as to say that God will "delight" in them, when the verses immediately preceding them clearly dismiss sacrifices.

Likely, a large portion of this psalm was written before the exile and preserved for hundreds of years with verse 17 standing as the psalm's last verse. After the exile, however, the prophetic books of Haggai and Zechariah tell the story of Israel's struggles to make Yahweh a priority in their worship. The rebuilding of the temple and walls was incomplete. As people sang this beloved psalm, some in the community likely feared that the psalmist's dismissal of the importance of sacrifice might be misinterpreted. The people of Israel were already not making a priority of the temple; a psalm of David that seemed to dismiss the importance of temple worship would not help their situation. As a result, well-meaning—and one can believe God-inspired—individuals added verses 18 and 19 to Psalm 51, asking God to rebuild the city and reminding the singers of the importance of temple worship. The community shaped the text to prevent it from misleading the faithful. God can be at work within the composition and preservation of the text over the centuries.

Translating Psalms (and the rest of the Bible)

Translation Philosophy

For obvious reasons, the overwhelming majority of Bible translations are done by large translation committees. Translating the entire Bible is a monumental task requiring expertise across numerous languages. When trying to translate more than 37,500 verses, it makes the most sense to divide and conquer!

This kind of translation has several strengths. A committee can involve specialists for specific sections of Scripture. Experts in the individual languages of Hebrew, Greek, Aramaic or specialists in epistles, poetry, prophets, psalms, etc. can be selected and provide their insight. In addition to diversity of skills, a theologically diverse translation committee can provide careful checks against ideological bias in translation. The New Revised Standard Version translation committee included men and women from Catholic, Greek Orthodox, mainline Protestant, and evangelical Protestant traditions. It even included a Jewish translator to provide expertise in the Old Testament. This kind of team can protect against "reading faith" into the text.

Unfortunately, strengths can also be weaknesses. Bible translations done by committee reflect the wording that the committee could agree on. As a colleague of mine once remarked, when a committee must agree on a color, it is always beige. Vibrant, "colorful" translations suggested by an individual have a hard time surviving the committee process. This is one reason Eugene Peterson's exceptional, individual translation[12] of the Bible, *The Message*, is so much more colorful than committee translations, like the *New Living Translation*, even though both share the philosophy of being more "readable."

While translation philosophy is a spectrum, two emphases emerge. A formal correspondence translation attempts to find exactly the right word in the target language to capture the sense of the word in the original language. The "form" of the translation "corresponds" as closely as possible

---

12. While *The Message* has been called a "paraphrase," Peterson worked from the original languages. In my opinion, a paraphrase works within the same language, like the original Living Bible. When one works across languages, it is more accurate to call it a translation.

to the original—in word choice and word order. This is the most common philosophy of translation. Some examples include the *King James Version*, the *New American Standard Bible*, the *New Revised Standard Bible*, and a host of others. These translations focus on form and trust that the reader will research historical and cultural issues to better understand the text.

Dynamic equivalence translations attempt to capture the meaning of the original text for early readers and translate that *meaning* to the target language. These translators will do more to "translate" the culture as well as the words. Many of these translations are marketed as "children's Bibles" because they are readable. Some examples include the *New Living Translation*, the *Contemporary English Version*, and *The Message*—with *The Message* probably being the most extreme commercial example of this philosophy of translation.

Compare these two philosophies side by side in their renderings of Psalm 100:4

NRSV	*The Message*
Enter his gates with thanksgiving and his courts with praise. Give thanks to him; bless his name. (Ps 100:4)	Enter with the password: "Thank you!" Make yourselves at home, talking praise. Thank him. Worship him. (Ps 100:4)

The Hebrew text has the words for "gate" and "thanksgiving" and "courts," and so the NRSV uses those English equivalents. In the ancient world, walled cities and siege warfare were a reality, and gates were a vulnerable point that controlled access to the city. One did not allow everyone to enter their city. Gates were only opened for trusted friends. In attempt to translate that cultural understanding to contemporary times, Peterson selects "passwords" as something that people would only share with someone they trust (like an open gate in the ancient world). While it lacks a certain majesty and "churchy-ness," it does elegantly translate the cultural expression of safety and trust that comes with God.

My Translation Philosophy

The translations in this book are my own. Most of them follow a broad, formal correspondence translation philosophy. This is partly because the paragraphs around the verse can provide the cultural translation for the reader and partly because of the familiarity many have with these verses.

> ## The Babylonian Exile
>
> While the last chapter of this book is dedicated to the Babylonian exile, it is important to take a moment to introduce the reality of exile at the beginning. To talk about the Babylonian exile in an introductory chapter on the Old Testament might feel like starting at the end, but in many ways, the exile is a beginning. It brought an end to the kingdom of Judah and the first temple, but it began the process of canonization. During that crisis, God's people began to ask what books needed to be preserved.
>
> The destruction of the first temple in 586 BCE motivated individuals to begin to ask the question "What should we be reading?" Prior to that moment, 2 Kings 22 tells a story of how it was possible to lose a book of Moses and not even be aware. The written word was not as important as public worship in the temple. Only after the exile did a new vocation of "scribe" became popular. This allowed the books to be transmitted from generation to generation. The Torah (Genesis–Deuteronomy) was the first collection to be set apart and recognized as special. Following the community's return from exile, Ezra the scribe read from this special collection of texts to the gathered community (Ezra 8:1-3).
>
> After Israel's return, the canonization process began in earnest. Stories were collected and selected as authoritative. Books were written to try to explain the theological significance of the exile. Joshua through 2 Kings were likely edited into their final form. These texts, along with the Writing Prophets (Isaiah through Malachi), were the second section of the Hebrew Scriptures to be canonized. By the second century BCE, an apocryphal text known as the Wisdom of Sirach (Ecclesiasticus) also recognizes the Prophets as special and authoritative.
>
> The last section of material to be officially canonized was what came to be known as the *Kethubim* or "writings." The Writings contain Job, Ecclesiastes, Ruth, Esther, Songs, Lamentations, Daniel, and Psalms. The final decision on which books remained in the Writings was debated even at the end of the first century CE.

Here are some of the choices I made in translation:

1. The Old Testament translations come from the Hebrew Masoretic Text (MT). The few New Testament verses use the United Bible Society's fourth edition Greek text. Though translations commonly amend the Hebrew text or follow a Septuagint reading for particularly difficult passages, these translations attempt to render the MT as it stands.

2. Since the psalms are musical compositions, they are filled with musical terms. Unfortunately, the exact meaning of these terms has been

lost to history, and etymology can only help so far.[13] Since the psalms are being used to understand other sections of the Hebrew Bible, these translations omit the transliterated terms like "Selah" or "Maskil."

3. Most Bibles translate the personal name for God (יהוה) as "the LORD." In this text, the word is untranslated and transliterated using the traditional vocalization "Yahweh."

4. The title of God *Yahweh Sabaoth* (יהוה צבאות) contains an ancient military metaphor. While "Yahweh of Hosts" or "Lord of Hosts" conveyed military associations in older English readings, the military associations have been lost in contemporary use of the phrase. The title emphasizes that the armies of the world and heaven fall under God's control. With that in mind and taking inspiration from Eisenhower in World War II, this text translates the title as "Supreme Commander Yahweh." This is the most "dynamic equivalence" choice made in these translations.

5. Since Israel and the nations around it were thoroughly patriarchal in their understanding of the world, most images of God in the Hebrew Bible are masculine—though remarkably, there are some exceptions. God is a tender mother in Hosea 11:3-4; a mother bear in Hosea 13:8; a mother bird in Deuteronomy 32:11-12; a woman who gives birth in Deuteronomy 32:18 and Isaiah 42:14; and a nursing mother in Isaiah 49:15. Since the word *Elohim* (יהוה) was used to generically refer to deities around the ancient Near East rather than using their individual names (e.g., the *Elohim* of Egypt or Canaan), *Elohim* is a pronoun. The practice is continued here, and these translations use "God" as the pronoun for the divine (and occasionally "the divine" as a pronoun for God).

6. In Genesis 2, the reader is introduced to the tree of the knowledge of *tov* and *ra'* (טוב and רע) These words are traditionally translated "good" and "evil," respectively. Unfortunately, English associates the word "evil" with moral failing, and *ra'* does not necessarily include that association. This must be the case because God performs actions that are called *ra'*.[14] Even so, this does not deter translators from using "evil" to translate the word.[15] Hebrew has a word that conveys moral failure (רשע, *rasha'*, or "wickedness"),

---

13. For a helpful attempt at understanding the terms, see Nancy DeClaissé-Walford, *Introduction to the Psalms: A Song from Ancient Israel* (Chalice Press, 2004), 151–55.

14. The plagues in Egypt and the exiles of Israel and Judah are two examples that are often referred to as the "*ra'*" that God did.

15. This leads to heartburn-inducing translations for people of faith like the King James Version's Exod 32:14 "and the LORD repented of the evil which he thought to do unto his people."

which, of course, God *never* has. With *tov*'s explicit association with created order and *ra'* so often standing as the opposite of that, these translations understand *ra'* as associated with chaos or destruction rather than "evil." These are moments when God's good, ordered creation is undone. This can happen because of the wickedness of humanity, or it can happen from God undoing what was previously done (like the flood).

7. Like many cultures, affection is expressed with a wide range of words. One significant word in the Hebrew Bible is God's *chesed* (חסד). It obviously conveys several elements. It is God's wondrous love associated with the covenant. It is also a word that conveys a love of "kindness." These translations lean into the "covenantal" aspect and God's choice to love, opting for "committed love."

8. Like most ancient cultures, the ancient Hebrews were not sure what the brain did. In the human body, most of the action seems to be happening elsewhere. As a result, reason and emotions were attributed to different organs. The heart, *lav* (לב), was thought of as the place of decision-making and usually associated with reason.[16] Emotions were felt in the gut or kidneys, *kilyoht* (כליות). These translations try to consistently associate the Hebrew word for "heart" with "mind" or "thinking" and the Hebrew word for "kidneys" with emotions.

Reading the Old Testament through the Psalms

When I was teaching in university full-time, our department had "help students read the Bible better" as our goal for the Introduction to the Bible classes.[17] That is the modest goal for this book. We will engage the Old Testament through the psalms. Often this will take the form of intertextual readings, noting where the psalms connect with the established Old Testament traditions. In other cases, the interpretation will be noting where the psalms are silent about a particular issue that is prominent elsewhere in the Old Testament. For example, what does it mean that the women in the ancestor stories play a prominent role in Genesis and are entirely absent in the Psalter? The psalms are also helpful for seeing the way the Old Testament assumes or expresses theological issues. For example, the issues of

---

16. In Hebrew, to "set your heart on" does not mean "desire." It means "to think about."

17. We had decided "help students read the Bible well" was too lofty a goal to achieve in a fifteen-week semester. We we just hoped we could move the needle a little bit to "better."

suffering and worship overlap a great deal in the biblical text (though rarely in contemporary Christian worship experiences).

This book is not comprehensive. Much more could be said on each topic; however, this approach covers significant issues that are helpful to gain an overall understanding of the Old Testament and, one hopes, read the Bible better.

QUESTIONS FOR FURTHER DISCUSSION

1. If, as seems likely, the text of the Bible came together over time as a result of composite authorship rather than a single author, does that challenge the authority of Scripture for people of faith? Or does belief in God's ultimate authorship and direction of the canonical process provide support for the authority of Scripture regardless of who put pen to paper?

2. The miracle of Pentecost proclaims that the gospel message can be translated. When it is translated, it remains "the gospel," not "the gospel in translation." When the Bible is translated from Hebrew, Aramaic, and Greek, it is called "the Bible," not "the Bible in translation," even though translations differ on the rendering of verses. How does a reader of faith reconcile the challenge of different translations calling themselves "the Bible"?

3. How does the musical origin of the book of Psalms affect how one reads the text? Does the "art" of the language affect meaning?

4. Did you find any choices the author made in his translation philosophy particularly interesting or challenging?

5. The early church used the Septuagint as their Old Testament, and the Septuagint was likely the basis of the New Testament quotations of the Old Testament. Contemporary Bibles, however, have Old Testaments translated from the language and canon of the Jewish Hebrew Bible sanctioned in the late first century CE. How should Christians process that complicated history?

The Old Stories (Genesis 1–11)

The story so far: In the beginning the Universe was created. This has made a lot of people very angry and been widely regarded as a bad move.

—Douglas Adams,
The Restaurant at the End of the Universe

Psalms and Creation

Creation is woven throughout the book of Psalms. The universe, the earth, and the sea are celebrated for their beauty and diversity in Psalm 104. Humanity is celebrated for its special place in the created order in Ps 8. Creation is a marvelous product, shaped by the hands of God in Ps 8, ordered in Ps 104, and also a violent act of God bringing order to chaos in Ps 74.

At their heart, creation stories in the ancient Near East were about kingship. Many ancient creation stories from the cultures surrounding Israel used creation stories to establish which god was supreme in the pantheon. The God who creates the universe is the god that is truly sovereign, and God's reign over Israel, the nations, and the universe is something the psalms celebrate in abundance.

Creation in the ancient Near East was also about defeating dragons. Oceans have always been scary and unpredictable. It does not take long at the beach to learn the lesson, "Never turn your back on the ocean." Many cultures in the ancient Near East personified their fear of the ocean by talking about frightening monsters, and creation was the defeat of these monsters. In Babylon, the "deep" was personified by the evil, saltwater, chaos dragon named "Tiamat." In Canaan, "Lotan" or "Leviathan" was an evil chaos serpent who served the god of the sea. "Rahab" was another chaos representation, possibly representing storms that terrify sailors at sea.

These "dragons" were part of the cultural understanding of the biblical authors as they told Israel's creation stories, and occasionally those dragons appear in subtle and, in the case of the exilic Ps 74, not so subtle ways in the text. In exile, the people of Judah had lost everything that was once certain and secure. Any of the characteristics of national identity could no longer provide comfort. In this time of crisis and hopelessness, the community sang songs of communal lament and despair.

In the middle of lamenting their situation and loss, the singers turned their attention back to God. With their lives in chaos, the exiled community of Judah remembered what their God, Yahweh, could do with chaos: "But my God, my king, is from ancient times, the one working salvation in the midst of the earth. You divided the sea by your might . . ." (74:12-13a). When faced with the smoldering ruins of the temple and of Jerusalem, Yahweh is affirmed as king. This is an important confession since Judah had lost their human king. This royal confession immediately moves the psalmist to celebrate God's creative power.

Genesis 1 has a similar royal view of God: "And God said, 'Let there be a great dome in the middle of the waters, and let it separate waters from waters'" (1:6). Genesis 1 does not give details on the means God uses for creation. Instead the text paints a royal picture of a transcendent, powerful God who can simply speak the universe into existence. Yahweh is king over all creation, and the powerful and unyielding chaos waters are not a problem for Yahweh. By strength in Ps 74 or by word in Gen 1, the seas were divided.

Psalm 74 echoes God's power, but, unlike Gen 1, it provides more exposition of the "how" of God's creation in surprising detail: "You [God] divided the sea by your might. You shattered the head of the dragon in the water. You crushed the head of Leviathan. You gave him as food for the people of the desert" (Ps 74:13-14).

In most contemporary faith depictions, creation is not expressed as a violent act. In Ps 74, however, creation is an act of extreme violence. The dragon and Leviathan have their heads broken, and the Leviathan is ground up for food. Why would the psalm portray creation as a violent act? Perhaps because the surrounding culture believed that "violent contest" was the nature of the creation of the universe. Consider this excerpt from tablet 4 of the Babylonian creation story, the *Enuma Elish*, where the Babylonian god Marduk celebrates his victory over the evil chaos water dragon,

Tiamat.[1] After his victory, Marduk uses her waters as the basis for creation of the universe:

> He split her up like a flat fish into two halves;
> One half of her he established as a covering for heaven.
> He fixed a bolt, he stationed a watchman,
> And bade them not to let her waters come forth.

While Gen 1 does not have an evil chaos dragon explicitly mentioned, it does seem to echo the aftermath of the battle in the *Enuma Elish*.

> And God said, "Let there be a great dome in the middle of the waters, and let it separate waters from waters." So, God made a great dome and separated the waters that were under the dome from the waters that were above it, and it was so. (vv. 6-7)

While not explicitly in Gen 1, chaos dragons and sea monsters do show up in other creation stories in the biblical text. Much like Ps 74, Ps 104 is a creation hymn that celebrates the power of Yahweh. While scholars do not know the precise original setting of the hymn, the text does have some of the same echoes of dragons:

> How many living things you have made, Yahweh!
> All them made with wisdom. The earth is full of your stuff!
> This is the sea! Great, spacious, and wide!
> There are creeping things and so many living things one can't count! Small and Large!
> There, the ships will sail, and the Leviathan that you shaped plays in it!
> (vv. 24-26)

Unlike in Ps 74, the Leviathan in Ps 104 is not scary or evil but celebrated as a creation of Yahweh. Leviathan is created to play in the sea with the other animals. Psalm 104 reminds readers that a watery chaos serpent might be scary to humanity, but Yahweh is not intimidated. In Ps 104, Yahweh is the creator of all things, including Leviathan. Yahweh is so powerful that Leviathan is a mere plaything. Psalm 148 goes even further and encourages the sea monsters to praise Yahweh: "Praise Yahweh

---

1. James B. Pritchard, "The Creation Epic," trans. E. A. Speiser, in *Ancient Near Eastern Texts Relating to the Old Testament (ANET)*, ed. James B. Pritchard, 3rd ed. with supplement (Princeton: Princeton University Press, 1969), 60–72. Hereafter cited as *ANET*.

from the earth, you dragons from the deep!" (v. 7). These are the same "sea monsters" that God created in Gen 1:21 and the same deep mentioned in Gen 1:2: "Now the earth was shapeless and empty. Darkness hung over the chaos waters, but the wind of God blew over the face of the deep."

Genesis 1 has several subtle allusions to the *Enuma Elish* story. The word translated "deep" shares an etymological connection to the name "Tiamat," and it is even in parallel with "sea monsters" in Ps 148:7. The "stormy wind" of Ps 148 and the "wind" or "breath" of God blowing over face of the waters in Gen 1 is also reminiscent of *Enuma Elish*, where Marduk blows an "evil wind" in the face of the watery chaos dragon.

> [Marduk] spread out his net and caught her,
> And the evil wind that was behind him he let loose in her face.
> As Tiamat opened her mouth to its full extent,
> He drove in the evil wind, while as yet she had not shut her lips.

Psalm 104 also connects the waters and the wind at the very beginning of the song: "You furnished the support of your chamber in the waters, and upon it, you made the clouds your chariot and ride on the wings of the wind" (v. 3).

In addition to the wind and waters, creation stories emphasize how the heavens came together as well. Following the defeat of the dragons and the Leviathan in Ps 74, the text reads in verses 16-17, "Truly, to you is the day and night. You established light and the sun. You fixed all the boundaries of the earth. You planned summer and winter." Likewise, in Psalm 104:19-20, we read, "God made the moon for seasons. The sun knows its setting. You make it dark and night comes, and in it, all the living things of the forest come creeping out."

Consider this passage from the *Enuma Elish*. After Tiamat was defeated,

> The stars, their images, as the stars of the Zodiac, he fixed.
> He ordained the year and into sections he divided it;
> . . .
> The Moon-god he caused to shine forth, the night he entrusted to him.
> He appointed him, a being of the night, to determine the days;
> Every month without ceasing with the crown he covered him . . . .

Also consider this passage in Gen 1:14-16, after the waters were divided:

> And God said, "Let there be lights in the dome of the heavens to separate the day from the night and to be signs to indicate seasons and days and years and let them serve as lights in the dome of the heavens to light the earth. And it was so. God made two great lights: the greater light to rule the day and the lesser light to rule the night and the stars."

The biblical text intentionally echoes earlier creation stories. The violent story of creation as expressed in the *Enuma Elish* was the common creation motif throughout the ancient Near East. Different cultures might change the names of the gods and specific details, but the elements in their stories would have been familiar to the general culture and to the biblical authors.

These connections between the biblical text and an older ancient Near Eastern text can make people of faith uncomfortable. It can feel like the Bible plagiarized the story of creation from a pagan source. It is helpful to remember that the authors of the biblical narratives were certainly not the first people to consider the creation of the universe. The authors of the biblical text were products of their culture and naturally took elements of the generally understood creation story and used them when "correcting" that culture's understanding of creation. The biblical stories of creation naturally share the familiar "creation narrative" form:

1. God defeats chaos.
2. God divides waters.
3. God creates sun, moon, and stars.
4. God creates humanity.
5. God rests.

The original author's audience expected these elements. Indeed, the author needed to include them for the story to have any credibility with the audience. An auto race begins, "Drivers, start your engines." A Star Wars film begins, "A long time ago, in a galaxy far, far away." A fairy tale begins, "Once upon a time." In the ancient Near East, a creation story had to include the waters being split. The wind or breath of God needed to play a role. What matters most is not the areas in which these creation stories agree but the theological correctives the biblical narratives offer in their differences. Psalm 74, 104, 148, and Genesis 1 and 2 are telling creation stories by alluding to the familiar stories of the surrounding culture and then *transforming* them as they talk about Yahweh, the God of Israel.

In the Sermon on the Mount in Matthew 5, Jesus spends a great deal of time correcting misunderstandings of the Torah in a series of *antitheses*.

Each of these begins, "You have heard it said . . . but I say unto you . . . ." In many ways the entire biblical text is a series of antitheses, as the Bible offers a different vision for humanity than the typical culturally accepted one. The biblical text could say, "You have heard it said about the flood, but I say . . ." or "You have heard it said about the Tower of Babel, but I say . . ." or "You have heard it said about kingship or wealth or power, but I say . . . ."

Genesis 1 and the other biblical creation stories provide dramatic contrasts to the rest of the ancient Near Eastern world's beliefs. Genesis 1 could easily have started, "You have heard it said that universe was created by the evil salt-water dragon, but I say unto you, a powerful sovereign God with mastery over all the universe simply spoke and the universe came into being." In the *Enuma Elish*, the universe is created as an afterthought—a trophy of war. In Genesis 1, a single god creates for no expressed reason. The God of Israel believed creation was better than "non-creation" and shaped a universe that is called "good" throughout the chapter.

In the same way, Psalm 74 affirms that it was Yahweh, not the Babylonian god Marduk or the Canaanite god El, who crushed the sea monster's heads and broke Leviathan into pieces as part of the creative process. The violent nature of the creative act would be particularly poignant when remembering the occasion of Psalm 74. With the exilic setting of the psalm, it is easy to understand. For Judah to come out of exile required God to work a miraculous, creative act. In the past, Yahweh was able to crush the ancient dragons, split chaos, and bring forth ordered creation. Now, Judah needed Babylon to be crushed, the smoldering chaos of Jerusalem reordered, and a new Israel to come out of exile.

Humanity: Creation and Fall

Psalm 8: A Little Lower than God

In *The Hitchhiker's Guide to the Galaxy*, Douglas Adams jokingly refers to humanity as the third most intelligent life form on earth, right behind dolphins.[2] Humanity rarely shares this opinion. The biblical text offers several opinions on where humanity fits in the hierarchy of the universe. Consider Psalm 8:4-8:

> What are humans that you remember them
> or human beings that you care for them?

---

2. Douglas Adams, *The Hitchhiker's Guide to the Galaxy* (New York: Balantine Books, 1980), 156–67.

> You made them slightly lower than God,
> and crowned them with glory and majesty.
> You have given them dominion over the deeds of your hands.
> You have set everything under their feet
> All of the sheep and cattle, even the beasts of the field.
> The birds of the heavens and the fish of the sea,
> and whatever passes through the currents of the sea.

In Psalm 8, humanity is crowned just lower than God (or the gods, depending on the translation)[3] and made ruler over the rest of creation. All human beings are royalty. This perspective on humanity echoes the royal perspective of humans found in Genesis 1: "And God blessed [humanity] and said to them, 'Be fruitful, multiply, and fill the earth. Subdue it and steward the fish of the sea and the birds of the sky, and over every living thing that moves on the ground'" (1:28).

To "steward" or have "dominion" makes humanity's royal calling explicit in Gen 1. God is ultimately sovereign, but the earth is a fiefdom for humanity to rule under divine supervision. Royal responsibility in the Bible, however, is evaluated differently than one might expect. Historically, most rulers view their positions as having supreme authority. The king gets what the king wants. In the Bible, however, good kings and bad kings are evaluated by how they use kingship and power. If a king uses his authority to improve his own position, he is considered a bad king for the nation (cf. Deut 17:14-20). If the king uses his position and authority to follow God's instruction, he is judged to be a good king for the nation. Needless to say, Israel and Judah had few good kings in their history.

Humanity's stewardship of creation is evaluated with that same understanding of kingship. If humanity wants to be faithful to the calling for which it was created, it cannot rule creation in an exploitive manner. This is made more explicit in the Gen 2 creation narrative: "The God Yahweh took the man and put him in the garden of Eden so that he might serve it and protect it" (2:15). The man in Gen 2 is commanded to serve and protect the garden, not exploit it. Ultimately, humanity's rule of creation should reflect God's rule of all creation. God is not a domineering bully. Humanity should not be either.

---

3. The Hebrew word "Elohim" can be a plural form for "gods" or a singular title for "God." Different translators will understand it differently.

Divine Image

Humanity's rule of this world should look like God's rule because humanity is directly subordinate to God. Humanity, however, has an even more basic reason to reflect God's rule. In Gen 1, humanity is said to be created in the "image of God." Later in the biblical story, the God of Israel is quite restrictive when it comes to images of the divine. In fact, humanity is the only image of God permitted in the world.

Like the Bible, other ancient Near Eastern creation stories connect the origin of humanity directly to the gods. Consider Tablet VI from the *Enuma Elish* where, after vanquishing Tiamat, Marduk says,

> "Blood will I take and bone will I fashion
> I will make man,
> I will create man who shall inhabit the earth"
> . . .
> They bound [Qingu] and held him in front of Ea,
> Imposed on him and cut off his blood.
> He created mankind from his blood,
> Imposed the toil of the gods on man and released the gods from it.

In the *Enuma Elish*, human beings have a special connection to the gods—having been created out of a defeated god's blood. Humanity's role in this story is one of servitude. The gods want to be at ease and impose their service on people. This stands in sharp contrast to the Bible's vision of human creation. The God of Israel rests following creation but only after trusting all of humanity with the rule of creation. To the God of Israel, humans are not servants but royalty.

Once again, the Bible speaks a countercultural message to its audience. In the rest of the ancient Near East, only kings had a royal responsibility. Human beings were merely servants, created to make the life of the gods easier. In Ps 8 and Gen 1, all of humanity is trusted with a royal calling. While the nations around Israel believed only the king bore the image of the divine, the Bible asserts that *all* of humanity, male and female, are made in the image of God. Where the Epilogue of the *Enuma Elish* encouraged humanity to rejoice in Marduk so that Marduk might make the land fruitful, the first words the God of Israel speaks to humanity contain a divine blessing. The God of Israel calls on humanity to be fruitful and fill the earth. Where Marduk has a transactional relationship with humanity—blessing comes as a reward for faithful service—Yahweh's blessing comes as an act of grace.

Genesis 3 and Psalm 104: Hard Workers

Life in the world is hard. Most ancient authorities have no problem explaining why life is so difficult. If the world was made from an evil chaos dragon, how good can one expect life to be? When "chaos" is the starting material, obviously suffering will abound in the world.

The Bible, however, does not accept the premise. Quite the opposite. The biblical text makes clear that when the God of Israel created out of the deep, creation was "good." In fact, in Gen 1:31 all of creation is said to be "very good." Creation was precisely what God intended to create. But if that truly is the case, why is life so hard?

Something changed after humanity's good creation in Gen 1. Psalm 104 reflects a similar change from the optimism of Ps 8. Where Ps 8 uses royal language when discussing humans and celebrates humanity as created just below the divine, Psalm 104 has a more ordinary description of people. After a long celebration of animals, mountains, and celestial bodies, humanity is finally mentioned in two passages:

> [God] You are the one causing grass to grow for cattle
> and plants for people to cultivate—to grow out of the earth.
> Wine to cheer the mind of humans, oil to brighten faces,
> and food to sustain the mind of humans. (vv. 14-15)
> . . .
> People go out to their work to labor until evening. (v. 23)

The royal responsibility of humanity is nowhere to be found in Psalm 104. In Ps 8, humans are created a little lower than God. In Ps 104, humanity is relegated to bringing plants out of the ground, eating and drinking to be made glad, and working and laboring unto evening. What has changed? Why does humanity now have to cultivate plants rather than be "given every plant for food" (Gen 1:30)? Why do humans need cheering up? Where does all this work and labor come from?

The occasion of Ps 104 is likely following the exile of Judah. The psalmist has seen the arrogance and disobedience of the people of God and the suffering it caused. After the exile, the psalmist still wanted to celebrate God as creator. The psalm, however, contains a reminder that while God is king over creation, humanity is simply a part of creation with a role to play like the rest of it.

In Genesis 3, humanity shows the same arrogance and disobedience that led Judah to exile. The idyllic perfection of creation and the garden does not last long in the biblical narrative. God desired to create creatures "after our likeness" in Gen 1:26 and certainly had a plan for how that would happen. Unfortunately, humanity decided that it wanted to "be like God" without consulting the divine. The image no longer wanted to reflect the divine but wanted to define good and evil on its own.

The punishments for disobeying God and consuming the fruit from the Tree of the Knowledge of Good and Evil explain why life can be difficult in this world. They also help make sense of the shift in the view of humanity from Ps 8 to Ps 104. In Gen 3:17b-18, we read that

> the ground is cursed because of you.
> In painful labor you will eat from it all the days of the life.
> it will bring forth thorns and thistles for you
> when you eat the plants of the field.

The behavior of Judah that brought about the exile likely reminded the psalmist of the actions of the first human beings. It might explain why, when speaking of humanity, the psalmist uses words that call to mind the divine punishments in Gen 3: "labor," "work," and "plants for people to bring forth food from the ground."

Biblical scholar James Sanders has said that the canon is self-correcting.[4] In other words, the Bible is good at keeping readers from taking passages out of context if they read all of it. One wonders if listing humanity in Psalm 104 among the rest of nature—just after birds, goats, and young lions and before the sea creatures and Leviathan—is a theological corrective to remind humanity not to misinterpret the "humanity is king" message. Humanity is entrusted with a royal responsibility over this world, but humanity is also part of the rest of creation with the birds, goats, young lions, and even Leviathan.

The strong anthropocentric view of creation in Ps 8 has been replaced by a more ecocentric view. Humanity is another group of creatures that must rely on God for sustenance. Psalm 104 comes from an occasion that remembers Israel and Judah's kingship as exploitive and self-centered. As a

---

4. James A. Sanders, *From Sacred Story to Sacred Text* (Philadelphia: Fortress, 1987), 7.

result, God sent them into exile. Genesis 3 remembers that the man and woman's plans were self-centered, and God exiled them from the garden.

HUMAN CREATIVITY AND THE IMAGE OF GOD

Psalm 33 and the Line of Cain

The Hebrew word translated "create" in Gen 1 is *bara'* (ברא). The word is only used with God as the subject, suggesting that *bara'* represents a type of creating only God can do. That word for creation, however, only occurs three times in Gen 1. The more common word for what God does in creation is the word *'asa* (עשׂה), which is often translated "made" or "work." This word is often used when talking about creation outside of Genesis. In Ps 33, "By the word of Yahweh, the heavens were made (*'asa*), and all their company by the wind of the divine mouth" (v. 6). In Ps 19, the heavens tell of God's deeds (*'asa*): "The heavens recount the glory of God, and the sky proclaims God's deeds (*'asa*)" (v. 1). In Ps 8:3, the sky is the work (*'asa*) of God's fingers: "When I see your heavens and the works (*'asa*) of your fingers —the moon and the stars that you have established . . . ."

God has created humanity with this creative ability as well. While only God can *bara'*, both humanity and God can *'asa*. Indeed, after celebrating what God has made in Ps 33, the psalmist moves on to humans: "[God] who forms together their minds also observes their deeds (*'asa*)" (v. 15). After fashioning humanity, God observes all their "deeds"—the same Hebrew word used of God's creative acts in Pss 8 and 19. Psalm 90 also reflects this same kind of creative ability in human beings. The psalmist in Ps 90 prays for God to prosper their creative efforts, the work of their hands: "May the favor of our Sovereign God be upon us. Establish the work of our hands for us! Establish the work of our hands!" (v. 17). Clearly, bearing God's image comes with a creative dimension. Perhaps humanity cannot create in the same way God "created" the heavens and earth. Humanity, however, does have the capacity to "make," "work," and "form." In fact, Ps 33 reminds the reader that God observes humanity's "deeds" or "works."

Humanity's creative impulse is on display in the genealogy of Cain. Consider Gen 4:17, 20-22:

> Cain knew his wife and she conceived and bore Enoch; and Cain built a city and named it "Enoch" after his son. . . . Adah bore Jabal who was the ancestor of people who live in tents and keep livestock. And his brother's name was Jubal who was the ancestor of everyone who plays the harp and flute. And Zillah had children as well: Tubal-Cain who

forged all sorts of tools made from bronze and iron. Tubal-Cain's sister was Naamah.

Cities, domesticated animals, music, and metalworking—the biblical text makes clear that all the makings of civilization were created by human beings. Cain is certainly not the hero of the story in Gen 4, but he and his line still reflect the creative impulse latent within the image bearers of God—even those whose lives are stained by sinful acts.

The Apkallu

Like the creation narratives, the biblical authors in Gen 4 are again correcting beliefs that are generally accepted in the surrounding culture. Many of those cultures believed in semi-divine creatures, commonly called "Apkallu," who were responsible for providing culture in the world.[5]

Assyrian art depicts the Apkallu with human, bird, or fish heads. They do the work of the gods in the world as messengers of the gods and advisers to the kings. Most ancient Near Eastern cultures believed the gods provided the forms of civilization—art, music, metalworking—to the Apkallu, and the Apkallu provided those aspects of culture to the kings. In other words, the wonders of culture are only available to those on whom the gods choose to show favor. Once the gods' kindness had been earned and patience had been bought, the gods provided the leaders of society the benefits of culture. The commoner would have to hope that, eventually, the benefits might trickle down.

Genesis 1 would have already confounded the ancient society's expectations of humanity by claiming that every human being bears God's image and has a royal calling to creation. That countercultural, prophetic message continues in Gen 4 with a radical, challenging, and beautiful word about humanity. The rest of the ancient Near East believed that civilization could only be established through strict obedience to the divinely appointed king and a god who *might* be inclined to look on humanity favorably. The Bible responds in the genealogy of Gen 4, and it makes clear that the gods do not give humanity culture, and the Apkallu do not deliver it. No one is withholding gifts from humans until their ego is satisfied. The God of Israel does not ration blessings, dribbling them out as humans earn favor with

---

5. For a more complete discussion of the Apkallu, cf. *Dictionary of Deities and Demons in the Bible* by Karel van der Toorn, Bob Becking, Pieter Willem van der Horst (2nd rev. ed.; Boston: Brill, 1998).

obedience. God shows grace from the beginning. God trusts humans with the working and protecting of this world. God gives all of humanity the divine image, and Gen 4 makes it clear that part of what the divine image grants is creativity.

Even more surprising, this empowering message regarding humanity comes from the genealogy of Cain. Even though Cain committed the first murder out of frustration with his own inadequacies, his genealogical line is the one that provides humanity culture. Historically, interpreters have struggled with this passage. Is music evil since it came from Cain's line? Is tentmaking a problem? Are cities bad? Is metalworking evil?

It seems clear that the Bible does not believe any of these things to be irredeemably evil. The apostle Paul was a tentmaker. Jesus and the disciples sang before leaving the last supper. In Revelation, heaven is depicted as a holy city. In other words, the ultimate destination of humanity is a redeemed picture of a human contribution to the world. Rather than a caution about the evil designs of Cain's line, this passage is more likely a sign of the powerful and far-reaching grace of God. Not even the selfish act of Cain and his fallen line could suppress the creative power of the image of God. God's image is still present in sinful humanity, and even fallen human beings can add substantively and creatively to the culture of the world.

While the rest of the ancient Near Eastern gods control and provide humanity with what they decide humanity should have, Ps 33 says that Yahweh "observes humanity's deeds." Where the ancient Near Eastern gods provide humanity with finished products, the God of Israel provides humanity with palette and paints and observes what humans will make. The gods of the ancient Near East want servants. Yahweh desires co-creators who shepherd this world.

Flood

Every culture in the ancient Near East told a story of a cataclysmic flood. It seemed to be part of the shared cultural memory. Curiously, as pervasive as the story of a global flood is outside the Bible, not much about it is discussed in the Bible outside of Gen 6–9. The flood story more commonly appears as subtle mentions throughout the texts. Like a composer subtly returning to themes later in a composition, the flood appears in allusions throughout the biblical text following its exposition in Genesis.

"Floods" of water are mentioned in several psalms. However, the word explicitly used for the global flood in Gen 6–9 occurs only once in Ps 29:10. Here it is used to celebrate God's sovereign relationship to creation:

"Yahweh sits upon the flood, Yahweh sits as king forever." The flood is associated with God's reign over creation. This is consistent with the Genesis narrative where the flood was a result of humanity's rejection of God's instruction.

More often, however, "flood" is only referenced in allusion. In Ps 18:13-15, the psalmist celebrates God's deliverance from a desperate situation using language that calls to mind the cataclysmic flood:

> Yahweh thundered in the heavens,
> and the Most High's voice spoke.
> Sending out arrows and scattering them
> and tremendous amounts of lightning and routing them.
> The bottom of the sea was seen
> and the foundations of the world were uncovered
> at your chastisement, O Yahweh,
> from the breath of your nose.

Psalm 88 uses images of flood in desperation. The psalmist is frustrated with God's lack of response to his repeated requests. He uses flood imagery to talk about God's wrath: "Your wrath has swept over and against me. Your terrors are ending me. Every day they sound me like water, altogether surrounding me" (vv. 16-17). Psalm 104:5-9, however, may contain a more explicit allusion to the flood in Gen 6–9:

> You laid the earth on its foundations,
> so that it will never shake
> You covered it with the deep like a cloak,
> so that the waters stood above the mountains
> The waters withdrew from your rebuke,
> at the thunder of your voice, they hurried away!
> The mountains rose up,
> and the waters went down the valley to the place you established for them.
> You set a boundary for them to not cross,
> and never return to cover the earth.

These verses are reminiscent of the global flood in Genesis. Though, as seen already, Ps 104 is a creation hymn. Rather than a discussion of flood, these verses could be interpreted as a poetic expression of the chaos waters in creation, which would be in keeping with the context of the rest of Ps 104. Is it flood? Is it early creation?

One difficulty in sorting out an interpretation is that the flood narrative itself is a creation story, or rather an un-creation story. Genesis 6–9 intentionally alludes to creation to show God un-creating. In Gen 1, God divides the waters. In the flood narratives, God allows the "waters above" to rejoin the waters below and "reboot" creation. God has decided to follow the classic bit of advice concerning technology: "Have you tried turning it off and back on again?" Creation has gone wrong, and the flood story is God starting over.

God is neither happy about nor eager for the reboot. Unlike other ancient Near Eastern deities, Yahweh is compassionate and patient. Much like in Ps 78:38-39, the flood narratives demonstrate Yahweh's longsuffering nature:

> God, being compassionate, forgives their iniquity,
> and does not destroy.
> Repeatedly restraining the divine anger,
> and not releasing all the divine wrath
> God remembered that they were flesh—
> a breath that passes and does not return.

Compare Yahweh's patience with Israel to the gods in *Atrahasis Epic*,[6] another ancient Near Eastern flood narrative:

> The god was disturbed by [humanity's] uproar.
> Enlil heard their clamor.
> (And) said to the great gods:
> "Oppressive has become the clamor of mankind.
> By their uproar they prevent sleep."

Humanity's noise was such a problem that Enlil tried an embargo (from the gods), plague, and drought to keep the noise down. When those plans failed, Enlil demanded the gods flood the earth so the gods could concentrate. Humanity was saved due to the unauthorized intervention of a god who warned Atrahasis of the coming cataclysm.

Another ancient epic, the *Gilgamesh Epic*, also contains a flood story that predates the biblical narrative. No explicit reason for the flood is

---

6. Pritchard, "Atrahasis," *ANET*, 104–106.

expressed in the Gilgamesh story; however, both the *Atrahasis Epic* and *Gilgamesh* end their flood narratives with the gods' desire to control the human population. This might imply that noise was the problem in the Gilgamesh story as well.

In this world of capricious and easily distracted gods, the Bible again offers a corrective when thinking about the flood. The biblical narrative is not trying to "prove" the flood. A universal flood was part of the cultural understanding throughout the ancient Near East. The biblical authors were saying, "When you think of the flood, think of it this way," in much the same way they did with the creation narrative.

In some ways, a polytheistic faith has an easier time explaining a calamity like a global flood. First, a malicious god can try to destroy the earth, and then a merciful god can save humanity. A monotheist, however, needs to explain how the god who brings the flood is the same god who saves the people.

The Bible diverges from the other ancient flood narratives by first changing the motives for the destruction of humanity. Yahweh's response is significantly different from the gods of Israel's surrounding culture. Where other ancient authorities tell of gods who are willing to destroy all of humanity because they cannot sleep or want to keep the population down, the Bible shows a god who is grieved that the situation has come to this.

> Yahweh saw the way the destructive acts of humans multiplied in the earth. Every inclination of their thoughts was only destructive every day. Yahweh regretted that humanity had been created on the earth and God grieved deeply. So, Yahweh said, "I will wipe out humanity, whom I have created, from the face of the ground—from humans to animals—from things that crawl to birds of the sky—because I regret that I made them." (Gen 6:5-7).

Humanity's immoral actions, not its noise, are so pervasive that God wishes creation would unmake itself.

The story in Genesis is similar to the trouble the divine has with Israel later in history: "How much [Israel] rebelled in the desert wilderness! They grieved God in the desert. They repeatedly tested God, and provoked the Holy One of Israel" (Ps 78:40-41). Like ancient Israel in the wilderness, all of humanity in Gen 6 has been testing God again and again. In fact, one specific provocation is discussed in one of the most enigmatic passages in the Old Testament.

> When human beings began to multiply on the face of the earth, daughters were born to them. When the divine beings saw the daughters of humans were beautiful, they took them as wives for themselves, whoever they chose. Yahweh said, "My spirit will not contend with humans forever since they are flesh. Their days will be one hundred and twenty years." The Nephilim were on the earth in those days and also after this. The divine beings came to the daughters of humans and they bore children to them. These were the mighty warriors from old. Warriors of fame. (Gen 6:1-4)

While the original audience might have known exactly what is meant by the term "Nephilim," subsequent interpreters are at a loss. The word occurs twice in the Hebrew Bible—once in Gen 6 and once in Num 13, when the unfaithful spies were likely invoking this story to frighten the people of Israel out of obeying Yahweh and taking the land of Canaan. The exact historical occasion referred to in this passage is unknown and likely unknowable. Some interpreters wonder if this passage and the Nephilim might somehow be connected to the Apkallu mentioned earlier, though what exactly the text is trying to say about them has likely been lost to history.

While the precise circumstances behind the passage are uncertain, the narrative function is clear. Human immorality is beginning to break down the barriers between human and divine. Wickedness is a cancer spreading through creation, and Yahweh needs to respond. The divine is under attack, and in many ways, the biblical account of the flood can be read as self-defense. In the midst of disobedience and sin, however, faith is found. Noah finds favor with God and is delivered, much like the psalmist in Ps 18:16: "God stretched out from on high and took me. God pulled me out of the mighty waters." By following Yahweh's instruction, Noah's family survived.

After the flood, God promises Noah never again to destroy the world by flood. This covenant is not a promise to be more creative in future punishments. It is a statement about Yahweh's commitment to creation. The flood was un-creation, and God resolved never to "un-create" again. God will not give up on humanity. Human beings do not have to live with the Sword of Damocles lingering over their heads—worried that the wrong action or wong word will cause God to abandon humanity and consign it to oblivion.

This is another contrast to the ancient Near Eastern stories. The other gods also promise not to flood the world, but they actually do decide to be more creative in their future punishments. Their primary desire seems to be to control human population. In tablet XI of *Gilgamesh*,[7] the gods promise never again to flood the earth. Rather, they promise,

> Instead of your bringing on the deluge, Would that a lion had risen up to diminish mankind!
> Instead of your bringing on the deluge, Would that a wolf had risen up to diminish mankind!
> Instead of your bringing on the deluge, Would that a famine had risen up to diminish mankind!
> Instead of your bringing on the deluge, Would that a pestilence had risen up to diminish mankind!

The God of Israel subverts cultural expectations again and does not desire to control human population. In fact, Yahweh blesses Noah and his family, showing the opposite concern in a direct connection to the first creation story in Gen 1 and in a direct refutation of the surrounding culture: "God blessed Noah and his sons and said to them, "Be fruitful, multiply, and fill the earth" (Gen 9:1). Humanity gets another chance, and it is clear that Yahweh is not going to give up on the relationship.

Tower

Much like the "flood," the Tower of Babel is not explicitly referenced in Psalms. The human pride and disobedience that led to the tower, however, are discussed often in the psalms. Unfortunately, they seem to be a common theme.

Throughout the Old Testament text, names give insight into character. If you know someone's name, you have insight into their character. The people in Gen 11 do not want God to define their character; rather, in verse 4, they want to "make a name for themselves." Humanity is supposed to be created in the image of God and reflect God's character—God's name. The psalmist recognizes the danger of wandering from the name of God and pursuing other gods to define character: "Whoever runs after another god multiplies their sorrow. I will never pour out their drink offerings of blood. I will never take their names on my lips" (Ps 16:4). The psalmist also recognizes that only God should define human character: "Yahweh is my chosen portion and my cup. You hold my fate" (Ps 16:5).

---

7. "The Epic of Gilgamesh," *ANET*, 95.

As discussed previously, one of the poetic features of the psalms is known as parallelism. Throughout the psalms, God's "name" is in synonymous parallel with "righteousness" (Pss 7:17; 89:16; 143:11), "glory" (8:1; 29:2; 66:2; 102:15), "good" (52:9; 54:6), "might" (54:1), "steadfast love" (109:21; 115:1; 138:2), "faithfulness" (115:1; 138:2), "help" (124:8), "creator" (124:8), and "gracious" (135:3). Obviously, God's name reflects quite a range of characteristics. These are the characteristics humanity was created to reflect by bearing God's image.

Unfortunately, humanity in Gen 11 has no desire to reflect the divine character. They have decided to go their own way: "And they said, 'Come, let us build a city for ourselves, and a tower with its top to the heavens. We will make a name for ourselves. Otherwise, we will be scattered over the face of the whole earth'" (v. 4). God has expressed a desire for humanity to "fill the earth." Apparently, humanity is not interested in that job. They have decided to settle in one place, define their own character, and attack God. The attack is implied by the height of the tower. The word for "heavens" is the same as in Gen 1:1 and implies that this tower will reach to the very edge of creation—right to the front door of God.

Humanity does not quite achieve those lofty goals, however. In fact, the Bible injects some humor in the story by implying that, although humans were going to build this tower to the edge of creation, God could not even see it: "Then Yahweh came down to see the city and the tower which humans had built" (Gen 11:5). God then puts humanity back on track to accomplish their divine calling to fill the earth, scattering them "from there over the face of the whole earth. So they stopped building the city" (11:8).

The Bible is again making a countercultural statement about what the surrounding culture believed. This story does seem to make a general statement about the common architectural feature of Babylon known as a ziggurat. These pyramid-like structures were often temples with dwelling places for the gods. It is also possible the Bible is more targeted in its critique. Consider this passage from the *Enuma Elish*:[8]

> The Anunnaki [lesser gods] opened their mouths and said to Marduk, their lord,
> "Now, O lord, thou who hast caused our deliverance,
> What shall be our homage to thee?
> Let us build a shrine whose name shall be called 'lo, a chamber for our nightly rest'; let us repose in it!

---

8. "The Creation Epic," *ANET*, 68.

> Let us build a throne, a recess for his abode! On that day that we arrive we shall repose in it."
> When Marduk heard this, Bright glowed his features, like the day:
> "Construct Babylon, whose building you have requested, Let its brickwork be fashioned.
> You shall name it 'The Sanctuary.'" The Anunnaki applied the implement;
> For one whole year they molded bricks.
> When the second year arrived,
> They raised high the head of Esagila equaling Apsu.
> Having built a state-tower as high as Apsu,
> They set up in it an abode for Marduk, Enlil, and Ea.

In the *Enuma Elish*, a tower with molded bricks is specifically mentioned as a dwelling place for the gods to rest now that creation is finished. The lower gods are celebrated by Marduk for this wonderful tower. While Marduk might enjoy this fixed dwelling, Yahweh does not. In fact, the tower in the biblical narrative is a direct assault on God and a rejection of God's calling for humanity to live into the divine character.

Conclusion

The Bible begins with images familiar to an ancient Near Eastern audience. Creation, the Great Flood, and the Tower would have been stories present within the popular consciousness of most ancient Near Eastern cultures. The Bible borrows these familiar concepts but offers correctives:

- "You have heard it said that a god created the universe after a battle and made people to be servants, but I say God created all of humanity in the divine image, with a royal responsibility, and all that God created was good."
- "You have heard it said that humanity is merely a servant of the king, reliant on the benefice of the gods for culture, but I say God created humanity with an ability, responsibility, and desire to create."
- "You have heard it said that an angry god flooded the earth due to humanity's noise, but I say God expressed sorrow at flooding the earth due to humanity's sin."
- "You have heard it said that the Tower in Babylon was celebrated, but I say it was an act of selfishness and defiance, and God took appropriate action."

Each of the stories uses elements from the traditions an ancient audience would have heard and recognized. Throughout the Near East, it was generally understood that creation came from the gods' organization of chaotic waters. Often a god's ultimate kingship over the other deities and the creation of the earth was the result when the hero god of the pantheon battled the evil god of the chaos waters.

Of all the classic stories, creation is what the psalms want to sing about. The psalms continue the Bible's different vision for the world, a world created "good" by a single God. That God, whom we discover in Gen 2 is named "Yahweh," created all of humanity in the divine image. Human beings serve and protect this creation, ruling over it as God rules over the universe. This God is merciful and longsuffering and has promised never to give up on a relationship with humanity. As a result of humanity's choices, however, God will change tactics in how that relationship is worked out in Gen 12.

Questions for Further Discussion

1. What does the fact that stories within the Bible are similar to, but predated by, other Near Eastern stories mean for the inspiration of the text?

2. In the flood narrative God "repents" that humankind was created by the divine. In the story of Cain and Abel, God encourages Cain to "choose what is right." From these and other passages in the Primeval History, what implications might one draw concerning the character of God?

3. Human beings often think a lot of themselves. What does the Bible's shifting perspective toward humans mean? After all of humanity's failures, why does God continue to trust them?

4. With the biblical understanding of "dominion" connected to "service" and "protection," what are the implications for humanity's responsibility to the world? For ecology? For humanity's relationship to one another?

5. How does the creative image of God work in contemporary vocations—beyond full-time ministry jobs?

Ancestors

> *"Fredo, you're my older brother, and I love you. But don't ever take sides with anyone against the family again. Ever."*
> —Michael Corleone, *The Godfather*

Psalms and the Ancestral Identity

The stories of Abraham, Isaac, and Jacob are not developed any further outside the book of Genesis. The names of the ancestors occur outside Genesis, but they are simply referenced in positive ways, appealing to the heroic and righteous understandings a reader might associate with them. They say that the secret to playing jazz well is knowing which notes not to play. Perhaps truth can be found in seeing what stories the psalms choose not to tell. That certainly provides interpretive possibilities when it comes to the ancestors.

"Abraham" is only mentioned four times in the psalms, and three of the references are in Psalm 105. Where Ps 104 focuses on Yahweh's creation of the cosmos, Ps 105 is a postexilic psalm that focuses on Yahweh's creation of a chosen people. The psalm is a historical survey of the people of Israel's journey from Abraham to Exodus with an overall emphasis on Yahweh's repeated faithfulness.

Even with the paucity of references, the ancestor stories provided identity for Israel. The strong tribal connection to identity provides the context for the biblical narratives. While twenty-first-century American society is always on the move, the first hearers of the biblical story were likely shocked that seventy-five-year-old Abram left the land of his father at the command of Yahweh.

In Genesis 12, God told Abram to go, and Abram went. The authority with which Yahweh spoke was certainly different than that of the local gods of the time, which more often reinforced cultural norms and understandings. Yahweh's authority was analogous to the authority Jesus displayed in the call of the disciples. In Matthew 4, when Jesus saw two men working in their family's fishing business and called them to follow, they left. No doubt the first hearers of the gospel story were shocked! Jesus conveyed such strong authority that individuals put aside the purpose and identity associated with family to follow him.

Though Abram defied his own tribal obligations in answering the call of Yahweh, the concept of tribal identity is still present throughout the story of the ancient Hebrews. The people of Israel identified themselves as exactly that—a group of people descended from a person whose name was changed from "Jacob" to "Israel." They sing about that tribal identity in Ps 22: "Everyone who fears Yahweh, praise God! All the descendants of Jacob, honor God! Every generation of Israel, stand in awe before God!" (v. 23). The ancient Hebrews wanted to remember "their people" in their songs and stories; however, some fascinating differences are apparent between the way Israel sang about their ancestors in the psalms and the way they told their stories in Genesis.

Tribal Identity

When I proposed to my wife, her family was not immediately supportive. I was from the Midwest, not Mississippi. Her mother objected, "We don't know his people!" In my mother-in-law's mind, my identity was tied to "my people." Did I come from alcoholics? Hard workers? Shiftless nobodies? She firmly believed if you knew "my people," then you would know me. Since she did not, she could not know what kind of person I was. It was not enough to meet me and talk to me. She wanted my wife to marry into a family where she would know "his people."

While my mother-in-law's reaction to me might be typical for parts of the American South, more often in contemporary culture, identity is more individualistic. It is something that one makes for themselves, not something tied to family or ancestors.

Identity in the ancient Near East, however, looked more like my mother-in-law's vision or the unquestioned loyalty to family in the film *The Godfather*. Family and tribe provided the window through which individuals were understood. An individual's first loyalty was always to the family and tribe. Tribal identities could be associated with geographical regions, but even nomadic groups understood identity through family and tribe. Familial allegiance could result in required participation in tribal disputes and even blood feuds.

The Covenant of Abraham

In Ps 105, Abraham is remembered as the bearer of the covenant. While the psalm focuses primarily on Yahweh faithfully bringing about these events, it uses a couple of unusual titles for the patriarchs: "[Yahweh] allowed no one to oppress them; [God] rebuked kings on their account, saying, 'Do not touch my anointed ones; do my prophets no harm'" (Ps 105:14-15). In Gen 20:7, Abraham is called a "prophet" by God in God's warning to Abimelech. In this psalm, however, all three patriarchs merit that title. (This also happens in 1 Chr 16:23, which quotes this psalm.) All three ancestors are also called God's "anointed ones," or *masiach*—the Hebrew root word for "Messiah." (The Greek translates *masiach* as "Christ." So, for example, to confess "Jesus Christ" is to confess "Jesus is the Messiah.") Clearly, the psalm has a wholly positive assessment of the patriarchs. They are superheroes of faith: ancestors of a chosen people, bearers of a divine covenant, prophets and messiahs.

The narrative of Genesis, however, tells a different story. Abraham does believe Yahweh's promises and is credited with righteousness, but he also has struggles of faith. Jacob's name can be translated in English as "con artist" or "manipulator," and even when his name is changed to "Israel," the etymology suggests that the new name means "one who strives or struggles with God." While the psalms portray the ancestors as superheroes, in the Genesis narrative a reader might struggle to understand how these flawed human beings could be the ones through whom God will work out the promise.

Yahweh's Covenant

After the failure of humanity at large in Gen 1–11, Yahweh decides to take a different approach. Rather than interacting with all of humanity at once, Yahweh decides to set apart a people who will build the bridge to bring the rest of humanity into relationship with Yahweh again. When the psalm remembers this event, all three patriarchs are recalled as the means through which Yahweh brought the covenant with Israel:

> God remembers the covenant and the things God commanded forever—
> for a thousand generations! God established the covenant God made
> with Abraham and the promise sworn to Isaac for Jacob as a statute for
> Israel as an everlasting covenant. (Ps 105:8-10)

The psalm remembers the covenant of the land of Canaan that Yahweh promised to the ancestors, saying, "To you I will give the land of Canaan as your portion for an inheritance" (v. 11). No doubt, the original exilic audience of Ps 105 desperately needed to hear these words as an encouragement in a time when they were without the land.

In addition to a specific promise of land, Yahweh made and confirmed several covenants in the stories of the ancestors. The psalmist's reference to "covenant" would likely call the original audience's attention back to all the promises Yahweh made to the ancestors. The first, then, came to Abram in Gen 12:

> Yahweh said to Abram, "Go from your land and from your relatives and from your father's house to a land that I will show you. And I will make you into a great nation. And I will bless you and I will make your name great, so that it will be a blessing. I will bless whoever blesses you, and I will curse whoever curses you. And all the families of the earth will find blessing by you." (vv. 1-3)

A few chapters later in Gen 15, the Gen 12 covenant is reaffirmed and given more specific details by Yahweh. Ten years passed in those chapters, and Abram had not seen an answer to the divine promise. When Abram asked Yahweh if his trusted servant Eliezer would inherit his wealth and the responsibility of the promise, Yahweh assured him that adoption was not the way the promise would be fulfilled.

> But suddenly the word of Yahweh came to him saying, "This one will not inherit, but instead, one who comes out from your own body will inherit." And [God] proceeded to bring him outside and said, "Look now toward the heavens and count the stars, if you are able to count them." And God said to him, "So will your descendants be." (Gen 15:4-5)

"Comes out from your own body" is Yahweh's not so delicate way of making it clear to Abram that he will biologically father a child. Though an accepted practice in the ancient Near East when a childless couple needed an heir, God would not use adoption as the means to manifest the promise. After this assurance, Yahweh orders Abram to

> And God said to him, "Bring me a heifer, goat, and ram, each three years old, a turtle dove and a young pigeon." And he took all of these and cut

them in two (though he didn't cut the birds in two). Then he set each half of the animals to sit opposite and correspond to each other. When the birds of prey came down upon the carcasses, Abram shooed them away. (Gen 15:9-11)

Though most English translations say that covenants are "made," the Hebrew uses the verb "to cut" when forming covenants. Covenants may have been "cut" because of the actions that occur during a covenant ceremony. When forming this covenant, animals are literally cut in half with the halves arranged facing one another. The party responsible for fulfilling the agreement passes between the animal halves as a way of sealing the covenant. The implication seems to be, "If I don't fulfill my part of the promise, let what happened to these animals happen to me." Gen 15:17-18a says, "When the sun set and it was dark, suddenly a smoking pot and a flaming torch passed between the pieces. On that day, Yahweh made a covenant with Abram . . . ."

In Gen 15, the text implies that Yahweh is the one passing between the animals. In other words, this ceremony assures Abram that Yahweh is the one who bears the responsibility of fulfilling the promise. In Gen 12, when Abram is seventy-five years old, God calls him to leave his family land and obligations, and without hesitation or question, Abram leaves. Ten years later with no visible answer to the promise, Abram has questions and needs more assurance that the promises of God will happen. Yahweh provides that assurance in the form of this covenant ceremony.

The most detailed expression of the covenant of Abraham over a decade after Gen 15 appears in Gen 17:1-8:

When Abram was ninety-nine years-old, Yahweh appeared to him and said, "I am God Almighty. Walk before me and be blameless and I will set my covenant between me and your offspring and I will make you exceedingly numerous." Then Abram fell on his face. God said to him, "Behold, for my part, this is my covenant with you: You will be the ancestor of a multitude of nations. Your name will no longer be 'Abram' but behold, your name is 'Abraham' because I have caused you to be the ancestor of a multitude of nations. I will cause you to be exceedingly and exceptionally fruitful. I will cause nations and kings to come from you. I will establish my covenant between me, you, and between your descendants after you for generations—to be an everlasting covenant—to be your God and your descendants' God after you. And I will give to you and to your descendants after you the land that you are wandering in and all the land of Canaan to be a permanent possession. And I will be their God.

This celebration of the covenant comes twenty-four years after Abram's initial call. Yahweh changes Abram's name from the ironic "Exalted Father" to "Abraham," which means "Father of Many." Abraham's wife Sarai also has her named changed to Sarah, though unfortunately, the nuance of the meaning change in her name is unclear.

The Genesis 17 expression of the covenant also requests a response from Abraham and his successive generations. In Gen 12 and 15, it seems that God's promises come without condition. In Gen 17, however, Yahweh asks Abraham to demonstrate his participation in the covenant with the sign of circumcision. Because of the ancient Near Eastern understanding of tribal identity, Abraham's tribe's participation in the sign of circumcision would reflect Abraham's commitment as well. Circumcision is an outward symbol of covenant identity and a tangible marker of faith. It makes clear who is part of the covenant and serves as a further act of faith for Abraham, considering what God will ask next of Abraham and circumcision's potential effect on Abraham's fertility.

God also assures Abraham in Gen 17 that he is not finished with his biological responsibilities. God tells Abraham that all these benefits of the covenant will come from the biological child of he and Sarah. Upon hearing that his post-menopausal wife will get pregnant, Abraham laughs (mirroring Sarah's response later) and offers a compromise to God in verse 18: "Abraham said to God, 'O, let Ishmael live before you!'" God promises to bless the child of Hagar but again makes clear to Abraham that he and Sarah will be parents, and that child—whose name will be "laughter," or Isaac, in honor of their response—will be the one who carries the promise.

Omissions from the Psalms: Hagar

Certainly, Abraham shows faith in his encounters with the divine. In Gen 17, when faced with the laughable idea of two senior adults having a baby, he is obedient in all the commands God gives him. It is logical to understand why the psalms celebrate this faithful ancestor as a prophet specially anointed by God.

Conspicuously absent in the psalms (and elsewhere in the Hebrew Bible), however, is any discussion of the struggles Abraham had in his journey of faith. His sojourn into Egypt in Gen 12:10-20 is missing from the psalms. The text does not make clear if God supported this attempt to avoid a drought in the new land Yahweh led him to. While in Egypt, Abraham lied about his relationship with his wife to save his life. When God intervened to punish Pharaoh for wanting Sarai for a wife, Abraham left Egypt a wealthier man than he entered. This sojourn in Egypt is likely where Abram's wife acquired an Egyptian servant who played an important role in another neglected part of the story, Hagar.

Though "Abram believed Yahweh" in Gen 15, the elaborate covenant ceremony was apparently not enough for Abram and Sarai to trust Yahweh to carry out the promise without help. Immediately following the covenant scene in Gen 15, Sarai decides to help God achieve this promise of a biological son. Abram and Sarai have been dealing with childlessness for years, so they turn their attention to a culturally acceptable practice, assuming Yahweh will use this to fulfill the promise.

In an agrarian society with no retirement plans, children were necessary for labor and security in old age. Within ancient Near Eastern culture, marriages were more about progeny than affection, and marriage contracts commonly contained provisions for acquiring heirs if a couple struggled with infertility.[1] Sometimes a surrogate was designated, often a handmaiden. After an agreed-on period of childlessness, the husband could have sex with the surrogate. If the surrogate became pregnant, the child from that relationship was legally understood as the primary heir of the husband. After learning of God's promise that Abram will biologically father a child, Sarai assumes that God must mean this sort of arrangement since she is past the age to conceive and forces her Egyptian servant, Hagar, to serve as a surrogate wife for Abram.

When Hagar becomes pregnant, it appears that God's promise to Abram is answered. In this patriarchal society, a woman's status was connected to her ability to bring forth children, and in this way, Hagar has now surpassed Sarai. Sarai struggles to deal with Hagar's elevated position, and her insecurity provokes Sarai to violate cultural convention and expel Hagar from the camp.[2] Though the promise of a biological heir seems to be fulfilled, the promise of God and societal expectation is not as compelling

---

1. One classic example of this practice is found in texts from an ancient city known as "Nuzi." The texts date from a later period than the one associated with the ancestors but could demonstrate that the practice existed within the culture. See "Real Adoption," *ANET*, 220.

2. The ancient Near Eastern texts specifically forbid the first wife from sending the offspring of this surrogate relationship away. The first audience of this text was likely shocked by Sarai's violation of social convention.

as the insecurity of his wife, and Abram allows Hagar's exile and certain death in the desert.

Although it was culturally scandalous, close readers might expect the exile of Hagar. God made clear to Abram in Gen 15 that it was the divine's responsibility to fulfill the promise. God even went so far as to pass between the slain animals to unambiguously make this point. Abram, however, interpreted this promise through his own cultural eyes and decided Sarai was correct to use the means at their disposal to "help God along" in fulfilling the promise. The Hagar episode seems to fall outside God's plan for establishing a chosen people (a fact that God confirms in Gen 17). Hagar is not mentioned in the psalms or in any other text outside of Genesis in the Hebrew Bible. The reader could easily dismiss her as an innocent victim—another unfortunate, marginalized woman in the ancient world who fell prey to those in positions more powerful than hers.

Throughout the Bible, however, Yahweh consistently cares for the rejected and outcast and brings judgment on all who do not do the same. In Ps 82:1-4, God reveals the expectation of the divine:

> God stands in the divine assembly.
> In the midst of the gods, God brings just rulings.
> How long will you offer judgments
> drunk up by your favorites that only honor the wicked?
> Offer true justice to the weak and the fatherless.
> Vindicate the oppressed and the poor.
> Secure the weak
> and deliver the needy from the hand of the wicked!

In Ps 82 the reader discovers what God expects of humanity because it is what God expects from the divine.[3]

Once again, the Bible shows that the character of God is defined by grace, and Yahweh surprises the reader and intercedes on Hagar's behalf. Though Hagar and her soon-to-be-born son, Ishmael, are not part of the covenant plan, God refuses to abandon them the way Abram and Sarai have. God meets Hagar in the desert and provides for her. In Gen 16:10, Hagar is given an honor only given to the men in the ancestor stories; she

---

3. For an interesting reading on Ps 82 and its definition of divine character, see J. Clinton McCann, "The Single Most Important Text in the Entire Bible: Toward a Theology of the Psalms," in *Soundings in the Theology of the Psalms: Perspectives and Methods in Contemporary Scholarship*, ed. Rolf Jacobson (Minneapolis: Fortress, 2011), 63–75.

is given an ancestral promise: "The messenger of Yahweh said to her, 'I will so dramatically increase your descendants it will be impossible to count them.'" Her offspring may not be the means through which Yahweh will work out the covenant, but she will be blessed. In addition to the ancestral honor, Hagar—the lowly Egyptian slave woman—is the only person in the Bible who gives God a name. Because of Yahweh's provision for her, Hagar names God "El-Roi," which is translated as "God sees" or "God provides."[4]

Once this encounter in the wilderness has taken place, Yahweh curiously asks Hagar to return to her abusive mistress. Several interpreters have struggled with this request by Yahweh.[5] Why would God return this woman to her abusers? Isn't this an act of cruelty? God, however, may be working within the cultural expectations that Sarai violated. While forcing Hagar to act as a surrogate for Abram might not have been part of Yahweh's plan, God does not allow Abram and Sarai to simply dismiss Hagar and pretend she does not exist. Since they decided to take on the responsibility of bringing a new life through a surrogate, God forces them to honor that responsibility. Returning Hagar to Abram and Sarai might be an act of culturally shaming them and compelling them to welcome her back into the camp. The Bible does not record any further abuse by Sarai until years later.

It is important to note that although the "unchosen" ones are not the ones through whom God will bring the promise, God loves them and consistently provides for them. One must reject the tendency to believe that "unchosen" means "rejected." The "chosenness" of Abraham's offspring is a vocational statement, not a statement of value. The children of the promise are the ones called to make possible the reconciliation of all humanity to God, just as God said to Abram in Gen 12:3.

Sarah may have been forced to welcome Hagar back into the camp, but she still had no love for Ishmael. Upon seeing that Ishmael is able "to make Isaac laugh," (Gen 21:9), she decides to send them away again. Ancient Near Eastern cultural traditions did allow that if the first wife was eventually able to have children, the surrogate and her child could be set free

---

4. Curiously, Hagar's name for God is remarkably similar to the name Abraham gives to the place of the offering of Isaac in Gen 22. Abraham names the site "Yahweh-Yirah" which is translated "Yahweh will see," often rendered idiomatically as "Yahweh will provide."

5. One compelling and fascinating interpretation of this account comes from Phyllis Trible, *Texts of Terror: Literary-feminist Readings of Biblical Narratives* (Philadelphia: Fortress Press, 1997).

with a financial severance. God assures Abraham that God will take care of Ishmael, and Abraham can do what Sarah asks. Sarah sets them free but apparently without compensation, in violation of cultural practice. Once again, God meets Hagar and Ishmael in the desert and provides for them. "Get up!" God says. "Lift up the lad. Hold his hand because I will make a great nation from him" (Gen 21:18). Once again, God shows grace to the outcast.

Omissions from the Psalms: Isaac and the Akedah

Isaac does not play a large role in Psalms. His name is only mentioned once in Ps 105, and only then in a list of the other patriarchs. In fact, Isaac is only ever mentioned outside of Genesis in the list "Abraham, Isaac, and Jacob." That likely should not be surprising, as Isaac does not play much of a lead role in the narrative of Genesis either. Most of Isaac's stories are told with him as the secondary figure, interacting with one of the other ancestors (i.e., Abraham and Isaac or Isaac and Jacob). Isaac does not even get to select his own wife in the story (Gen 24). His one solo story in Genesis echoes his father's lying about his relationship to his wife to protect himself (Gen 26:6-33). The story shows that Isaac makes the same kinds of mistakes his father did. Even Isaac's solo story does not seem to be about Isaac! Psalm 105 likely refers to these two stories of God's protection of Abraham from Pharaoh and Isaac from Abimelech:

> When they were small and few in number, and strangers in it,
> Walking around from nation to nation,
> from one kingdom to another people,
> God did not allow anyone to oppress them
> and corrected kings on account of them.
> "Do not touch my anointed ones!
> And do not destroy my prophets!" (vv. 12-15)

A story in Genesis involving Isaac acts as the climax of the Abraham story. It is known as the "Akedah," or "Binding." In Gen 22, after Ishmael is officially disinherited in Gen 21, God comes to Abraham and says, "Take your son—your only son Isaac—whom you love and go to the land of Moriah and offer him up there as a burnt offering on one of the mountains there that I will indicate to you" (v. 2). While human sacrifice was not uncommon in the fertility religions that surrounded Abraham, he never anticipated this request from Yahweh, particularly after it took more than twenty-five years to fulfill the promise of offspring.

If Abraham has reservations about this request, the text never reveals them. Abraham shows the same obedience to this request in Gen 22 that he showed at the beginning of the journey in Gen 12. Again, God tells Abraham to go to a destination that will be specified later. This time, however, Abraham must offer Isaac as a sacrifice. Without question or protest, Abraham goes.

The story in Gen 22 is painful to read. The conversation between Isaac and Abraham is tender and difficult. Isaac addresses Abraham as "Father," and twice Abraham calls Isaac "My son." The conversation is made even more tragic upon realizing that, in the Genesis narrative, Abraham and Isaac never speak again after this conversation. Why would God put Abraham through this kind of test? What does it prove? After interceding to prevent the sacrifice, God reveals the motivations at the end in verse 12: "[The messenger of Yahweh] said, 'Do not harm the boy! Don't do anything to him! Because now I know that you truly fear God. You did not withhold your son—your only son—from me.'"

To this point in the story, Abraham's obedience has been connected to God's promises of reward. God's tasks for Abraham always have a reward for obedience. "Go . . . and you will be a great nation." "Believe . . . and your descendants will have the land." God has also declared that Isaac is the person through whom the rewards of the promise will come. In Gen 17:21a, Yahweh explicitly says, "But I will establish my covenant with . . . ."

In asking for the sacrifice of Isaac, Yahweh is not merely asking Abraham to give up a son—which would certainly be difficult enough! Yahweh is asking Abraham to also surrender the benefits of the promise: land, great name, and great nation. Abraham is asked to demonstrate in this test whether he is following Yahweh for the promised blessing or whether he is following Yahweh simply because God is worthy of obedience. Obedient faith with no concern for reward is known as "disinterested piety."

DISINTERESTED PIETY

Disinterested piety is faith that follows God no matter where it leads. If an individual is following God for personal reward, that individual is no different from the trained dolphin who jumps for the reward of fish. In being asked to offer Isaac, Abraham is asked to demonstrate that his obedience is stronger than a dolphin's. Abraham shows that it is. Even if the call of God requires Abraham to give up the promised blessing and his beloved son, Abraham shows in Gen 22 that he is willing to do that.

The psalms do not specifically reference the Akedah or this test of Abraham, but they do celebrate faith that does not seek a reward. In fact, Sigmund Mowinckel, a twentieth-century psalm scholar, believed that one quality of all the psalms defined as "hymns" was that those psalms reflected disinterested piety.[6] The singer, overcome by the awesome nature of God, offers praise without thought of reward.

Psalm 150 is the best representation of this kind of faith. At the end of a celebratory doxology of psalms, 146–150, Ps 150 offers an abundant call to praise:

> Praise Yahweh! Praise God in the holy sanctuary.
> Praise God in the expanse of the firmament
> Praise God for divine might!
> Praise God for surpassing greatness!
> Praise God with the sound of the trumpet!
> Praise God with harp and lyre.
> Praise God with tambourine and dance!
> Praise God with strings and flute!
> Praise God with loud cymbals.
> Praise God with joyful cymbals!
> Let everything that breathes praise Yahweh.
> Praise Yahweh! (vv. 1-6)

Psalm 150 is the only psalm that does not offer any specific reason to praise Yahweh.[7] Israel calls on the hearers to praise Yahweh only because Yahweh is worthy of praise—not because of victories, answers, or blessings. Other psalms might praise Yahweh for a celebration of deliverance or healing, but Ps 150 simply offers praise.

Abraham shows this kind of faith in offering Isaac. Abraham had been promised land, a great name, and a nation, coming through Isaac. After all the years with their ups and downs, Abraham had learned it is not about the reward. It is about Yahweh.

---

6. Sigmund Mowinkel, *The Psalms in Israel's Worship* (trans. D. R. Ap-Thomsa; 2 vols; Nashville, Abingdon Press, 1962), 181.

7. Walter Brueggemann, "Bounded by Obedience and Praise: The Psalms as Canon," in *The Psalms and the Life of Faith* (Minneapolis: Fortress Press, 1998), 189–213.

Omissions from the Psalms: Jacob the Scoundrel

Jacob is not exactly omitted from the psalms. In fact, Jacob's mentions far exceed Abraham's. "Jacob" is mentioned thirty-four times to Abraham's four,[8] and that number does not include the mentions of "Israel" when used to refer to the person, "Jacob," like in Ps 22:23:[9] "Everyone who fears Yahweh, praise God! All the descendants of Jacob, honor God! Every generation of Israel, stand in awe before God!" What is missing from the mentions of "Jacob" in the psalms is any reflection of his controlling and manipulative personality. Like Abraham, Jacob is remembered in a positive manner in the psalms. In fact, he is apparently included in Ps 105's celebration of the ancestors as "prophets" and "messiahs."

One possible reason for this might be because by the time the psalms were written, "Jacob" was understood more commonly as a metonym for the nation of Israel.[10] Two examples can be seen in Ps 14:7—"Who will bring deliverance for Israel from Zion? Yahweh restores the fortunes of God's people, Jacob will rejoice. Israel will be glad!"—and in Ps 44:4: "You are my king, O God. You command the deliverance of Jacob." In neither of these examples does it seem likely that the psalmist is referring to the ancient patriarch. Rather, "Jacob" means "the nation."

Jacob even outdoes Abraham for custody of Yahweh. Although Abraham is often regarded as the "father of the faith," the psalms prefer to use the phrase "God of Jacob" to refer to Yahweh,[11] as in Ps 20:1: "May Yahweh answer you on your day of trouble. The name of the God of Jacob will exalt you." While the psalms never mention Jacob's colorful personality, for the psalms to use the name "Jacob" at all is an interesting reminder of Jacob's difficult past. Much of the period of the patriarch's life when he was known as "Jacob" is associated with manipulative control and trickery. Though his name was changed to "Israel" twice near the end of his story,

---

8. Pss 14:7; 20:1; 22:23; 24:6; 44:4; 46:7; 46:11; 47:4; 53:6; 59:13; 75:9; 76:6; 77:15; 78:5, 21, 71; 79:7; 81:1, 4; 84:8; 85:1; 87:2; 94:7; 99:4; 105:6, 10, 23; 114:1, 7; 132:2, 5; 135:4, 146:5; and 147:19.

9. Note also Pss 46:7, 11; 75:9; 76:6; 81:1, 4; 84:8; and 94:7.

10. A metonym is when a word is used to represent something else with which it is connected. One classic example is to use "Washington" to refer to the United States federal government.

11. Pss 20:1; 24:6; 46:7, 11; 75:9; 76:6; 81:1, 4; 84:8; 94:7; 114:7; 146:5.

the psalms are content to use the name "Jacob" more often when remembering the tricky patriarch.

Jacob's name is changed to "Israel" on two occasions in the Genesis narratives: once by the man he wrestles in Gen 32:28 and once by God in Gen 35:9. Unfortunately, in both cases, the name change does not stick. He never seems to effectively live into his name change. He is called "Jacob" in texts immediately following both naming events.

Jacob seems to be the only person in the biblical text for whom this is an issue. "Abram" is universally known as "Abraham" after his name is changed. The text and readers remember Hoshea as "Joshua" and Simon as "Peter." Jacob, however, remains "Jacob" long after both attempts to change his name. Even Yahweh seems to prefer "Jacob" when reminding Moses of the ancestors in the Exodus story: "You should say this to the children of Israel, 'Yahweh sent me—the God of your fathers, the God of Abraham, God of Isaac, and the God of Jacob'" (Exod 3:15).

The secret might be in each name's meaning. As already discussed, names give insight into character in the Hebrew Bible. When Esau and Jacob were born, their parents named them based on their obvious traits. Esau was "covered in red hair," so they named him a combination of "red" and "hairy." Jacob was given his name after being born holding his brother's heel. His parents made a verb out of the word "heel." The idiomatic sense of Jacob's name would be "one who trips someone up" or, more idiomatically, "con artist." One wonders if "Israel" never really stuck because "Jacob" better captured his personality.

Not all of Jacob's actions were "tricky." Often, Jacob used every opportunity to stay in control of his destiny—occasionally with deceit. In Gen 25, Jacob trades a bowl of soup with a hungry Esau for the right to be considered the firstborn. Then he would not only inherit two-thirds of his father's wealth but would also be responsible for the administration of the family—deciding where to graze the animals, what and where to plant crops, who marries whom, etc. Early in the story, the reader can clearly see that Jacob is more suited to those responsibilities than Esau. Esau is called a hunter and a "man of the field." Jacob, on the other hand, is called a "civilized man, living in tents." The ancient reader would no doubt hear the echoes of Gilgamesh, the civilized king, in the person of Jacob, while Esau is reminiscent of Enkidu, the wild, hairy man. Jacob's acquisition of the birthright did not involve much "trickery." The terms were simple and understood. Much like the reader, Esau recognized that he had no desire to lead the family and "despised his birthright."

Jacob did live up to his name, however, by stealing his father's blessing from his brother. At the urging of his mother, Jacob dressed as his brother Esau to trick his father into blessing him in Gen 27. Vows and oaths were important in the ancient Near East. When someone invoked a divine being in a promise, that promise was understood as unbreakable. In other words, once Isaac asked God to bless Jacob (ostensibly believing him to be Esau), Isaac could not take back that blessing. It was a signed contract. When Jacob's deception was revealed, Isaac's only option for blessing Esau was to offer a blessing that roughly translated to "Life for you will be hard, but eventually, it will be okay."

For fear of his life, Jacob fled from his family and the promised land. After no doubt being weaned on the stories of the faith of his grandfather Abraham, Jacob must assume that in his attempt to secure the promise, he had lost it. In a beautiful moment of divine reassurance, Yahweh meets Jacob at Bethel. In a dream, God comes and provides an illustration of the bridge his descendants would be to the divine. God then makes a promise to Jacob in Gen 28:13-15:

> And suddenly, Yahweh stood above it and said, "I am Yahweh, God of Abraham your father, and the God of Isaac. The land which you are lying on I will give to you and to your descendants. And your descendants will be as the dust of the earth. And you will break forth to the west and the east and the north and the south. And all the families of the earth will be blessed by you and your descendants. And behold, I am with you and I will protect you everywhere you go. And I will return you to this land because I will never leave you until I have done what I have spoken to you.

After a theophany that provided this kind of divine assurance, one might assume Jacob would awaken to a new faith. Surely, now that God had appeared and provided this word of comfort, Jacob would leave on his journey with a new confidence in God's provision. Jacob, however, had a persistent need to control every situation, and upon waking, he "took a vow":

> If God will be with me, and protect me on this journey which I am taking, and give me food to eat and clothes to wear, and return me in peace to the house of my father, then Yahweh will be my God. And this stone I have placed as a sacred pillar will be the "House of God" and I will surely give a tenth to you from all you give me. (Gen 28:20-22)

This confession is not exactly the faith of his grandfather Abraham. God spoke to Abraham, and Abraham went. God spoke to Jacob, and Jacob began lengthy contract negotiations to make sure the divine would honor God's part of the bargain. Jacob makes it clear that only after God meets Jacob's list of expectations will Yahweh be Jacob's God.

Jacob does safely reach his uncle's land, and after a twenty-year sojourn with his uncle/father-in-law, Jacob discovers firsthand which side of the family his personality comes from. Laban tricks Jacob into marrying Leah, the older daughter, rather than Rachel, the daughter Jacob truly wants to marry. Jacob then manipulates the breeding of Laban's flocks so that Jacob can build his own flocks. By the end of Jacob's time with his uncle, he has demonstrated the administrative skills the reader knew would make him the preferred choice for "firstborn" at the beginning of the story.

In the same way the Akedah is the narrative climax of the Abraham story and is neglected by the psalms, Jacob's wrestling by the ford of the Jabbok River is neglected by the psalms as well. In Gen 32, Jacob lives an event that serves as a metaphor for his entire life.

> And Jacob was left alone. Then a man wrestled with him until the dawn. But when he saw that he couldn't overcome him, he struck his hip socket, and dislocated Jacob's hip. And he said, "Release me! It's dawn." And he said, "I will not release you until you bless me." And he said to him, "What is your name?" And he said, "Jacob." And he said, "Your name will no longer be Jacob, but Israel because you have never backed down with God and with men, and you have overcome." (Gen 32:24-28)

Throughout his life, Jacob has attempted to maintain the upper hand in all his negotiations with humans and with God. After Jacob confesses his name to the man, which would be a confession of character—"I am a con artist"—the man reframes Jacob's life journey with a name change. No longer is Jacob "the con artist who trips people up"; now he is "Israel" or "the one who asserts themselves with God." In other words, the man has taken Jacob's relentless desire for control and reframed it as a desire never to give up.

The Bible does not give any details about the identity of the "man" who wrestles with Jacob by the Jabbok. Tradition has connected the man to a divine being because of Jacob's name for the place. "And Jacob called the place 'Peniel, because I have seen God face to face and my soul was delivered'" (Gen 32:30).

The divine nature of the "man" is somewhat problematic. One might assume that the God of all creation could defeat Jacob in a wrestling match! A likely explanation is that seeing the "face of God" is metaphorical for Jacob. The wrestling match forced him to confess and own his character throughout his life journey. If the term is metaphorical, the Bible might be providing a clue to the identity of the "man" in the next chapter.

Following Jacob's difficult night, he goes out to meet Esau in Genesis 33. Unsure of how Esau might react, Jacob lines up his wives and children in the order of his preference so that his favored wife and son can have the best chance to escape should Esau respond violently. Likely to everyone's surprise, Esau receives Jacob with remarkable grace and forgiveness. After Jacob tried to buy Esau's favor, Esau asks Jacob to keep his gifts because he became wealthy during Jacob's absence. Jacob, however, insists Esau keep the gifts and says, "No—please, please—if I have found grace with you then take my presents from my hand, because truly, I see your face as *the face of God* since you have accepted me" (Gen 33:10). Seeing Esau was seeing the "face of God." One wonders if the Bible is trying to give the reader a subtle clue to the identity of the man who refused to give his name by the river Jabbok. It may have been that after twenty years, Esau and Jacob wrestled out their problems by the Jabbok. Perhaps it was Esau himself who provided the reframing of Jacob's name into Israel as an act of forgiveness.[12] Regardless, as Yahweh had promised at the beginning of his journey, Jacob was brought back home after twenty years and reconciled to a now wealthy Esau and aged (but still alive) father.

JOSEPH

While not an ancestor of the entire nation of Israel, Joseph is often included among the ancestor stories since he is considered the father of two of the largest tribes in the northern kingdom, Ephraim and Manasseh. Indeed, because of the tribe's power and position in the northern nation, "Joseph" is often used as a metonym for the entire northern kingdom. In Ps 78, another historical psalm, "Joseph" and his son "Ephraim" are used to refer to the northern kingdom while discussing God's exile of the northern

---

12. That possibility would add another interesting parallel to the ancient Gilgamesh/Enkidu story. Gilgamesh and Enkidu wrestled until Gilgamesh "turned his knee with his foot on the ground" and won the match. Once he did, Enkidu's "fury abated," and the two became close friends.

tribes: "God rejected the tent of Joseph and did not choose the tribe of Ephraim" (v. 67).

The way the story of Joseph is told in Genesis also contrasts with the primary ancestor stories. The stories of Abraham, Isaac, and Jacob provide the reader small glimpses into individual episodes in the lives of the ancestors, like "Abraham and Pharaoh," "Isaac and Abimelech," or "Jacob and Esau." The Joseph narrative is more cohesive in the way story unfolds. The story has been called a "novella" (or little novel) since it has a narrative flow with character development and drama.

Psalms provides more depth to the Joseph narrative than to the other ancestor stories. In fact, in Ps 105 Joseph's entire story arc is told in brief:

> God summoned a famine upon the land
> and broke every staff of bread.
> God sent a man before them, Joseph,
> who was sold to slavery.
> His feet were afflicted with shackles.
> Iron was placed around his neck.
> Until the time about which he spoke came.
> Yahweh's word proved him right!
> The king sent for and released him.
> The ruler of the peoples set him free.
> He was made master of the king's house,
> and he ruled all his possessions,
> To teach his officials however he liked,
> and his elders however seemed wise to him. (vv. 16-22)

Naturally, the psalm does neglect some of the precise details of Joseph's life in favor of a broader survey. It is interesting, though, when considering the lack of detail on the lives of the primary ancestors, that a general overview of Joseph's entire story is found in the psalm.

Additionally, the psalm provides a theological interpretation of Joseph's experience in Egypt. In 105:17, the psalmist says God sent Joseph to Egypt ahead of the famine. Apparently, Joseph's sojourn into Egypt was part of a divine plan to provide for Egypt through the famine and to provide for Egypt's instruction. Joseph's status in Egypt gave the family of Jacob a unique opportunity. Psalm 105:23-34 shares the result of this: "Israel came to Egypt, and Jacob lived as a stranger in the land of Ham. God made his people exceedingly fruitful, and mightier than their foes."

Joseph serves as a transitional character from the primary ancestors to the need for an exodus. In Ps 105, the Joseph story serves the same purpose as the psalm moves to celebrate Yahweh's creation of a nation, brought up out of the land of Egypt.

OMISSIONS FROM THE PSALMS: FORGOTTEN WOMEN

Of the omissions from the lives of the ancestors in the book of Psalms, the most troubling might be the women. While there is little mention of the patriarchs outside the book of Genesis, the women who play significant roles in their stories are mentioned even less.

In Gen 16, Hagar was given an ancestral promise and allowed to name the divine. Unfortunately, she has no other mention in the Hebrew Bible. Sarah played a role in the promise in showing both faith and doubt, and her part in the story is also forgotten in the worship life of Israel. Rebekah played an active role in trying to ensure the promises of God were observed, and she is omitted from the biblical story outside of Genesis as well. Much like Sarah and Rachel, Rebekah dealt with the issue of barrenness. After finally getting pregnant, Rebekah was told by God that her younger son would be favored over the older: "And Yahweh said to her, 'Two nations are in your womb. For two divided nations will come from your belly. One people will be stronger than the other. The older will serve the younger" (Gen 25:23).

Upon hearing this oracle, Rebekah used what agency she had to defend the word of God when she saw this oracle threatened in Gen 27. When Isaac planned to bless his favored child Esau and (perhaps unknowingly) upset the plans of God, Rebekah arranged for Jacob to impersonate Esau to secure the blessing. Rebekah was also the one who suggested that Jacob should flee to her brother's house in Northern Syria until Esau calmed down. She then manipulated Isaac into suggesting that Jacob travel to Laban's house. Much like Jacob, Rebekah was always in control, though she was always working to defend the promises of God she heard while she was pregnant.

Of all the matriarchs, Rachel's legacy is the most enduring outside of Genesis. In Gen 35, Rachel died in childbirth with Benjamin near Bethlehem. As a result, Rachel became a representative figure for mourning the loss of children. While she is not mentioned in the psalms, she is found in the powerful poetry of Jer 31. Rachel provides a mother's voice lamenting the exile of the nation in verse 15: "Thus Yahweh says, 'A voice is heard in Ramah, wailing and bitter weeping. Rachel weeps for her children, and refuses comfort over her children because they are no more.'" In Matt 2, when Herod orders the death of children under two in an attempt to kill the young Christ, the Jeremiah passage is also quoted, and Rachel becomes a partner in sorrow.

Leah, Rachel's sister, is not mentioned outside of Genesis except for a brief mention in Ruth 4. So the reader is left to decide, is it better to be remembered for sorrow or not to be remembered at all? In Leah's heartbreaking story, she hopes each time that her ability to bear a son will cause Jacob to love her. While she is never favored by Jacob, she is favored by God. God always regards the "unchosen" ones. God "opens her womb" and allows Leah to bear six of Jacob's twelve sons. Her children become the ancestors of half the tribes of Israel. Her son, Judah, would be the tribe of David and later of Jesus. The text does not give any reason for Leah's favored status beyond the fact that Jacob favored Rachel. In other words, God is once again on the side of the marginalized, choosing Leah to be the mother of a special part of the promise. As difficult as Leah's story is, it does have a positive ending. Since Rachel dies in childbirth and is buried near Bethlehem, Leah is the wife Jacob buries with him in the "Tomb of the Patriarchs" in Hebron. In death, Leah finally becomes the favored wife.

CONCLUSION

This book has operated under the premise that the psalms contain every important theme in the Hebrew Bible. The ancestor stories have certainly challenged that thesis! While the Psalter does reference the patriarchs, important (even crucial) aspects of the ancestral narratives are missing: Abraham's struggles of faith, the Akedah, Jacob's colorful personality, and all the important contributions made by the women. What is to be made of these omissions? Why is it that when Israel sings, they sing only of the men, and they only sing of them as "prophets" and "messiahs"?

Certainly, the book of Psalms is not afraid to discuss difficult parts of life. The book remembers the sinfulness of the great king David in Ps 51. Half of the psalms contain lament characteristics, many from the mouth of the David. The book of Psalms is consistently a real book about real people who often struggle in real ways. Yet the psalms show no interest in remembering the "real" (i.e., difficult) lives of the ancestors, only their callings as "prophets" and "messiahs."

The psalms, however, were sung in a different time and spoke to a different need than Genesis. Psalm 105, which gives the most complete story of the ancestors in the Psalms, highlights four important lessons from the ancestor stories:

1. God promised the ancestors and their descendants the land.
2. God protected the ancestors when they were outnumbered and wandering from "nation to nation."
3. God protected Joseph during his slavery.
4. Joseph rose in power and was a blessing to Egypt.

As always, the occasion of the text is important. Psalm 105 likely finds its place in Book IV after the exile. The nation of Judah had been destroyed, and the people of God were scattered throughout the ancient Near East with communities in Babylon, Egypt, Israel, and elsewhere. The faithful were trying to understand their place in a world where their lives looked much like those of their "wandering" ancestors. In that context, it is not as important to remember the humanity of the ancestors. The reality of the exiles' own humanity was likely enough. It was far more important to remember what Yahweh did for and with the ancient ancestors. When the faithful once again find themselves as a minority among the nations, they should hold fast to Yahweh. Yahweh will protect them and raise them up to be a blessing to the nations. Then, they can be "prophets" and "messiahs."

Questions for Further Discussion

1. In narratives that are from a thoroughly patriarchal era (and that are themselves often patriarchal), women play a large and sometimes remarkably active role. There is surely no neat answer to this seeming contradiction, but what is a possible explanation?

2. The psalms omit several stories that have historically been important to people of faith. It also adds titles to the ancestors not normally associated with them (like "messiah"). What might account for these selective choices?

3. Why might God have wanted Hagar to return to Abraham to fulfill a responsibility that God never commanded (i.e., the child with Hagar)?

4. Where might one find more tribalistic identity in contemporary society? Where might one find more individualistic identity? What are the cautions and blessings of each?

5. The Bible consistently shows that "unchosenness" does not mean "rejection." The individuals who do not carry forward the chosen line find great blessing (e.g., Ishmael and Esau). What does this mean regarding the way Christians talk about "chosenness?"

The Exodus

This is not a moment, it's the movement / Where all the hungriest brothers with something to prove went / Foes oppose us, we take an honest stand / We roll like Moses, claimin' our Promised Land…

—Alexander Hamilton,
Hamilton by Lin-Manuel Miranda

Exodus and the Psalms

The story of the ancient Hebrews' exodus from Egypt has resonated with groups throughout history. Shortly after signing the Declaration of Independence, a committee was commissioned to design the first national seal, and Benjamin Franklin proposed Moses standing on the shore with his hands spread over the Red Sea.[1] The exodus narrative was a central metaphor for liberation theologians fighting for social reform in Latin America.[2] Black spirituals regularly contained exodus images and references to Moses. Songs like "Go Down, Moses," "Wade in the Water," and "Bound for Canaan Land" resonated as individuals longed for freedom and justice. The Civil Rights Movement of the 1960s drew on the same story in songs like "We Shall Not Be Moved" and in the speeches of Martin Luther King Jr.[3] Lin-Manuel Miranda even used a reference to Moses and Exodus in the

---

1. Derek Davis, *Religion and the Continental Congress, 1774–1789: Contributions to Original Intent* (New York: Oxford University Press, 2000), 138.

2. The work that began the movement is usually associated with Gustavo Gutiérrez, *A Theology of Liberation: History, Politics, and Salvation* (Maryknoll, NY: Orbis, 1988).

3. Martin Luther King Jr.'s final speech "I've Been to the Mountaintop" presciently associates the end of his ministry with the death of Moses on the day before his assassination. See "Martin Luther King's Final Speech: 'I've Been to the Mountaintop,'" ABC News, April 3, 2013, https://abcnews.go.com/Politics/martin-luther-kings-final-speech-ive-mountaintop-full/story?id=18872817.

song "My Shot" in his award-winning musical *Hamilton*, first performed in 2015.

Part of the appeal of the exodus narrative is this ability to speak into different contexts. God's deliverance of Israel is not a spiritual deliverance consigned to some ideal future "out there" somewhere, nor is the exodus exclusively a political action. The exodus is both spiritual and political. God disapproves of Pharaoh's unjust treatment of the children of Israel in history, and God intervenes to miraculously affect that history. For some the exodus forms the central salvation metaphor for the Old Testament story. Yahweh demonstrates both power and love for the people of Israel, tangibly acting in history on behalf of a powerless people under an unjust and oppressive regime.

While the psalms might be selective when it comes to the ancestors' stories, the psalms overflow with exodus imagery, particularly in the second half of the book. For the psalms, beginning in Book III (Ps 73), the exile provides the historical occasion, and the people of Judah desperately desired for God to work a new exodus. This story of liberation became formative as the people in exile in Babylon began to collect their stories. Israel's understanding of itself and its origins were shaped by an exilic people looking for a story to speak to their situation. The story of the exodus was the story that they preserved. The hope of political restoration and spiritual forgiveness shaped their worship life and songs they sang.

As seen in the previous chapter, Ps 105 provides a helpful introduction to the exodus narrative:

> Then Israel came to Egypt,
> and Jacob lived as a stranger in the land of Ham.
> God made his people exceedingly fruitful,
> and mightier than their foes.
> God turned their mind to hate the people,
> to deal treacherously with God's servants. (vv. 23-25)

After Jacob's family moved to Egypt, Israel multiplied quickly and soon outnumbered its foes. The psalm says that the foes responded to this threat by dealing treacherously with Israel. In this way, it resonates well with Exod 1:7-10:

> But the children of Israel were fruitful, increased abundantly, and became
> numerous. Their presence strengthened, and the land was filled with

them. A new king arose over Egypt who did not know Joseph. He said to his people, "Look, these people—the children of Israel—are numerous and stronger than we are! Come, and let us be clever, otherwise they will multiply and in a time of war, join also with our enemies, fight against us, and escape from the land."

The Exodus passage does provide an additional reason for the oppression. In Exodus, Egypt's insecurities lead to the oppression of the Hebrews. In Ps 105:25, Yahweh intervenes, causing the foes to bring violence on God's people. The "minds God turned" against the people in the psalm calls to mind the "hardening of Pharaoh's heart" mentioned in Exodus, which brought about the exodus out of the land. The action of Yahweh causing the original decision of the Egyptians to oppress the ancient Hebrews likely represents the exilic occasion of the psalm, especially considering the suffering of the people in Ps 105:25. The prophetic message to Israel (from Joshua to Malachi) explains exile as God's judgment for the people's disobedience. The postexilic occasion of Ps 105 shows how this theological belief found its way into the worship life of Israel in the retelling of the exodus story.

The occasion of exile also helps to interpret Ps 106's telling of the story. Psalm 105 tells the story of Yahweh's creation of a chosen people with an emphasis on God's faithfulness. Psalm 106, however, tells the story of Israel's rebellion despite God's continued love and mercy for the children of Israel. When Psalm 106 mentions Israel in Egypt, it reinforces the "Egyptian oppression as God's judgment" theory:

> We sinned like our ancestors.
> We have committed iniquity and wickedness.
> Our ancestors in Egypt did not consider your deeds.
> They did not remember the abundance of your committed love.
> They rebelled at the sea, the Red Sea. (vv. 6-7)

Prior to the exile, Israel seemed to understand their national origin story as the deliverance of a small, powerless, faithful people from Egyptian oppression by the God of Israel. Prophetic voices challenged the understanding of the "faithful people" part of that story. Ezekiel reflects this shift in perspective in his preaching immediately prior to the destruction of Jerusalem. He challenges Israel's national story by claiming they were unfaithful, even in Egypt:

> [Israel] rebelled against me and were not willing to obey me. They did not throw away one of the detestable things their eyes beheld. The did not forsake the idols of Egypt. So I decided to pour out my wrath and full anger upon them in the midst of the land of Egypt. I acted so that my name would not be profaned in the eyes of the nations who were there, in whose sight I was made known in bringing them out from the land of Egypt. So, I led them out from the land of Egypt, and I brought them to the desert wilderness. (Ezek 20:8-10)

For Ezekiel, the oppression in Egypt was judgment for the idolatry of the ancient Hebrews. God's deliverance of them was simply for God's glory. In the same way, the story in Psalms comes from remembering the exodus through the painful reality of exile.

MOSES

The name "Moses" occurs only eight times in the book of Psalms.[4] They are grouped from Pss 77–106 in the psalms that likely came together during Israel's struggle with the reality of identity in exile. James Sanders once remarked that "in crisis situations only the old, tried and true, has any real authority."[5] In the time of exile, the psalmists turn to an ancient figure with the authority to help Israel through a desperate situation.

Moses's voice is the logical choice to shepherd Israel through exile. In Jewish tradition, he is the archetype for a prophet. A prophet's job is to bring God's word to the people, and in the Old Testament, no one did that better than Moses. Moses speaks outside of the Torah in the only psalm associated with him in the canon, Psalm 90, which speaks directly to the crisis moment in the story of the psalms and the life of Israel. Indeed, Pss 90–100 have been called a "Moses book" for their numerous allusions to Moses and the exodus story.[6] In a time of crisis when the people have lost confidence in the institution in which they had placed their trust, they turn their attention to one who came before David.

Much like the Psalter's memory of the patriarchs, when it sings of Moses, it sings of him only in positive ways. The superscription of Ps 90 calls him "the man of God." Ps 99:6 identifies Moses and Aaron as Yahweh's "priests." In Ps 105:6, they are both called God's "chosen." In Ps 106:23,

---

4. Ps 77:20; Ps 90's superscription; Pss 99:6; 103:7; 105:26; 106:16, 23, 32.

5. James Sanders, "Adaptable for Life: The Nature and Function of Canon," in *From Sacred Story to Sacred Text* (Philadelphia: Fortress, 1987), 21.

6. Marvin Tate, *Psalms 51–100* (Dallas: Word Books, 1990), xxvii.

Moses is called the "chosen one." Even Moses's failure in Numbers 20 is remembered in Ps 106:32 as the fault of the faithless congregation of Israel, not Moses.

In addition to omitting any negative images, the psalms also neglect to mention any historical context of Moses. The psalms say nothing of Moses's adoption into the royal court in Egypt, the murder he committed, his marriage to a Midianite woman, or any of the situations that led to Moses's unique qualifications for the role of deliverer. The psalms simply think of Moses as the one Yahweh "chose" and "sent."

The Call

When the Bible tells the story of an individual called by Yahweh, the narrative often follows a similar formula, or "type scene."[7] Typically, the experience follows this pattern:
1. God appears (theophany).
2. God offers a commission.
3. The individual objects.
4. God offers reassurance.
5. A sign confirms God's word.

Not every call experience has every element, but this list represents the generally understood formula when telling the story. Different individuals respond to God in different ways. For example, Ezekiel does not have an objection to God's call. Jeremiah objected that he was too young to be taken seriously. In Isa 6:5, Isaiah's objection was simply that he "was a man of unclean lips." Moses, on the other hand, sets a record for most objections to God's call:
- "Who am I?" (Exod 3:11)
- "Who are you?" (Exod 3:13)
- "What if they don't believe me?" (Exod 4:1)
- "I don't talk well" Exod (4:10)
- "Send someone else." (Exod 4:13)

In nearly half (3) of the occurrences of Moses's name in the Psalter, he and his brother Aaron are on equal footing. This close association likely comes from remembering Moses's call experience. It took two chapters of

---

7. For the classic discussion of the prophetic call type scene, see N. Habel, "The Form and Significance of the Call Narratives," *ZAW* 77 (1965): 297–323.

convincing, two miraculous signs, and a promise Moses would not have to speak to people directly before he finally decided to acknowledge God's call. God answered each of Moses's objections and offered reassurance throughout the conversation. Aaron was the final part of God's reassurance to Moses after Moses begged God to send someone else. Though apparently frustrated by Moses's attempts to circumvent his call for two chapters, Yahweh agreed to send Aaron to speak as the intermediary for Moses. Moses was God's prophet, and Aaron was to serve as Moses's "prophet" to Pharaoh and the people. This association is likely why the psalms talk about "Moses and Aaron" together as often as they do.

The Divine Name

The most significant act of reassurance Yahweh offers Moses is giving him the divine name. When Moses objects, "When they ask me, 'What is [God's] name?' what shall I say to them?" God responds with "אהיה אשר אהיה," pronounced "Ehyeh asher Ehyeh." Unfortunately, this phrase is difficult to render elegantly into English. God's name appears to be in the first person and connected to the Hebrew "to be" verb; however, biblical Hebrew does not have the same sense of "tense" that English does. Any English tense could be meant by the conjugation of God's name. When the translators of the Septuagint rendered the phrase in Greek, they needed to pick a tense. So they rendered it into the present tense, giving the English phrase "I Am who I Am." Since the early Christian church used the Septuagint as their Bible, the "I am" sayings in the Gospel of John are a direct allusion to the Septuagint's translation of this passage to reference Jesus's claim to divinity.

The present tense is not the only translation option, however. It would be possible and grammatically appropriate to render each אהיה ("Ehyeh") into any English tense of the verb "to be." In other words, "I was," "I am," or "I will be" are faithful renderings of the Hebrew. The word occurs twice around a relative pronoun, which would mean all the permutations, e.g., "I will be what I was" or "I am what I will be," are appropriate translations. To further add to the linguistic fun, some scholars believe that the divine name is the "causative stem" of the Hebrew verb "to be." In other words, the divine name could be translated as "I cause to be" or, idiomatically, "I am creator." If names give insight into character, it is interesting that God's name is difficult to get a comprehensive picture of beyond God's "being."

Another fascinating choice Yahweh makes with the divine name is that it is conjugated. In other words, God says the divine name is the first person "I am" but then tells Moses to identify the divine to the people in Egypt in the third person, e.g., "'He is' has sent me." This third person conjugation of the name is what is often transliterated "YHWH" and known as the "tetragrammaton" or "four letters." This Hebrew word is rendered by most Bible translations as "the LORD," though unfortunately that can hide its distinctive character. Yahweh is the name that distinguishes the God of Israel from any of the gods of the other nations. Other nations could have "Elohim" (gods), but only one "Yahweh" exists. This can be seen in Psalm 83:18: "So let them know who you are. Your name—Yahweh alone—is the Most High over all the earth." Unfortunately, the exact vocalization of the tetragrammaton has been lost. After the exile, the people of Israel avoided speaking the divine name for fear of misusing it and thereby breaking the third commandment. As a result, the ancient pronunciation has been lost to history. A postexilic Jewish settlement in Elephantine, Egypt, apparently pronounced the tetragrammaton as "Yahu."[8] Most contemporary pronunciations, however, have settled on "Yahweh."

When the medieval Jewish scribes developed a written vowel system for biblical Hebrew, they faced a problem. They revered the divine name and did not want to aid anyone in speaking it, but once vowels were added to the consonants of written Hebrew, they could not prevent its pronunciation. Their solution was to change the vowels. These scribes, called Masoretes, took the existing consonants for the divine name (YHWH in English) and added the vowels of the word "Adonai."[9] This move safeguarded the divine name and guaranteed it would not be pronounced accidentally or maliciously. This combination of letters went through numerous transliterations in numerous Bible translations throughout history to finally create the name "Jehovah." "Jehovah" is the transliteration of a name created by Masoretic Jews in an effort to guarantee the mispronunciation of the divine name.

OMISSION FROM THE PSALMS: MOSES THE MIDIANITE

Before arriving in Egypt as the ancient Hebrews' liberator, Moses has an encounter with God in the Exodus story that is not found in Psalms. It is

---

8. The "Yahu" pronunciation survives in some names in the biblical text. The "jah" or "iah" at the end of biblical names like Jeremiah is a shortened form of the divine name. With Jeremiah and Elijah (and others) in Hebrew, the ending is vocalized as "Yahu." Prime Minister of Israel, Benjamin Netanyahu, reflects this same tradition.

9. "Adonai" is traditionally translated as "Almighty" and is the word spoken when a devout Jewish reader encounters the divine name in a manuscript.

omitted from Psalms; it is omitted from every biography of Moses; and it is omitted from every movie ever based on the exodus.

After Yahweh spends two chapters convincing a stubborn Moses to go to meet Pharaoh, Moses finally relents and begins his journey. The Exodus story shocks the reader with this enigmatic passage in Exod 4:

> On the way at a lodging place, Yahweh met him and sought to kill him. But Zipporah took a flint and cut her son's foreskin and touched it to his feet and said, "Because you are a bridegroom of blood to me." So God withdrew from him. She said "a bridegroom of blood," referring to circumcision. (vv. 24-26)

Questions abound about these three verses. Why would Yahweh spend all that time and effort trying to convince Moses to go to Egypt only to try to kill him when he started his journey? What does it mean that Yahweh "sought" to kill Moses? Shouldn't the God of Creation be successful in the attempt? What is the purpose of this strange ceremony? How did Zipporah know what to do? Why would what Zipporah did appease Yahweh?

This story appears to be a symbolic "re-circumcision" of Moses.[10] After fear that he would be discovered as a murderer in Egypt, Moses fled into the wilderness and spent a generation working for the Midianites. Now, as he leaves for his call, Moses is apparently trying to bring his Midianite life along with him, which includes his Midianite wife and uncircumcised son. Moses has spent this generation living as a Midianite. This strange ceremony provides Moses the opportunity to rededicate himself to the Hebrew people that he has been separated from for a generation.

Apparently, Zipporah, being from a priestly family, recognized the need and acted accordingly. Ironically, her actions to save Moses may have resulted in her own exile. The reader does not hear anything more from Zipporah until she returns after the Exodus. In Exod 18:2, the Bible says that Jethro meets the people of Israel and returns Zipporah after she had been "sent away." This verb in Hebrew for "sent away" can also carry the meaning of "divorced." In this patriarchal culture without social assistance, a divorced wife would likely return to her family of origin in the hopes that her family would support her after this dishonor. Zipporah being brought

---

10. The word "feet" can, on occasion in the Old Testament, be used as a euphemism to avoid saying "genitals." See also Judges 4:27; Ruth 3:4-8; Isaiah 6:2; and perhaps Isaiah 3:16. This is not a common use (most times "feet" just means "feet"), but on occasion, to be delicate, the authors use this euphemism.

into the camp by Jethro might support the "divorce" interpretation. It is possible that after this ceremony in Exod 4, part of Moses's rededication to the task of being a Hebrew included divorcing his foreign wife. After the exodus when she and Jethro confess Yahweh, they are allowed to stay in the camp, and Jethro becomes a trusted advisor to Moses.

Plagues

Often in Psalms, specific details from narratives are omitted. One can't sing a whole story! This is the case with the plagues. Most psalms simply reduce the event to God "working wonders" in the land of Egypt. While Psalm 135 specifically mentions the last plague, it offers this more general survey of how God worked in Egypt: "God sent signs and wonders in your midst, O Egypt, against Pharaoh and all his servants" (v. 9).

Psalms 78 and 105, however, break this convention by providing recitations of the plagues in surprising detail.

Ps 78:43-51	Plague # in Exodus
44 [God] transformed their rivers to blood, and they could not drink from their streams.	1
45 God sent among them swarms which consumed them!	4
and frogs which destroyed them.	2
46 God gave their produce to the caterpillars	?
and their labor to locusts.	8
47 God destroyed their vines with hail. And their fig trees with frost.	7
48 God also destroyed their cattle with hail and their flocks with lightning bolts.	
49 God sent against them burning anger, wrath, hostility, and trouble: a company of destructive messengers.	
50 God made a path for anger, and did not spare their souls from death. God gave their lives over to the pestilence.	10?
51 God struck all the firstborn in Egypt, the first fruits of their power in the tents of Ham.	10

Ps 105:28-36	Plague # in Exodus
28 God sent darkness and caused it to be dark! The darkness did not disobey God's words.	9
29 God turned their waters to blood and caused their fish to die.	1
30 Their land swarmed with frogs, even in the rooms of their kings.	2
31 God spoke, and a swarm came. Gnats were throughout their borders.	4 / 3
32 God gave them hail for rain with fiery lightning in the land.	7 / ?
33 God withered their vines and their fig trees. God shattered the trees within their borders	7
34 God spoke, and locust came —young locusts that couldn't be counted!	8
35 They consumed all the vegetation in the land. They consumed the fruit of their ground.	
36 God struck down the firstborn in their land— the first fruits of their power	10

Each psalm shows stylistic freedom when discussing the plagues. Psalm 78 adds both "caterpillars" to the locusts and "frost" to the hail. It also omits the plagues of "gnats," "boils," and "pestilence on the cattle," though the plague of hail does seem to be focused primarily on the cattle in Ps 78. In Psalm 105, the first plague mentioned in the psalm is darkness, which was the ninth plague in Exodus. Poetically, "darkness" effectively sets the tone for the plagues that follow. The "fiery lightning" in Ps 105:32 is difficult to connect to any specific event in the Exodus narrative. It may be associated with the hailstorm.

As in the creation psalms, rigid understandings of "order" are not important. The psalmist feels free to shift the order, add and delete elements, and provide theological interpretation within the understanding of Yahweh as the director and champion. Wherever the plagues are discussed, however, the climax is always the same. Both psalms finish with the firstborn in Egypt being struck down. Indeed, in the Exodus allusion in Psalm 135, the death of the firstborn is the only specific plague that is mentioned (135:8).

Psalm 78 offers an interesting theological interpretation of the final plague and apparently attributes the death of the firstborn to a "company of destructive messengers." This stands in direct contrast to Exod 11:4 where Yahweh says, "I, myself, will go out in the midst of Egypt." Ps 78 is the only psalm to offer this level of administrative protection to the divine. Ps 135:8 reads more like the Exodus account: "[God] was the one who struck down the firstborn in Egypt, both human and animals. God sent signs and wonders in your midst, O Egypt, against Pharaoh and all his servants." Ps 136:10 also has no problem attributing the tenth plague directly to the divine, remembering Yahweh as the one "who struck Egypt through their firstborn."

God and Violence

The tenth plague provides an opportunity to speak to the "God of Violence" in the Old Testament (a topic that will be revisited in Joshua). One of the greatest hermeneutical challenges facing a Christian who reads the Old Testament is the apparent difference between Yahweh, the God of Israel, and the New Testament Jesus, whom Christians believe is the full revelation of that same God.

For some, the disjunction is too much to reconcile. Early church heretics believed there must be two Gods in the Bible: the god of creation who is violent and legalistic and the father of Jesus who believes in grace and mercy.[11] In practice, many people of faith do not formally reject the Old Testament, but they spend their time reading parables and Paul's epistles, only visiting the Old Testament to read an occasional psalm.

Two things create the problem for the contemporary reader. The first is that Yahweh (and Jesus) meet people where they are in time and culture. An individual does not have to change to meet the divine—a character trait of God that culminates in the miracle of Pentecost. The gospel speaks everyone's language. Second, readers have lost the original occasion of the text. Contemporary readers view the text through the lens of their own culture. This is not surprising, but it does mean that a meaning intended for an ancient culture with a significantly different worldview can be lost.

In its original occasion, the statement "I myself will pass through Egypt and kill the firstborn" contains a powerful quality of mercy. At the beginning of the Exodus account, Pharaoh attempts to control the Hebrew population by killing *all* the Hebrew boys. According to the later Torah

---

11. F. F. Bruce, *The Canon of Scripture* (Lisle, IL: InterVarsity Press, 1988), 134.

that God would soon give the Israelites, an individual may reciprocate to the degree that party has been injured. In other words, if someone pokes your eye, you are allowed to poke theirs, but you are not permitted to respond any further. According to Torah, since Pharaoh's attack was on all of God's male children, God would be permitted to kill all of Egypt's male children. Fair is fair. God defies this expectation, however, and only kills the firstborns of the Egyptians. To a contemporary reader, any death is unfathomable. An ancient audience, however, would hear this as the story of a God of mercy. The God of Israel did not escalate violence but showed restraint. When God's children were threatened with genocide, God did not respond in kind. Christians find the ultimate example of God's desire for humanity expressed in Christ and Christ's teaching. Unfortunately, the ancient Hebrews did not have the cultural context to hear "Love your enemies, and pray for those who persecute you." As a result, God met the people where they were and attempted to move the conversation in Christ's direction. Without a sensitivity to these relational concerns of God and the original occasion of the text, God will come off looking bad to the contemporary reader.

Yahweh vs. "Pharaoh"

As part of its attack on Pharaoh, the Bible never names the pharaoh of the exodus. Yahweh gives Moses the divine name to accompany the message, but no pharaoh is named in the story—neither the pharaoh of the oppression nor the pharaoh of the exodus. To add to the insult of omission, the two midwives to the Hebrews in Exod 1—individuals at the bottom of the social ladder—are named Shiphrah and Puah. Not naming Pharaoh in the story is a clever theological statement as well. When Moses first confronts Pharaoh with the simple request to allow the ancient Hebrews a few days to worship Yahweh, he responds in Exod 5:2, "Who is Yahweh that I should obey and release Israel? I don't know Yahweh, and so I will not release Israel." Pharaoh does not know Yahweh, and now, because of his pride, the reader does not know Pharaoh.

This concept of "knowledge" plays an important role in the contest between God and Pharaoh. The Hebrew word translated "to know" carries a much closer connection than is usually associated with "knowledge" in English. The Hebrew word is deeply relational, implying an association and intimacy that allows the word to be used as a euphemism for sex. "To know" is not simply to be aware of or have some mental recall of something. It is to be deeply connected to it.

When the pharaoh who "did not know Joseph" first increases the burden on the children of Israel at the beginning of Exodus, the text finishes chapter 2 with a powerful statement: "God heard their groaning and remembered the covenant with Abraham and Isaac and Jacob" (v. 24). God saw the children of Israel, and *God knew*. God was not merely aware of the suffering of the covenant community; God was connected to them in their suffering. God confesses this in the next chapter when calling Moses: "And Yahweh said, 'I have truly seen the affliction of my people who are in Egypt. I have heard their cries from the oppression of their taskmaster. I know their sorrows'" (Exod 3:7). The ancient Hebrews did not believe in a dispassionate God who was isolated and remote. The God of Israel hurt for them and with them.

Yahweh demonstrates "knowledge" by sharing precisely how the story will unfold with Moses at the call:

> Yahweh said to Moses, "When you return to Egypt, see that you do all the wonders which I have placed in your hand before Pharaoh. I, myself, will harden his heart, and he will not release the people. You will say to Pharaoh, 'Thus says Yahweh, Israel is my firstborn son. So I have said to you, release my son so that he can worship me. But you refused to release him, so see now, I myself will kill your firstborn son.'" (Exod 4:21-23)

Pharaoh's contest with Yahweh creates a similar interpretive problem to God's violence in the plagues. In several passages in the Exodus narrative including this one, God is said to "harden Pharaoh's heart."[12] This statement has caused readers difficulty throughout history.[13] How does one balance justice and mercy if Pharaoh is a mere puppet?

Once again, cultural context is important. Egyptians believed that after death, humans appeared before Osiris and had their hearts weighed against a feather from the god of "truth."[14] The deceased would then have to recite a list containing behaviors they had avoided in their life. For example, "I

---

12. God explicitly hardens in Exod 4:21; 7:3; 9:12; 10:1, 20, 27; 11:10; 14:4, 8; Pharaoh hardens his own heart in Exod 8:15, 32; 9:34; Pharaoh's heart is said to harden without reference to who hardened it in Exod 7:13, 14, 22; 8:18; 9:7, 34.

13. A survey of how different groups have struggled with the text can be found in Claire Mathews McGinnis, "The Hardening of Pharaoh's Heart in Christian and Jewish Interpretation," *Journal of Theological Interpretation* 6 (Spr 2012): 43–64.

14. Michael D. Coogan, "The Weighting of the Heart," *A Reader of Ancient Near Eastern Texts: Sources for the Study of the Old Testament* (New York: Oxford University Press, 2013), 150–54.

have not blasphemed a god" or "I have not done violence to a poor man."[15] If the heart of the deceased was heavier than the feather, the deceased would not be allowed into the afterlife, and their heart would be consumed by a god of destruction, a half-crocodile/half-hippopotamus. One of the words translated in English as "harden" is also the Hebrew word for "to make heavy." For Yahweh to "make Pharaoh's heart heavy" is to deny Pharaoh's position as god over Egypt in the afterlife.

Egyptians believed Pharaoh was a god incarnate, not simply one who bears the divine image. The battle between Yahweh and Pharaoh in Exodus would not be understood by an ancient reader as a battle between a god and a man but as a battle between the God of Israel and the gods of Egypt. Yahweh makes clear from the beginning it is not going to be a contest.

"Hardening Pharaoh's heart" might reflect a belief that Yahweh would control Pharaoh's moral decision-making, but it may more likely be that Yahweh correctly predicts what Moses's commands will provoke. Yahweh speaks a word of prophecy to Moses. Yahweh gives Moses this sign of what will happen, and repeatedly, Moses sees that, as Yahweh predicted, Pharaoh's heart is hardened. This statement might be an act of reassurance by the divine to Moses. Though, to be fair, one does not necessarily need omniscience to know that when ordered about and threatened by a member of a slave-class, Pharaoh will become stubborn and reject the requests.

However one understands the phrase, "hardening Pharaoh's heart" makes it clear that Yahweh is in complete control in the Exodus account, and the battle between the God of Israel and the gods of Egypt will be no contest. God knows how it is going to go.

Natural or Supernatural?

When I first began teaching "Introduction to the Old Testament," the department required John Tullock's *The Old Testament Story* as the textbook. In it, Tullock suggested that the plagues might be connected to naturalistic explanations.[16] In other words, the plagues might not be "supernatural" events but natural events with convenient timings. The idea challenged my students of faith. Some felt that Tullock was removing God from the story and replacing any divine action with easily explained "scientific"

---

15. These forty-two "Negative Confessions" are contained in chapter 125 of the Egyptian "Book of the Dead" funerary text.

16. John H. Tullock and Mark H. McEntire, *The Old Testament Story* (Boston: Prentice Hall, 2012), 68–69.

explanations. Were the plagues miracles? Or were they simply byproducts of the regular flooding of the Nile and sandstorms?

The "natural" or "supernatural" debate is not one an ancient reader would understand. Enlightenment "Deistic" interpretations of the world, where a creator god set the world in motion but then withdrew from being involved in its working, would not have been recognized. For the ancient reader, God controlled everything. All "natural" occurrences were actually "supernatural." If the plagues could be interpreted as byproducts of what a contemporary reader would call "natural phenomena," an ancient reader would have attributed their timing and effects to the divine.

If one could provide naturalistic explanations for the plagues, the Egyptians are more sympathetic characters. If the plagues are dramatic, onetime, miraculous events with no possible explanation in the natural world, Pharaoh looks like a prideful idiot. If, however, the Egyptians could dismiss the plagues as a familiar phenomenon, Pharaoh's unwillingness to credit Yahweh makes sense.

Psalm 77 might offer some support for Tullock's reading of the plagues. In the psalm's celebration of the crossing of the sea, it says,

> Your way was in the sea.
> Your path was in the abundant waters.
> Yet your footprints were not known.
> You led your people as a flock of sheep
> by the hand of Moses and Aaron. (vv. 19-20)

While the psalm credits Yahweh with the miracle at the sea, Yahweh remained anonymous in its working—"yet your footprints were unseen." Yahweh chose instead to lead the people "by the hand of Moses and Aaron." While Israel could see Yahweh at work, the divine presence was hidden from the Egyptians.

The Sea

The one image consistently associated with the exodus is the splitting of the sea. That is the event on which movies spend most of the special effects budget. It is the image that Ben Franklin wanted on the national seal to capture the story of "exodus." In fact, Moses's first mention in Psalms occurs in the context of the parting of the sea. In Psalm 77:16-20, the psalmist writes,

> Waters saw you—God—
> when the waters saw you they were afraid.
> Indeed the deep trembled.
> The clouds poured out water and the skies thundered.
> Truly, your arrows flashed everywhere.
> Your thunderous voice was in the whirlwind.
> Lightning lit up the world.
> The earth trembled and shook.
> Your way was in the sea.
> Your path was in the abundant waters.
> Yet your footprints were not known.
> You led your people as a flock of sheep
> by the hand of Moses and Aaron.

Throughout the psalm, the psalmist blends both creation images and Exodus images in telling the story. Exodus does the same. The Exodus narrative has numerous creation allusions as well:

> Moses stretched his hand over the sea,
> and Yahweh walked the sea back all night with a mighty East wind.
> God made the sea dry land and divided the waters.
> The children of Israel came in the midst of the sea on dry ground
> and the waters were a wall on their right and on their left.
> (Exod 14:21-22)

The "wind/spirit/breath" (all three words are legitimate translations of the Hebrew word *ruach* [רוח]) of God blowing over the sea remembers when the same thing happened in Gen 1. In Ps 77:16, the "deep" trembles, using the same word from Gen 1. Again, the waters were "split" and dry ground appeared. The deliverance of Israel is an act of creation, and both the psalm and Exodus allude to that.

As important as the image of the creation of the "nation of Israel" is to the Red Sea narrative, equally important is the destruction of the armies of Egypt. The image of deliverance is frequently followed by the fate of the Egyptians. In Ps 78:

> Then God led the people like sheep,
> and drove them like a flock in the desert wilderness.
> God guided them to safety so they would not be afraid.
> But the sea overwhelmed their enemies. (vv. 52-53)

And in Ps 106,

> God rebuked the sea
> and it became dry,
> God led them through the deep,
> but it was like a desert.
> God delivered them
> from the hand of the ones who hated them,
> redeemed them from the hand for their enemy.
> Then the waters covered their adversaries.
> Not one from their company was left. (vv. 9-11)

The destruction of the Egyptians at the sea seems to be as important as the crossing itself in both Exodus and Psalms. Exod 14:28 says, "The waters returned and covered the chariots and the horsemen—the entire army of Pharaoh that came after them. Not even one of them remained." The psalm implies that Pharaoh might also have been a victim! God is

> the one who made Israel pass through, in the midst,
> because God's committed love is forever
> And shook Pharaoh and his army in the Red Sea
> because God's committed love is forever. (Ps 136:14-15)

The Song of the Sea

Fittingly, the crossing of the sea ends with a psalm. Exodus 15 contains both the song of Moses (vv. 1-18) and his sister Miriam (v. 21). While Moses's song does mention "planting" the people, the primary focus of the song is God's victory over the Egyptian army and the reputation among the nations of God as a warrior who fights for Israel. Miriam's song is only one line, and Yahweh's victory is all she wants to sing about: "Miriam sang to them, 'Sing to Yahweh! God has triumphed gloriously! Horse and rider God threw into the sea!" (v. 21).

The singing of the songs is even remembered in Ps 106:11-12:

> Then the waters covered their adversaries.
> Not one from their company was left.
> They trusted in God's words and sang God's praise.

Moses's song closes by establishing an important aspect of Yahweh's relationship with Israel: "Yahweh reigns forever!" (Exod 15:18). Yahweh's kingship over Israel is directly connected to Moses and Exodus from the birth of the nation. In the exilic psalms of Book IV, after the people of God have lost their king, "Yahweh reigns" is the theme of the entire book, and maybe of the entire book of Psalms.

Conclusion

From the context of exile, the psalms highlight several aspects of the exodus:
1. Sin brings judgment.
2. God knows the people's suffering.
3. God is more powerful than the nations.
4. God's name means deliverance.
5. Yahweh reigns.

Each of these would be an important message to an exilic audience, but "Yahweh reigns" might be the most significant theological emphasis to come out of the exodus for the book of Psalms. James Mays argued that "Yahweh reigns" is the central message of the entire book of Psalms.[17] Though "Yahweh reigns" is one verse in Exodus 15, it is the metaphorical and literal "center" of the book of Psalms. Psalms 93–100 contain the theme. Each of these psalms also shares numerous connections to the crossing of the sea, Moses, and the Exodus.[18] For the psalmist, God's kingship and Exodus go hand in hand.

In 1 Samuel 12, when God grudgingly permits Israel to set up a human monarchy, Samuel accuses Israel of forgetting God's kingship in a speech referencing the exodus and Moses. Over the centuries that followed, that human monarchy was idolized by the people, ultimately failing in exile for both the northern kingdom of Israel and the southern nation of Judah. Psalm 99 reminds Israel of Samuel's position by opening the psalm with "Yahweh reigns" and then highlighting that "Moses and Aaron were among God's priests. Samuel was among those who called on God's name. They all called to Yahweh, and God answered them" (v. 6).

The psalmist appeals to two authorities who proclaimed Yahweh as king without equivocation: Moses in Exodus 15 and Samuel in 1 Samuel 12. In exile, the psalmists remind their audience to be like Moses and Samuel and remember that Yahweh is king.

---

17. *The Lord Reigns* (Louisville: Westminster John Knox, 1998).

18. Robert Wallace, *The Narrative Effect of Book IV of the Hebrew Psalter* (StBL 112; New York: Peter Lang, 2007).

Questions for Further Discussion

1. How does reading the plagues of Egypt as either "natural" or "supernatural" events affect the story?

2. Moses was uniquely qualified for the role of deliverer, yet Moses was equally certain he was the wrong choice. What does that mean for the evaluation of callings?

3. Where might the Exodus narrative speak most directly in contemporary culture? Who most needs to hear the message of deliverance?

4. "Yahweh reigns" was the first proclamation of the ancient Hebrews on the other side of the Red Sea. Yet it came in a place and time when they were not properly "a nation" but simply a "wandering people." What does "God's reign" mean to a people without a country? What does it mean that God was displeased that humanity wanted to set up an analogous "human reign" on earth?

5. Pharaoh "does not know Yahweh." Yahweh "knows the sorrows" of the people. How does the intimate understanding of the word "know" offer deeper meaning to the text.

Chapter 5

Torah

> *This is one of the goals of the Jewish way of living: to experience commonplace deeds as spiritual adventures, to feel the hidden love and wisdom in all things.*
> —Rabbi Abraham Heschel,
> *God in Search of Man: A Philosophy of Judaism*

The Psalms as Torah

How can a contemporary reader relate to the love the psalms show for "law"? In contemporary society, laws are usually believed to be, at best, necessary evils. They are required for social order, but society should keep them to the barest minimum to allow for human freedom. In that context, one would find it odd to sing a song that celebrates the "law." So the psalms are odd. The "hymnbook of ancient Israel" sings about law throughout the text. One example in Ps 40 says, "I delight to do your will, O God. Your Torah is inside me" (v. 8).

The law, or more accurately Torah, is a central focus for the psalms. Psalm 1 introduces the book by calling the reader to "meditate on Torah" (Ps 1:3). The center of Book I (Ps 19) is a Torah psalm, and the center of Book V (Ps 119) is a Torah psalm. Even the canonical shape of the psalms mirrors the Pentateuch. The division of the Psalter into five books has been read as an intentional allusion to Torah. A rabbinic commentary on the psalms, known as the *Midrash Tehillim*, introduces Ps 1 by saying, "Moses gave Israel five books, and David gave Israel the five books of Psalms." Psalms is a musical expression of the Torah.

One of the first interpretive obstacles for contemporary readers is understanding the word "Torah." When the Hebrew text was translated into Greek, the Septuagint translators used the Greek word that is commonly rendered "law" (*nomos*) to translate Torah. Later translations have followed this convention, and most English Bibles use the word "law" when translating "Torah."

Torah, however, carries a far more nuanced meaning than the word "law" might suggest. The root of the word "Torah" is a word that means "teaching" or "instruction." (The Jewish Publication Society's translation prefers the word "instruction.") Occasionally, the "teaching" sense of the word comes through even in translations that prefer "law." Consider the New Revised Standard translation of Ps 78:1: "Give ear, O my people, to my *teaching*; incline your ears to the words of my mouth." Although the word in verse 1 is literally "Torah," most English translations render the word "teaching" or "instruction." Psalm 78 gives a recitation on the history of Israel, and the psalmist wants the reader to listen and learn from this history.

Any time a reader finds "law" or "Torah" in the Old Testament, they could benefit from mentally translating these words as "Yahweh's teaching." Consider Psalm 19's celebration of Torah:

> Yahweh's Torah is perfect,
> restoring the soul.
> Yahweh's decrees are trustworthy,
> giving wisdom to the naïve
> Yahweh's precepts are right,
> making one joyful.
> Yahweh's commandments are pure,
> enlightening the eyes . . . . (vv. 7-8)

If contemporary understandings of "law" seem to limit human behavior, Torah leads to human flourishing. God's Torah is the guide to a full life.

Fear of the Lord

"Fear" is not a contemporary virtue, so contemporary readers might struggle with the Old Testament command to "fear Yahweh." Hymns like "What a Friend We Have in Jesus" or worship songs like "Come as You Are" seem to run against the theological narrative of "fear." Some translations soften the notion of "fear" to "revere" to help a contemporary Christian ear. The psalms, however, clearly define what "Fear Yahweh" meant to an ancient reader. Continuing the parallelisms from verses 7 and 8, Psalm 19:9 says,

> The fear of Yahweh is pure,
> standing forever.
> Yahweh's justice is true
> and wholly righteous.

The same connection between Torah and fear of Yahweh is made in Psalm 112:1: "Praise Yahweh! Blessed is the one who fears Yahweh, who excessively delights in God's commandments."

In both psalms, fear of Yahweh is in parallel with, and apparently analogous to, following God's teachings. In other words, fear of Yahweh is obeying God's teaching or instruction rather than following human concerns. Fear of the Lord is, at a basic level, a proper recognition of humanity's position in the cosmos. It is to acknowledge that Yahweh is God, and humanity is not God. Yahweh's teachings are the way to a flourishing life. Fear does not have to be connected to anxiety, but a recognition of Yahweh's position in the universe should bring humility. Fear of Yahweh reflects a respect that leads to obedience, analogous to the type of fear one has for a beloved mentor or teacher. Psalm 111:10 highlights the "teaching" aspect of this fear by connecting it to "wisdom": "The fear of Yahweh is the beginning of wisdom. Understanding comes to all who do good. God's praise stands forever."

"Fear of Yahweh" is something that is "done" in the mind of the psalmist. Practicing it leads to understanding and wisdom. In Jewish tradition, it was not uncommon to think of Torah as "God's wisdom." This psalm provides support for that tradition.

GIVING OF TORAH

Following the crossing of the sea, Yahweh directed the ancient Hebrews to a holy mountain in the desert. Two traditions exist for the name of the mountain. In one it is called "Sinai" and in the other "Horeb." Both are reflected in the psalms. Psalm 106:19 remembers the mountain as "Horeb" in connection with the golden calf story. Psalm 68:8 and 68:17 remember the mountain as "Sinai" in connection with God's dramatic presence on earth. More often, the psalmist prefers to use the more ambiguous phrase "holy mountain," which allows the reader to combine of the images of Zion and temple with Sinai/Horeb and tabernacle.[1]

> Extol Yahweh, our God!
> Worship on God's holy mountain
> because Yahweh our God is holy! (Ps 99:9)

---

1. This play on words seems intentional in Ps 15:1; 43:3; and 99:9;

Covenant

One unfortunate byproduct of translating Torah as "law" is the natural move the reader makes to a legalistic reading of the relationship between Yahweh and Israel. The Old Testament covenant is too often understood as a legalistic relationship focused on limiting the behaviors of Israel in exchange for Yahweh's favor. Israel's understanding of its relationship to Yahweh was binding; however, it was not legalistic. The Torah was how Israel properly remembered the works of Yahweh:

> God established a decree in Jacob.
> In Israel, God placed the Torah,
> which commanded our ancestors to teach their children.
> So that they might know, and the generation after them,
> children who will be born would rise up and recount it to their children.
> So they would place their confidence in God,
> and not forget the practice of God,
> and keep God's commandments. (Ps 78:5-7)

Torah needed to be taught to the children so they would not forget God's words.

This concern for children is seen in the Torah itself. The book of Deuteronomy records Moses's final speeches to the second generation that came out of Egypt. In it, he emphasizes the need for these children to pass on the teachings to subsequent generations. A significant passage in which he does this is known as the "Shema," named for the first word of the passage, meaning "Hear" or "Heed":

> Hear, Israel! Yahweh is our God! Yahweh alone! And you shall love Yahweh our God with all your mind and all your soul and all that makes you, you. These words which I myself am commanding you today must be on your mind. You should teach them to your children. You should talk about them when you sit in your house and when you walk on the road, and when you lie down and when you rise. You should tie them on your hands as a sign. They should be a sign between your eyes. You should write them on the doorframes of your house and on your gates. (Deut 6:4-9)

This passage is still recited in synagogues every Sabbath, and copies of it are placed on the doorframes of the homes of the devout. Israel needed to teach their children and literally bind themselves and their homes to Torah so that they would not forget the mighty works of Yahweh: "Guard yourself, lest you forget Yahweh who brought you out of Egypt, from the house of slavery" (Deut 6:12). The Torah is how one remembered the great works of God. This connection of Torah to Yahweh's deliverance is important from the beginning. When Yahweh first gives the Torah to Israel in Exodus 20, "God spoke all these words, 'I am Yahweh, your God, who brought you out from the land of Egypt from the house of slavery. You are never to have other gods in my presence'" (vv. 1-3).

The Ten Commandments and subsequent Torah are given because of God's actions in Egypt. Like Ps 78 reflects, these commandments in Exod 20 are the proper response to the salvation that had taken place. In other words, salvation came by Yahweh's grace for Israel, and now, the Torah is the way Israel demonstrates that salvation. Torah is God's instruction on how to be a saved people. Obedience to these instructions is the thank-you note that Israel writes with their life.

The covenant ceremony at the holy mountain was analogous to a wedding ceremony. God is saying, "I will be your God," and Israel is saying, "We will be your people." The Torah is the way in which Israel conforms their behavior to reflect that covenant relationship. This change is not a legalistic decision, in the same way that relationship with a spouse should not be legalistic. One should not think of marriage as, "This is what I must do to become or stay married." Rather, the choices an individual makes in a marriage relationship should reflect, "This is the way I live because I am married." Israel's covenant with God works the same way.

The New Testament tells the same story of salvation with a simpler Torah. Consider this summary of the salvation story in Ephesians 2:8-10: "For by grace you are saved through faith, and this is not from you. It is a gift of God, not from works so that someone might boast, for we are God's works of art, created in Christ Jesus for good works, the ones God prepared so that we might walk in them." In the New Testament, salvation comes by grace, and the "good works" of the Christian life reflect what Christ, quoting Deut 6:5, called the greatest commandment. The Torah may look different, but salvation always comes by grace. Once salvation comes, the saved one's life should look like it.

The Decalogue

While specific Torah instructions are not typically mentioned in the psalms, Psalm 81 has a direct allusion to the Ten Commandments, or "Decalogue," explicitly in verses 9 and 10:

> Listen, my people while I correct you!
> O Israel, if only you'd listen to me.
> There will not be a strange god in your midst,
> and you will not bow down to a foreign god.
> I am Yahweh, your god, who brought you up from the land of Egypt.
> Open your mouth and I will fill it! (vv. 8-10)

Psalm 81 directly alludes to the *Shema* by commanding Israel to "Listen!" Then the psalm connects to Exod 20 when it connects exclusive commitment to Yahweh with the divine deliverance of Israel from captivity in Egypt. In other words, "Israel, be faithful to Yahweh because it was Yahweh who delivered you."

Curiously, the giving of the Decalogue in Exodus 20:1 does not use the Hebrew word for "commandments" but rather a generic term, "words" or "things." This leads to the association of Yahweh's "words" with Torah. This association is likely what motivates Ps 119's frequent use of the "words of God" to highlight its celebration of Torah.[2] The psalmist of 119 does not spend any time discussing the Torah's origins. The psalm has no explicit exodus or mountain images. Torah is simply celebrated as God's word and how one remains close to Yahweh.[3]

Lex Talionus

In a key moment in the movie *The Untouchables*, the character of Jim Malone (Sean Connery) explains to Elliot Ness (Kevin Costner) how he can get Al Capone: "You wanna get Capone? Here's how you get him. He pulls a knife, you pull a gun. He sends one of yours to the hospital, you send one of his to the morgue. That's the Chicago way! And that's how you get Capone."[4] The "Chicago Way" is familiar to anyone with a sibling.

---

2. Psalm 119 uses "word" to refer to God's teachings in Ps 119:9, 16, 17, 25, 28, 42, 43, 49, 57, 65, 74, 81, 89, 101, 105, 107, 114, 130, 139, 147, 160, 161, and 169.

3. The Septuagint's translation of the Hebrew for "word," as "logos" may provide the gospel of John the opportunity to apply the same imagery to Jesus.

4. Dir. Brian De Palma, Paramount Pictures, 1987.

Retributive violence is always escalating. Every punch is harder, and every response is bigger. Usually, this continues until something (or someone) breaks, and an adult gets involved. Escalating violence seems to be part of human nature. If someone were to walk up to a gang leader today and punch them in the nose, that person (and likely their entire family) would be killed. For the sake of honor and pride, the violence is escalated. People in the ancient Near East were no different. A simple honor violation could result in tribal blood feuds.

Yahweh speaks directly to this tendency of humanity to escalate violence with perhaps the best-known individual instruction in the Torah: *Lex Talionus*, or the "Law of Retaliation" in Exod 21:23-25: "If there is any harm, you will give life for life, eye for an eye, tooth for a tooth, hand for a hand, foot for a foot. Burn for burn, wound for wound, bruise for bruise." This instruction places limits on retaliation. Victims can only respond to the degree they have been wounded. If someone loses an eye, they can take the perpetrator's eye, but they cannot avenge themselves on the perpetrator's life, family, or tribe. *Lex Talionus* places limits on what is considered an acceptable response to violence. Yahweh's mercy in the Exodus account, however, demonstrates that *Lex Talionus* was a not a legalistic duty. One could show mercy. The text suggests that God desired Israel to reflect the character of the divine and be merciful, but at least, they should only respond to the degree they had suffered.

God's implicitly expressed desire for mercy in the Hebrew text is made explicit by Jesus in the New Testament. In Matthew 5, Jesus preaches in the antitheses:

> You have heard it was said, "An eye for an eye" and "a tooth for a tooth." But I, myself, say to you, do not respond to an evildoer. If anyone strikes you on your right cheek, turn the other to them as well. If anyone wishes to sue you to take your coat, allow them also to have your garment. And if anyone compels you to go one mile, go with them two. (vv. 38-41)

Unfortunately, rather than hearing a message of mercy, people had heard *Lex Talionus* as entitlement. "I only can respond by taking an eye" became "I get to respond by taking an eye." The message of mercy was lost in favor of a legalistic understanding of vengeance. It would seem the children of Israel were not able to answer a call to mercy in a world of violence—though *The Untouchables* makes it clear that Israel is not alone in that struggle.

SHARED LEGAL TRADITIONS

As in the creation stories, the ancient Hebrews were not alone in believing that law codes came from the gods. Perhaps the most famous of the law codes is Hammurabi's. Also like the creation stories, this law code likely predates the Torah instruction of the biblical text. The dating is significant since several passages in the Law Code of Hammurabi resonate directly with the Bible.[5] One example is an echo of *Lex Talionus*: "Law 196: If a man has destroyed the eye of a member of the aristocracy, they shall destroy his eye. 197: If he has broken another's bone, they shall break his bone." In addition to the broad philosophical idea of *Lex Talionus*, some specific rules show great similarity. Compare Hammurabi with Exodus:

Law Code of Hammurabi	Exodus 21:28-29
250 If an ox, when it was walking along the street, gored a man to death, that case is not subject to claim 251 If a man's ox was a gorer and his city council made it known to him that it was a gorer, but he did not pad its horns or tie up his ox, and that ox gored to death a member of the aristocracy, he shall give one-half mina of silver.	When an ox gores a man or woman and they die, the ox shall surely be stoned, and do not eat its meat. But the master of the ox will not be held responsible. But if an ox gored someone previously, and the ox's master had been warned before and had not restrained it, and the ox then kills a man or a woman, then the ox must be stoned and the master also put to death.

The code of Hammurabi and the Torah often deal with similar issues.[6] The parallels are close enough that it is hard to consider them coincidental. The similarities might be direct borrowing, or it's possible that the similarities in the two codes may come from the cultures dealing with similar issues in similar settings, e.g., dealing with the consequences of domesticating oxen in the Levant.

Regardless, the Torah is again an example of Yahweh meeting Israel where they are culturally. Israel may have been aware of certain principles,

---

5. "The Code of Hammurabi," *ANET*, 60–72.

6. Some close parallels, e.g., Exod 21:2 and Law 117; Exod 21:15 and Law 195; Exod 21:18 and Law 206; and Exod 21:22 and Law 209.

or even specific laws, that existed in famous law codes. Yahweh worked within that culture to select instruction that revealed the character that God wanted Israel to reflect at that time. Unfortunately, the specific occasions of the texts have been lost. As a result, the distinctive way in which these teachings might show the character of God that Christians understand as fully revealed in Christ has been lost. That loss of original occasion can explain why Yahweh can appear to a contemporary reader more legalistic and crueler than the original readers of the text would have understood.

LEX TALIONUS AND THE IMPRECATORY PSALMS

Imprecatory psalms might on the surface seem to have little to do with a chapter on Torah. The imprecatory psalms, or "cursing psalms," are a specific type of lament psalm in which the singer asks Yahweh to curse his enemies.[7] The enemies can be societal, national, or personal. The imprecatory psalms provide a hermeneutical challenge for Christians who have been told to love their enemies and pray for those who persecute them.

The curses might simply be, "Rise up, God, strike down the wicked." Other times the imprecation is more specific. Psalm 109 offers a list of accusations the "wicked" offer against the psalmist in 109:6-19. These include a negative finding in court, death, the begging of his children, and the seizure of his wealth. The psalmist responds to these curses in verse 20: "May this be the reward to my adversaries from Yahweh. The ones who speak destruction over my soul." So the psalmist responds to these curses by asking God to throw each one back at the accuser.

The most shocking of the imprecations comes from the communal lament of Ps 137. In exile, when the people are asked to sing a song of Zion by their Babylonian captors, the psalmist sings,

> Daughter of Babylon, the destroyer,
> Blessed is the one who fulfills
> and repays you for your deeds to us.
> Blessed is the one who grabs
> and then shatters your child against the rocks. (vv. 8-9)

It is difficult to believe that one can work infanticide into a worship song, but Israel managed to accomplish it! How can a contemporary reader find grace in the imprecations? Through the canonical process, these words to

---

7. Pss 5, 10, 17, 35, 58, 59, 69, 70, 79, 83, 109, 129, 137, 140 have imprecatory characteristics.

God have become words from God. These were songs sung to God that God felt needed to be in the canon. They have something to teach and cannot simply be dismissed.

In the imprecatory psalms, the psalmists ask Yahweh to be the avenger. They do not ask for the ability to enact vengeance themselves. The psalms recognize that feelings like these against an enemy are not an uncommon part of the human experience. The imprecatory psalms provide a model for how to process those feelings. They need to be brought to the divine.

The imprecatory psalms also provide an affirmation of Yahweh's desire for righteousness and justice in this world. The psalms are asking Yahweh bring justice on behalf of the psalmist. God is not neutral or distant in the life of Israel. God is on the side of justice, and the psalmist is reminding God that action needs to be taken. Clint McCann says it this way:

> In the face of monstrous evil, the worst possible response is to feel nothing. What must be felt is grief, rage, outrage. In their absence, evil becomes an acceptable commonplace. To forget is to submit to evil, to wither and die; to remember is to resist, be faithful, and live again.[8]

Finally (and the reason the imprecatory psalms are in a chapter on Torah!), no matter how difficult the situation is for the psalmist, the imprecatory psalms never exceed *Lex Talionus*. In other words, the psalmists are only asking for the same punishment for their enemy that the psalmists have suffered at the hand of the enemy. The psalmist of Ps 137 had seen children killed by the Edomites and the Babylonians. The psalmist of 109 had received a list of slanders from his accuser and wished them back on his enemy. The psalmists did not escalate vengeance but only sought the justice that God permitted them in the Torah.

As difficult as the imprecatory psalms are for a contemporary reader, for individuals in marginalized communities, they may provide a helpful model for how to process the feelings of injustice.

Clean vs. Unclean

Frequently in the Torah, the text mentions "clean" and "unclean" restrictions. Certain foods and activities can make one clean or unclean. Only a "clean" individual would be permitted to worship Yahweh. Israel was camping near a holy God, and in that context, failure to maintain holiness

---

8. J. Clinton McCann, Jr., *A Theological Introduction to the Book of Psalms: The Psalms as Torah* (Nashville: Abingdon, 1993), 119.

could come with serious consequences.⁹ Psalm 19:9 uses the word for "clean" in connection with "fear of Yahweh": "The fear of Yahweh is pure [clean], standing forever. Yahweh's justice is true and wholly righteous."

Torah observance makes ones "clean." The list of clean and unclean requirements can be tedious for a contemporary reader; however, an important principle is at work in the lists that can speak to a contemporary situation. The clean and unclean restrictions extend to all areas of life. Certain actions, animals, and foods were considered unclean, and performing those actions or eating unclean foods rendered one unclean. Food, skin diseases, clothing, how one handled mold, who one married—all could render a person unclean. The Torah makes clear that worship of God affects every area of life. One cannot simply be concerned with what is done in temple or tabernacle. Even the handling of one's moldy garments reflected worship. Israel was required to commit every area of life to Yahweh. Since Yahweh is a holy God, Israel should be a holy people.

In the Old Testament vision, clean things can be corrupted by unclean things.¹⁰ The psalmist remembers the sins that led to exile in Ps 106 by connecting them to Israel's "uncleanliness": "They were unclean in their actions, and prostituted themselves with their deeds" (v. 39). What makes something "clean" or "unclean"? It is hard to say, though much has been said.¹¹

Some believe that the clean and unclean rules reflect hygiene concerns. Certainly, hygiene does come into play for several of the Torah instructions. Israel is camping together in the wilderness, and having a neighbor with leprosy (Lev 13:2-23) or a house with mold (Lev 13:34-53) could have serious consequences for the community. Unfortunately, hygiene and health fail to answer all the issues. Hygiene is often cited as the reason for pork's classification as an unclean food. Certainly, trichinosis, among other diseases, would have been a risk from undercooked meat. Most food, however, can be dangerous if improperly prepared. Several cultures around

---

9. Aaron's sons, Nadab and Abihu, met with a quick end when failing to maintain holiness in their duties as priests in Lev 10:1-3.

10. In the New Testament, Christ "cleanses" unclean things. When Jesus touches things that by Old Testament rules would have rendered him "unclean" (people with leprosy, dead bodies, etc.), the unclean things are cleansed.

11. One scholar lists at least fourteen difference explanations for the clean/unclean animals. See Jiří Moskala, "Categorization and Evaluation of Different Kinds of Interpretation of the Law of Clean and Unclean Animals in Leviticus 11," *Biblical Research* 46 (2001): 5–41.

Israel apparently consumed pork without severe consequences, so while "hygiene" might explain the Torah instructions like leprosy and mold, the Torah concerning unclean animals is less clear.

Distinctiveness is also popular theory for the clean/unclean distinctions. Excavations have shown that pigs were a popular part of the diet of the Philistines. Israel could demonstrate their distinctiveness by abstaining. Some Torah instruction may be calling Israel to abstain from the practices of other cultures, and the food would be a part of that call to be a separate people.[12]

One of the more creative explanations suggests that the Torah for clean and unclean is connected to creation.[13] Clean things function as they were created to function. Unclean things are consequences of sin's corruption of the created order. For example, fish should have scales, so fish without scales, like catfish, are unclean. Things with legs should walk on the land, so animals with legs in the water (like shrimp or lobsters) are unclean. This extends to other rules as well. Blood belongs in the body, so when blood is outside the body, even during menstruation, it renders one unclean. The creation explanation is sometimes broadened to focus on life and death. In other words, clean things contribute to life, and unclean things contribute to death. The bleeding and high risk of death during childbirth might explain why that activity rendered one unclean. Like hygiene, creation theology answers some questions but unfortunately does not provide a comprehensive answer for clean and unclean activities.

If a single unifying principle existed that comprehensively explained the clean and unclean distinctions, it has unfortunately been lost to history. Though ultimately unsatisfying, "Because God said," might be the best answer for a contemporary reader.

Justice

The reader has already seen God's concern for the marginalized and the vulnerable in the narrative portions of the Torah. Concern for the vulnerable is an essential part of the divine character that is seen throughout the poetic texts as well. Consider Psalm 146:

---

12. The prohibition of cooking a baby goat in its mother's milk (Exod 23:19; 34:26) and making blended clothing (Deut 22:11) may have been prohibitions of specific Canaanite worship practices.

13. Mary Douglas, *Purity and Danger: An Analysis of Concepts of Pollution and Taboo* (London: Routledge & Paul, 1966), 51–57.

> God is the one who make justice for the oppressed
> and gives food to the hungry.
> Yahweh releases the prisoners.
> Yahweh gives sight to the blind.
> Yahweh raises up the one who is bent.
> Yahweh loves the righteous.
> Yahweh protects the foreigner.
> God upholds the fatherless and the widow,
> and cripples the way of the wicked. (vv. 7-9)

It is not surprising that Yahweh commands the people who wear the divine name to reflect the same character. Throughout the Torah, Yahweh connects Israel's need to show justice to both God's character and Israel's experience in Egypt. Leviticus 19 says,

> You should never take vengeance
> or bear a grudge against any of your people.
> And you should love your neighbor as yourself.
> I am Yahweh. (v. 18)
> . . .
> You should rise up for the gray haired!
> You should honor the face of an older person,
> then you shall fear your God.
> I am Yahweh.
> And when a strange foreigner dwells with you in your land,
> Do not wrong them.
> The strange foreigner should be like a native-born to you.
> You shall love the strange foreigner as yourself,
> because you were strange foreigners in the land of Egypt.
> I am Yahweh.
> You should not cheat a just measure,
> in length, weight, or amount.
> You should have just weights and just scales—
> a just ephah and just hin.
> I am Yahweh, your God,
> who brought you from the land of Egypt. (vv. 32-36)

All of these commands for just living come from two reasons: one, because their God is Yahweh, and Yahweh looks after the vulnerable, so they need to look after the vulnerable; and two, because they were once vulnerable, so they need to look after the vulnerable.

Because Yahweh, your God, is God of Gods, and Sovereign Lord. The great God, mighty and awesome, who is unbiased and never takes bribes. The one who brings justice for the fatherless and the widow. The one who loves the foreigner and gives clothing and food. So you must love the foreigner because you were foreigners in the land of Egypt. (Deut 10:17-19)

In a time without social support programs, Yahweh insisted Israel conduct themselves in a manner that provided for the most vulnerable among them. Israel was commanded not to completely harvest their fields but to leave what was unharvested for those who had need:

Whenever you reap a harvest in your field and forget a sheaf in the field, do not return to get it. It will be for the foreigner, the fatherless, and the widow so that Yahweh, your God will bless all the work of your hands. When you beat the olive tree, do not go over the branches again; let the foreigner, the fatherless, and the widow. When you gather your grapes, do not harvest again, but let the foreigner, the orphan, and the widow. (Deut 24:19-21)

Even the portion of the required tithe meant to support the Levites was to be shared with the vulnerable: "When you finish tithing all your tithe of your produce in the third year (the year of the tithe), you must give to the Levites, the foreigner, the fatherless, the widow so that they may eat their fill in your gates" (Deut 26:12).

Nothing makes Yahweh as angry as those who violate the third commandment and "take the divine name in meaninglessness." The harshest words of judgment in the biblical text are directed at the religious who misrepresent what it is to follow Yahweh. Making God look bad brings swift judgment. Yahweh even judges "the gods" in Ps 82 because they do not take care of the vulnerable:

God stands in the divine assembly.
In the midst of the gods, God brings just rulings.
How long will you offer judgments drunk up by your favorites that only honor the wicked?
Offer true justice to the weak and the fatherless.
Vindicate the oppressed and the poor.
Secure the weak
and deliver the needy from the hand of the wicked

who do not know and do not understand. They wander around in darkness while all the foundations of the earth are shaken.
I thought, "You are gods.
You are children of the Most High!
All of you!"
However, you will die like a human,
and fall like any prince. (vv. 1-7)

Even connections to the divine do not exempt one from showing justice. If the gods cannot escape judgment, it should not be surprising to read in Ezekiel that humanity is not exempt from this standard. In a passage that should make any person of faith nervous, God reveals to Ezekiel the reason Sodom and Gomorrah were destroyed:

> See, now, this was the iniquity of your sister, Sodom, and her daughters: majesty, abundance of food, prosperous ease, but they did not strengthen the poor or the afflicted. They were supremely arrogant and they did abominable things before me. So, when I saw it, I destroyed them. (Ezek 16:49-50)

This Ezekiel passage provides important context through which to read Genesis 19. Initially, Sodom's selfishness is shown in Lot being the only person to offer hospitality to the divine messengers when they arrive at the city. The reader finds that Lot warns the messengers of God against spending the night outside in the public square. Apparently, Sodom will not provide shelter for the traveling strangers. Sodom's selfishness and insufficiently welcoming attitude is then fully on display when they want to publicly humiliate Lot by attacking his guests. In an honor/shame culture, they want this outsider to "know his place." Though many faith traditions have read the Genesis 19 text and connected city's destruction to specific sexual behavior, Ezekiel clarifies that the city's destruction came from their selfish regard for their own and their failure to look after the vulnerable.[14]

From Isaiah to Malachi, the prophets understood regard for the most vulnerable as a proper interpretation of God's instruction. In Isaiah, when the people of God selfishly kept God's blessing for themselves, God brought judgment:

---

14. The sexual behavior was a way of "shaming" Lot. By allowing his guests to be attacked in such a way, he would be considered a "bad host" and publicly shamed.

> Woe to you who enact unjust policies and
>> who write troubling decrees,
> allowing you to turn aside from the fair treatment of the poor,
>> and to deprive the oppressed of my people of justice,
> to make the widows your spoils
>> and the orphans your plunder!
> What will you do on the day of judgment,
>> in the devastation that will come from far away?
> To whom will you flee for help?
>> Where will you abandon your wealth . . . (Isa 10:1-3)

Torah demonstrates the proper response to God's salvation. Part of what that means is to take on the character of God, and an essential part of that character is justice. In Psalm 68:5, the psalmist asserts, "God, in the holy dwelling place, is father to the fatherless, and an advocate to widows."

The Psalms and Sacrifice

The part of the Torah that seems the most distant to a contemporary Western reader is the detailed sacrificial system. The book of Leviticus offers in graphic detail the way the priest is to conduct the numerous live animal sacrifices for Yahweh.[15] Each sacrifice served a specific function, and the parts of the animal were treated differently depending on the sacrifice.

The psalms seem to be of two minds about sacrifice. On the one hand, the psalmists encourage individuals to make God a priority in sacrifice. For example:

> Sacrifice righteous sacrifices and trust Yahweh! (Ps 4:5)

> May God remember all your offerings and accept your sacrifices? (Ps 20:3)

> With a freewill offering I will sacrifice to you.
> I will give thanks to your name, Yahweh, because it is good. (Ps 54:6)

---

15. The primary offerings are "The Whole Burnt Offering" (Lev 1:1-7), "The Grain Offering" (2:1-16), "The Well-Being Sacrifice" (Lev 3:1-17), "The Purification Offering (Lev 4:1–5:13), and "The Guilt Offering" (Lev 5:14–6:7). Several of these offerings could be adapted to additional circumstances. The "Well-Being Sacrifice," for example, could be modified to be used as a "Thanksgiving Offering" if it was given with unleavened bread and the meat was consumed in a specific time frame.

When the psalmist celebrates a return from exile, part of the joy of the return comes in Yahweh allowing the people to offer thanksgiving sacrifices again: "And let them offer thanksgiving sacrifices and tell of God's deeds with a shout of joy!" (Ps 107:22). The "thanksgiving sacrifice" is likely a direct allusion to the offering specified in Leviticus 7:11-18 that includes both the proper handling of an animal sacrifice and the inclusion of an unleavened cake.

The psalms are not universally positive toward sacrifice, however. Some psalms imply that Yahweh is not interested in sacrifices at all: "You do not desire sacrifice or offering, but an open ear. You don't ask for burnt offering and sin offerings" (Ps 40:6). Psalm 50 clarifies God's position. While it has a sharp rebuke of poor sacrifices, the psalm makes clear that Yahweh does not object to the sacrifice itself. The people are the problem. The psalm echoes the Shema in Deuteronomy once again and takes a prophetic tone by opening with "Hear!" or "Take heed!":

> Hear, my people, I will speak.
> Israel, I will warn against you. I am God, your God.
> I am not condemning you because of your sacrifices
> or your burnt offerings which are continually before me.
> I don't need a bull from your house
> or a goat from your herds.
> Because all that lives in the forest,
> the cattle on a thousand hills, is mine.
> I know all the birds of the hills
> and the creeping things in the field are mine.
> If I were hungry, would I not tell you?
> But the world and everything that fills it is mine.
> Do I consume the flesh of bulls
> or drink the blood of goats?
> Offer a sacrifice of thanksgiving to God.
> Fulfill your vows to the most high. (Ps 50:7-14)

Unlike the rest of the gods of the ancient Near East, Yahweh does not need to "feed" on the sacrifices. Yahweh states that sacrifice is not Israel's problem. The problem is that the "wicked" are members of the covenant community whose lives do not reflect Torah: "But to the wicked God says, 'How can you recite my statutes or take my covenant on your lips? You truly hate constraints and cast my words behind you'" (Ps 50:16).

In Ps 50:18-20, the wicked steal, commit adultery, and bear false witness. The sacrifices are not magical ways of covering sins; rather, they should reflect an appropriate attitude. When sacrifice reflects a commitment to God's covenant and thanksgiving, God hears: "Those who offer a sacrifice of thanksgiving honor me. To those who are set in my way I will show the salvation of God" (Ps 50:23).

As already discussed, perhaps the most confusing psalm on the issue of sacrifice is Ps 51. Famous for being the psalm David sings after the Bathsheba incident, Ps 51 advocates both positions on sacrifice within two verses of one another!

> Because you do not delight in sacrifice,
> if I were to give a burnt offering, you would not accept it.
> Godly sacrifices are humble spirits.
> God will not despise a humble and repentant mind. (vv. 16-17)

Echoing Ps 50, this psalm reminds the reader in verses 16 and 17 that sacrifice is not a magical cover-up for sinful behavior. If sacrifice is not an outward reflection of a heart committed to Torah, then God takes no delight. Yahweh does not delight in sacrifice but in a heart focused on God . . . at least until verses 18-19, when the psalmist sings,

> Do good and show Zion your favor,
> build the walls of Jerusalem.
> Then you will delight in right sacrifices and whole offerings.
> Then bulls will be offered on your altar.

After the beautiful statement of God's lack of regard for sacrifice, the psalm now celebrates God's delight in sacrifice. How could the psalmist advocate two positions in the same psalm?

Psalm 51 provides a nice reminder that communities preserved and composed the biblical text over time, and the texts of the Bible are products of composite authorship. Communities shaped texts. Likely, the first seventeen verses of Ps 51 were composed early in the history of Judah. The psalm survived the destruction of the temple, the destruction of the walls of Jerusalem, and the exile. After Israel returned from exile, the people delayed in rebuilding the temple. In the book of Haggai, the prophet complains that the people had made a priority of rebuilding their own luxurious houses, but they had left God's house, the temple, in disrepair. Some faithful singers likely wanted to preserve this psalm but worried about singing it. If the people heard that "God does not desire sacrifice," it might lead them to continue to devalue the temple and worship. The temple might never get rebuilt. To remind the people that God truly did value sacrifice, perhaps the last two verses were added to the psalm to prevent a dangerous misunderstanding for the people in the postexilic community.

Conclusion

This book breaks little new ground in suggesting the psalms are connected to Torah. In many ways, it stands in a long tradition of reading the Psalms as Torah—as "instruction." Psalms is a teaching book. It teaches about Israel's history. It teaches how to come into worship of God. It teaches what do with frustration, despair, and enemies.

The psalms also teach the Torah instruction that came following the exodus. A failure to "fear Yahweh" and follow God's instruction repeatedly led to problems. Humanity ignored God's instruction in the garden, and it resulted in their exile. Israel ignored their responsibility to look like a "saved" people by following Torah, and it resulted in their exile.

Questions for Further Discussion

1. Torah is the proper response to God's salvation of grace. Not following Torah would equal "taking God's name in vain." Moving the story forward, how does a Christian avoid "taking God's name in vain"?

2. At the center of the Torah (literally and figuratively) is justice. People are shown to be followers of God by how they treat the most vulnerable in society. The Old Testament lists those as the orphan, the widow, or the immigrant. Who would fit that category in contemporary settings? What should a follower of God's response be?

3. "Cursing psalms" are not at home in contemporary worship contexts—even in contexts where injustice suffered might suggest they should be! If one takes seriously God's inspiration of the canon, then these texts are here because God wanted them to be. What might they teach about the nature of acceptable prayer to God?

4. If the sin of Sodom and Gomorrah was arrogant inhospitality, as Ezekiel says, what does that mean for reading that text? What does that mean for how the text has historically been read by the broader culture?

5. The "sacrifices" to God showed culturally understood expressions of complete commitment to and faith in God. In a contemporary society, without animal sacrifice, what would be an analog that might convey the same?

Chapter 6

WILDERNESS

> *It is in the deserts and high places that religions are generated. When men see nothing but bottomless infinity over their heads, they have always had a driving and desperate urge to find someone to put in the way.*
> — Terry Pratchett *Jingo*

THE PSALMS AND THE WILDERNESS

The wilderness is a place of temptation and rebellion; however, the wilderness is also a place of creative potential. God created the nation of Israel out of the wilderness. The covenant that brought order and flourishing to Israel was created at Mt. Horeb/Sinai in the wilderness. The prophet Elijah mysteriously entered the narrative of 1 Kings from the wilderness, and the wilderness was a place of refuge for him in 1 Kings 19. As difficult as life is in the wilderness, Ps 63 remembers it as a place of refuge for David as well.

The desert is the dry land analog to chaos waters. In Job 40, the "Behemoth" is a personification of chaos on land in the way that Leviathan is a personification of watery chaos. While chaos is always dangerous and overwhelming to humanity, it is also always subject to the creative power of the divine. Indeed, in what might be an allusion to the crossing of the sea and the wilderness period, Ps 29 celebrates Yahweh's voice as superior to the sea and the desert:

> The voice of Yahweh is heard upon the waters.
> The glory of God thunders, Yahweh upon many waters! (v. 3)
> . . .
> The voice of Yahweh shakes the desert wilderness.
> Yahweh shakes the wilderness of Kadesh. (v. 8)

Most English Bibles choose the more romantic sounding "wilderness" when translating the Hebrew word for the area of wandering following the exodus. This "wilderness" is a parched, barren, and rocky area that would more precisely be translated as "desert." When reading the word "wilderness" in modern Bibles, readers should avoid images of the "Pacific Crest Trail" that the word might convey. In the wilderness of the Bible, death is an ever-present reality. The sacrificial system in Leviticus even uses the ravenous nature of the wilderness to the people's advantage. The sins of the people are placed on a goat that is then led into the wilderness. The desert literally consumes the sins of the people.[1]

The people's victory and faith leaving Egypt is quickly followed by their failure and doubt. The ink on the covenant is not dry, and Israel begins corrupting their worship of Yahweh with the practices of local fertility gods in the golden calf story.[2] Israel perverts God's plan for worship and repeatedly fails to trust in God's provision. Perhaps unsurprisingly, the psalms remember the time in the desert as a difficult one:

> How much they rebelled in the desert wilderness!
> They grieved God in the desert.
> They repeatedly tested God,
> and provoked the Holy One of Israel.
> They did not remember God's hand,
> nor the day when God redeemed them from their adversary.
> When God did signs in Egypt
> and marvels in the fields of Zoan. (Ps 78:40-43)

The desert narratives would appear to be a model for how not to conduct oneself in relationship with Yahweh. Though, ironically, Yahweh remembers the wandering period differently. Apparently, according to Yahweh, the desert was the honeymoon period in Israel and Yahweh's relationship. In Jeremiah, God is even wistful about it:

> [God said,] "Go, declare in the hearing of Jerusalem, 'Thus Yahweh says, I remember your committed love in your youth—your love as a bride. You followed me in the desert wilderness—in a land which couldn't be farmed.' Israel was holy to Yahweh—the first fruits of a harvest to God. Everyone who tried to consume them was found guilty and destruction came on them," declares Yahweh. (Jer 2:2-3)

---

1. See Lev 16:1-34.
2. See Exodus 32.

Yahweh later accuses the nation of forgetting God after the wonderful time in the desert together. If Judah's sin prior to the exile reached the level where the desert wandering appeared to be faithfulness, it gives a perspective on the seriousness of Judah's situation.

To be fair, however, Yahweh's idyllic perception of the desert period in Jeremiah is a minority position. While God might have romantic remembrances of Israel's time in the wilderness, even Yahweh acknowledges the desert is hard and barren. Later in Jer 2:31, Yahweh asks if Judah's faithlessness was because Yahweh was a desert:

> This generation, see the word of Yahweh. "Have I been a desert wilderness to Israel? Have I been a land of darkness? Why do my people say, 'We are free to wander and not come to you anymore'?"

When the psalms remember the desert wandering, the songs sing the details of the story in a different order from the narrative version. The psalmists often start with Israel's behavior in the wilderness and relate it to the consequence of "forgetting" what Yahweh did in Egypt. As seen above, Ps 78 follows this pattern and tells the story of the exodus only after highlighting Israel's experience in the wilderness.

Psalm 106 also makes clear that the people's sin comes from forgetting. In the first section of the psalm, the psalmist's current, exilic sin is analogous to the first generation's forgetting God:

> We sinned like our ancestors.
> We have committed iniquity and wickedness.
> Our ancestors in Egypt did not consider your deeds.
> They did not remember the abundance of your committed love.
> They rebelled at the sea—the Red Sea. (vv. 6-7)

The punishments in the desert were a consequence of quickly forgetting Yahweh's mighty works:

> But quickly, they forgot God's works,
> and did not wait for God's plans.
> They had an insatiable craving in the desert wilderness,
> and tested God in the wastelands.
> God gave them what they asked for,
> and sent a wasting in their soul. (vv. 13-15)
> . . .

> They forgot the God of their salvation,
> the one who did great deeds in Egypt—
> Works in the land of Ham, and
> Awesome things by the Red Sea. (vv. 21-22)

The psalms are not employing hyperbole with the phrase "quickly, they forgot." Israel begins complaining immediately after the crossing of the sea. Moses sings the song of God's victory over the Egyptian armies and proclaims Yahweh as king in Exodus 15. Then, at the beginning of Exodus 16, Israel cries out,

> The whole congregation of the children of Israel grumbled against Moses and against Aaron in the desert wilderness. And the children of Israel said to them, "If only we'd been killed by the hand of Yahweh in the land of Egypt where we sat by pots of meat and had our fill eating bread—because you have brought us out to this desert wilderness to kill this whole assembly with starvation." (vv. 2-3)

God provides for Israel's hunger through "manna." Though various attempts at naturalist explanations have been provided for manna over the years, the mysterious bread has no explicit origin beyond Yahweh.[3] However manna might have manifested in history, the Bible is clear that manna comes directly from God:

> God commanded the skies above,
> and the doors of the heavens opened.
> It rained manna upon them to eat.
> And God gave them the grain of the heavens.
> Humans ate the bread of the mighty.
> God sent them food to satisfy them. (Ps 78:23-25)

Immediately following Israel's demand for food in Exod 16 came Israel's demand for drink in Exod 17:

> The people quarreled with Moses and they said, "Give us water to drink!" And Moses said to them "Why do you quarrel with me?! Why do you test Yahweh?" But the people were thirsty for water there and murmured

---

3. The word itself offers no clue since its etymology is connected to the Hebrew question, "What is it?"

against Moses. "Why would you bring us up from Egypt to kill us and our children and animals with thirst?!" (vv. 2-3)

Once again, God answers Israel's quarrel and challenge to Moses's leadership, this time by miraculously producing water from the rock. Much like bringing dry land out of the chaos waters is an act of creation, bringing water out of the parched land manifests God's creative abilities.

In both examples of the people's doubt, the source of Israel's sin is "forgetting." When Ps 105 sings of God's provision of meat, bread, and water for Israel, the psalmist does so in the context of God's "remembering:"

> They asked, and God brought quail.
> And caused them to be satisfied with the bread of heaven.
> God opened a rock, and water flowed out,
> going through the wastes like a river.
> Because God remembered the holy word to Abraham, the divine servant.
> (vv. 40-42)

Analogous to the way creation is remembered in the psalms, the psalmist feels free to creatively engage with the order of the events in the exodus story as well. Though in the exodus narrative the miracle of manna precedes the miracle of water, the psalmist in Ps 78 reverses the story:

> They spoke against God, and they said,
> "Is God able to arrange a banquet table in the desert wilderness?
> Even though the rock was hit and the waters flowed out, and torrents overflowed,
> can God also able to give bread or prepare meat for the people?"
> (vv. 19-20)

Though contemporary readers are often fastidious about the order of events in the biblical text, the psalmist clearly felt the ancient reader would not have any trouble reordering the events for the purposes of the story or the song.[4]

---

4. This might be analogous to the creative chronology the Gospel of John uses in, for example, moving the narrative of temple cleansing to the beginning of Jesus's ministry and the day of the crucifixion with respect to Passover. Later readers have sought ways to harmonize John's differences with the Synoptic Gospels when it seems clear the Gospel writer did not feel the same compulsion.

In the psalms, the wilderness narratives act as prophetic warnings to contemporary audiences. Ps 95 provides the clearest example:

> Today, if only you would listen to God's voice!
> Do not harden your thoughts as you did at Meribah,
> as on the day of Massah in the desert wilderness.
> When your ancestors tested me and asked me for proof,
> when they had seen my deeds!
> Forty years I felt a loathing for that generation,
> and said, "These people's minds wander about, and they do not know my ways!"
> So I swore in my anger, they will not come to my rest! (vv. 7b-11)

Psalm 95 likely has an exilic occasion. For the psalmist, Israel has entered another time of testing that they must see though. Marvin Tate puts it this way: "The hardening of the hearts and the test of God, as at Meribah, cannot be relegated to the past and left there. The matter still lives and the congregation is at Meribah again. Massah ("testing") is now."[5] If a new exodus out of the exile is to begin, the people must learn the lessons of the first one.

TABERNACLE

Once while I was teaching, a student said, "You use a lot of metaphors about bad relationships when you talk about God." I said, "It works well because God is in a dysfunctional relationship, and unfortunately, the signs of the dysfunction occur from the beginning."

One early warning sign comes at the start of the relationship. In Exod 24:3, Moses reports to Israel the requirements of the covenant: "Moses came and he recounted to the people all the words and ordinances of Yahweh and. Then all of people answered in one voice, 'We will do all the words that Yahweh spoke.'" After receiving this affirmation of commitment from the people, God begins describing the building of the tabernacle, which literally translates to "dwelling." The tabernacle serves as Yahweh's portable "manifesting location." In a dramatic, countercultural move, Yahweh desires to dwell with the people. In the ancient Near Eastern cultures surrounding Israel, gods were believed to live on specific mountains or have clearly defined regions for which they were responsible. Jacob reflects this understanding in Gen 28:16 when he is surprised to discover

---

5. Marvin Tate, *Psalms 51–100*, 502.

Yahweh at Bethel: "Surely Yahweh is in this place, and I did not know it!" Yahweh, however, continues to defy that cultural expectation and makes plans to travel with the people. The tabernacle is a tent for God's presence to manifest with built-in safeguards to protect an unholy people from the holiness of God.

By the time the psalms were written, a fixed temple on Mt. Zion had replaced the portable tent. The two images are often conflated:[6] "Send out your light and your truth! Let them lead me. And bring me to your holy hill, to your dwelling [tabernacle]" (Ps 43:3). The joining of the two buildings is also reflected in the more generic word "tent": "O Yahweh, who may abide in your tent? Who may dwell on your holy hill?" (Ps 15:1).

Contemporary society often has a difficult time hearing how radical the message of a god who desires to travel with humanity would have been to the ancient Hebrews. The psalmist in Ps 68 recognized that when Yahweh marched in front of the people, it was a terrifying and creative force:

> God, when you went out before your people,
> when you marched through the desert

Syncretism

Syncretism is the most insidious sin that can be committed. Its danger is connected to the ease with which one succumbs to it and its appearance as faith. Syncretism is a reversal of what God desired in human relationships from the beginning.

Throughout the Bible, Yahweh meets people where they are. God walks with the man and woman in the garden and goes camping in the wilderness the children of Israel. God literally walks with humanity in the miracle of the incarnation of Christ. For the church, this impulse is realized in the miracle at Pentecost in Acts 2 where the gospel is spoken in the different languages of the people celebrating the holiday in Jerusalem. Individuals do not have to perform priestly acts, gain special knowledge, or learn special languages to meet God. God meets humanity where they are. Unfortunately, in a syncretistic faith, people believe that where they are reflects who God is. Instead of Yahweh speaking their language, they believe their language captures Yahweh.

---

6. The psalms contain numerous references to "tabernacle" though a casual reader might miss them since most translations opt to translate the word to capture its sense of "dwelling." Likely the word's conflation with the temple motivates this choice. The word "tabernacle" occurs in Ps 26:8; 43:3; 46:5; 74:7; 78:60; 84:1; 132:5; 132:7, and "tent" conveying God's dwelling place occurs in Ps 15:1; 27:5-6; 61:4; 78:60.

the land shook and the heavens poured down
before the God of Sinai—before God, the God of Israel. (vv. 7-8)

Unfortunately, while Moses was on the mountaintop getting the instructions for the tabernacle's construction and further instructions of the covenant from Yahweh, Israel grew impatient. The people decided that rather than waiting on Yahweh's teaching on how worship should be done, they would implement their own plan. In the golden calf story, Israel combine the worship of Yahweh with the worship forms of local fertility religions. This combination is known as "syncretism" (see page 117).

Golden Calf

In the golden calf story, Israel syncretizes the worship of Yahweh with the worship forms of local fertility religions. Fertility gods were often represented with bulls, and Israel decides that Yahweh can be represented with the bull as well. In the minds of the people, Yahweh is no different from any of the other gods in the world. The similarities do not stop at appearance, and Israel even decides to worship Yahweh in the manner other fertility religions would be worshiped. After the people declare in Exod 32:4, "These are your gods, O Israel, who brought you up out of the land of Egypt!" Aaron decides to hold a festival to Yahweh with the golden calf. At the festival, the people participate in a feast and then "rose up to play" or "revel." This phrase is likely a euphemism for the sexual acts associated with fertility religions. Since the calf was created after the exodus from Egypt, the people did not believe inanimate objects were the source of their liberation. They did believe, however, that this calf could represent the source of their liberation. The worship of Yahweh was combined with other deities until it was indistinguishable. Israel believed Yahweh looked like the other gods.

The Bible often uses phrases like "turned aside to other gods." For example, in Ps 40:4: "Blessed is the one who makes Yahweh their trust and does not turn to the proud and to false gods."

In these cases, the sin of Israel is analogous to the golden calf incident. Israel syncretized Yahweh worship with the worship forms of other gods. Throughout the Old Testament, this practice leads to a faith that is unrecognizable. In 1 Kings 19, Elijah feels that the perversion of the covenant is so serious that he is the only one left in Israel who speaks for Yahweh. And the prophet Hosea laments, "Hear the word of Yahweh, children of Israel: Yahweh has an indictment against people who dwell in the land because there is no faithfulness. There is no committed love. There is not even knowledge of God in the land!" (Hos 4:1).

Isaiah and Jeremiah indict the people for their lack of knowledge as well. They are particularly critical of the religious establishment whom one would think should know better.[7] The syncretism of faith was so pervasive that an eighth century BCE inscription found at Khirbet el-Qom in Israel refers to "Yahweh" and implies that Yahweh has the same wife as the local Canaanite fertility god.[8] If Israel can give thanks to God and God's wife, then "Our God is Yahweh alone" of Deut 6:4 has been lost.

Psalm 106 remembers the beginning of Israel's problems and recounts the story of the golden calf:

> They made a calf at Horeb.
> And they worshiped a molten image.
> They exchanged their glory
> for the form of an ox that eats grass.
> They forgot the God of their salvation,
> the one who did great deeds in Egypt,
> works in the land of Ham,
> awesome things by the Red Sea.
> God planned to destroy them, but Moses,
> God's chosen, stood in the breach before him,
> to turn God's wrath from destroying them. (vv. 19-23)

Though many of the narrative elements are present in the text, Ps 106:23 fails to capture the rage God shows in the Exodus account. God does not simply desire to destroy this generation; God is prepared to start the story over. According to Exod 32, the progress made since Abraham is going to be undone:

> Yahweh spoke to Moses, "Go! Go down! Because your people that you brought from the land of Egypt are acting perversely!" . . . Yahweh said to Moses, "I see this people and, look now, they are a people of stiff necks. Now, leave me, and my anger will burn against them and consume them, and then I will make a great nation with you." (vv. 7-10)

---

7. See Isa 5:13; Isa 45:20; Jer 10:14; 14:18; 51:17.

8. Judith M. Hadley, "The Khirbet el-Qom Inscription," *VT* 37 (Jan 1987): 50–62.

The fury is understandable when one remembers the nature of Israel's betrayal. Israel and Yahweh have metaphorically been standing at a marriage ceremony. God has said, "I will be your God." Israel has responded, "We will be your people." Now, after signing the marriage license, one partner has found the other in the closet with another wedding guest. Furious, God wants to start over. This generation will be destroyed, and God will bring a new nation from Moses.

The betrayal with the golden calf interrupts the narrative in Exodus. It comes between God's description of the tabernacle plans and Israel's building of the tabernacle. This highlights the direct contrast between Israel's plans for their relationship and God's plans for Israel's fellowship with God.[9]

1. Israel is trying to create what God has already provided.

2. The tabernacle represents God's plans and initiative. The calf is motivated by humans.

3. For the tabernacle, generous offerings were requested. Aaron demands gold for the idol.

4. The tabernacle requires elaborate preparation using the entire community's gifts. The calf has no planning.

5. The long process of tabernacle construction contrasts with the quick construction of the calf.

6. The tabernacle is designed to safeguard divine access and access is provided on God's terms. The golden calf provides immediate divine access on human terms.

7. The invisible God of the tabernacle is made visible and easily controllable with the golden calf.

8. The personal God who desired fellowship with the people is now an impersonal object that is easily controlled.

Psalm 106:23 makes clear that Moses was the only thing that stood between Israel and destruction. This resonates well with the Exodus account:

> But Moses begged before Yahweh, his God, "Why, Yahweh, should your wrath burn against your people whom you brought out from the land of Egypt with great power and a strong hand! Why? Because the Egyptians will say, 'For destructive purposes did God bring them out—to murder

---

9. Terence Fretheim, *Exodus* (Louisville: Westminster John Knox, 2010), 279–80.

them in the mountains and to finish them off—off the face of the ground!' Turn from your burning anger, and relent from this destructive action against your people. Remember Abraham, Isaac, and Israel your servants—whom you swore by your own self—how you said to them, 'I will multiply your descendants, like the stars of the heavens and this land which I said I will give to your descendants will be their inheritance forever.'" (Exod 32:11-13)

After a slightly humorous (and almost parental) exchange in which Yahweh and Moses disagree over who brought Israel out of Egypt, Moses reminds God of the covenant with the ancestors and God's reputation in the world. Moses uses surprising language with Yahweh. In this passage, Moses implores God to "Turn!" and "Reconsider!" These two words in Hebrew are translated "Repent!" in other contexts. Literally, Moses begs God to repent twice. What might be even more surprising is that Moses's request works: "So Yahweh relented from the destructive action that was planned for the people" (Exod 32:14). Yahweh's mind is changed, and Israel avoids destruction.

In the only psalm in which Moses appears in the superscription, Moses uses the same language as Exodus 32: "Turn, Yahweh! How long? Have compassion [reconsider] on your servants" (Ps 90:13). With the number of parallels in the language between Exod 32 and Ps 90, some scholars read Ps 90 as a poetic expression of the golden calf narrative.[10] Its position at the beginning of Book IV evokes an interesting interpretation in light of the exilic context of Book III (Pss 73–89). Book III has dealt with the reality of the loss of temple, land, and kingship. Psalm 89 passionately expresses confusion over the loss of the Davidic monarchy. In the midst of this despair, Ps 90 enters the exilic occasion and remembers another time when Israel's existence was threatened. For the reader coming out of Book III, this psalm of Moses and allusions to Exod 32 can be read as an ancient authority once again interceding on behalf of an exiled people.

An emotional god who can be talked into and out of decisions can make contemporary readers nervous. The ancient readers, however, had no problem understanding God as an emotional being. This should not be surprising since humans are emotional beings, and they are created in the divine image. While contemporary readers often think of a dispassionate God, sitting on a large throne thoughtfully moving the chesspieces of this

---

10. See, for example, David N. Freeman, "Other than Moses . . . Who Asks (or Tells) God to Repent?" *BR* 1 (1985): 56–59.

world, the Bible tells the story of a God who is relationally present in the moment with the people in their story.

Failure to Take the Land

The generation that came out of Egypt failed at Sinai with the golden calf incident. Their ultimate failure, however, came when they failed to trust Yahweh to give them victory in the promised land. Psalm 95 remembers the story this way:

> When your ancestors tested me and asked me for proof,
> when they had seen my deeds!
> Forty years I felt a loathing for that generation,
> and said, "These people's minds wander about,
> and they do not know my ways!"
> So I swore in my anger,
> they will not come to my rest! (vv. 9-11)

The spies who investigated the land in Num 13 reported that the military strength of the Canaanites was too much, even for Yahweh. They appealed to the enigmatic "Nephilim" mentioned in Gen 6 in an effort to incite the people against Moses (and Yahweh). Yahweh's response in Num 14 is identical to Exod 32. God wants to destroy the people and make a nation from Moses:

> And Yahweh said to Moses, "How long will this people despise me?! How long will they refuse to trust me?! Even after all the signs I have done in their midst?! I will strike them with a plague and disinherit them. And I will make a great nation from you—one even mightier than them!" (Num 14:11-12)

In this complaint in the wilderness at Kadesh, Yahweh uses the phrase "How long?" which is a typical way to introduce a lament. God opens this speech by lamenting to Moses about the people. It might be this lament that Ps 29 refers to when it remembers: "The voice of Yahweh shakes the desert wilderness. Yahweh shakes the wilderness of Kadesh" (v. 8). It was this "voice of Yahweh" that the people ignored in Ps 106:

> Then they rejected the desirable land,
> and did not trust God's word.
> They grumbled in their tents,

> they did not listen to the voice of Yahweh.
> So God took a vow:
> God would make them fall in the desert wilderness.
> God would make their descendants fall among the nations,
> God would scatter them over the earth. (vv. 24-27)

Ps 106 remembers more severe consequences for the people's disobedience than a failure of that generation to take the land. Indeed, verse 27 implies that the later exile came as a direct punishment of the people's lack of faith in Num 14. In Exod 32, Moses reminded God that Israel was brought out of Egypt with a "mighty hand," and God "swore by God's own self" when the promises were made to the ancestors. In Ps 106, God raises the divine hand again and this time swears never to let this people enter the land.

Moses once again intercedes for the people. This time he appeals to more than God's reputation. He appeals to God's character of forgiveness. In this speech, Moses does not use the Hebrew word "repent," but he does beg God to reconsider these terrible actions. He reminds God,

> Yahweh is slow to anger and full of committed love, forgiving iniquity and transgression. Never leaving the wicked unpunished but seeing the iniquity of parents visit the children upon the third and fourth generations. Forgive this people now, according to the greatness of your committed love, as you have forgiven this people from Egypt until now. (Num 14:18-19)

God does relent and does not destroy the people. As Ps 95 alludes to, God forbids anyone over age twenty to enter the promised land. The only exceptions are the two spies who showed faith: Joshua from the tribe of Ephraim and Caleb from the tribe of Judah.

Problematic Numbers

The English name of the book of Numbers comes from the Septuagint's title of the book. The Septuagint's title was likely inspired by the census data of the tribes from Num 1:1–4:49 and Num 26:1-65. According to the first census, most translations report 603,550 men of fighting age. Unfortunately, this traditional translation of the census numbers is hard to reconcile with other parts of the Old Testament narrative and what is known from historical sources. This many fighting men would imply that two to two and a half million people came out of Egypt.

Several places in the narrative indicate that the number is problematic. Only two Hebrew midwives met Pharaoh at the beginning of the story in Exod 1. Two midwives would be inadequate to attend to the needs of a population of two and a half million people. If one takes seriously the number seventy for the children of Jacob who settled in Egypt (Gen 46:27) 430 years prior to the exodus, then biologically, one might reasonably expect approximately ten thousand ancient Hebrews.[11] While the book of Exodus says Yahweh made the Israelites exceedingly fruitful, 25,000 percent more fruitful than normal seems high! Additionally, if Israel's army was six hundred thousand men, then Israel's crushing defeat in the promised land is confusing. At the town of Ai in Joshua 7:4, "about thirty-six men" were killed. For an army of six hundred thousand, thirty-six men would not seem to be a significant enough loss to "melt the hearts of the people and turn them to water" after the battle.

Historically, the numbers cause difficulty as well. If Israel's army was six hundred thousand men, the impact of the exodus story is diminished. The exodus is not a story about a God who took a large number of people with an enormous army and guided them out of Egypt. Two million people could travel wherever two million people wanted to go without waiting on deliverance. An army of six hundred thousand men would vastly outnumber Egypt's army at the time. For comparison, immediately prior to the best date understood for the exodus, Ramses II engaged the Hittite army at the battle of Kadesh. In this battle, Ramses committed a force of twenty thousand men to win the day.[12] With an army thirty times the size, Israel could have left Egypt whenever they wanted.

Why would the biblical text have a number that causes such difficulty in interpretation? In truth, it might not. The difficulty may come in the translation of the number. The Hebrew word traditionally rendered "thousand" (אלף, "*alef*") has several meanings associated with it. The word can mean "thousand," but it can also be "clan" or "unit."[13] In other words, instead of translating Num 1:21, "Those enrolled of the tribe of Reuben were 46,500," the passage could be understood, "Those enrolled of the tribe of Reuben were forty-six military units, totaling five hundred men."

---

11. A. Lucas, "The Number of Israelites at the Time of the Exodus," *PEQ* 76 (1944): 164–68.

12. Mark Healy, *Qadesh 1300 BC: Clash of the Warrior Kings* (Oxford, UK: Osprey Publishing, 1993), 32.

13. George Mendenhall offered a compelling argument for this understanding of the word in "The Census Lists of Numbers 1 and 26," *JBL* (Mar 1958): 52–66.

Translating the text this way would help make sense of several problematic passages.

A variety of suggestions have been made through the years to reconcile the numbers with reason and the overall biblical narrative. Unfortunately, none of the solutions is completely convincing. The numbers could be hyperbole. They could represent numbers from a later census. Or, as was suggested, it is possible the word "thousand" has been imprecisely translated throughout the years. It is also possible that the ancient readers understood the occasion of the text in a manner that made these numbers more understandable. Contemporary readers may have to learn to be comfortable with "the numbers are problematic."

MOSES IN THE WILDERNESS

The wilderness was a difficult time for all the heroes in the exodus narrative. The story of the book of Numbers is a story of rebellions. Miriam and Aaron challenge Moses's leadership. The people reject God's call to take the land. And, ultimately, Moses rebels against God's teaching. When Ps 106 remembers this story, it does soften Moses responsibility:

> They made God angry by the waters of Meribah.
> God punished Moses because of them.
> Because they made Moses's spirit bitter,
> and he spoke rashly with his lips. (vv. 32-33)

Moses's "rash words" came after Israel complained again about lacking water. In Num 20, God promised to meet their need for water just as it was met in Exod 17, but this time Moses's role in the miracle would look different. Rather than hitting the rock with his staff to bring water like in Exod 17, Yahweh commanded Moses to speak to the rock. Instead of following Yahweh's commands, Moses spoke to the people, saying in Num 20:10, "Listen, you rebels, shall we bring water for you out of this rock?" and then used the method that had worked before, hitting the rock twice with his staff.

The psalm's remembrance of this story assigns more of the blame for this sin to the people, which corresponds well to Moses's report of the event in Deuteronomy:

> And I pleaded with the Lord at that time, saying, "O, Sovereign Yahweh! You have begun to show your servant your greatness and your strong

hand! What god in the heavens or on the earth could do your works and mighty deeds? Please, now, allow me to cross over that I might see this pleasant land on the other side of the Jordan—the fair mountains and Lebanon." But Yahweh was angry with me *because of you*, and did not listen to me. Yahweh said to me, "That's plenty from you. Do not speak to me again about this." (Deut 3:23-26)

Numbers, however, does not shift the blame; God makes clear who is at fault:

Yahweh said to Moses and to Aaron, "Because you did not trust in me, to show my holiness to the children of Israel, therefore you will not bring this assembly to the land which I gave to them." (Num 20:12)

This one mistake is enough to keep Moses out of the promised land. If this punishment seems too harsh, recall that in Num 12, Yahweh chastised Miriam and Aaron for challenging Moses's leadership:

And God said, "Hear, now my words. If there are prophets with you, I, Yahweh, make myself known in visions. I speak to them in dreams. Not so with my servant Moses. He is trusted with all my house. I speak to him directly, and not with riddles. He looks on the form of Yahweh. Why were you not afraid to speak against my servant, against Moses?" (vv. 6-8)

Moses's special relationship with God meant that Miriam and Aaron should have known better than to challenge his leadership. In the same way, because of Moses's special relationship with God, Moses should have known better than to act in a way contrary to God's teaching. If Moses was afraid the people doubted his leadership to the point that they might take life—which is likely considering their murmuring—Moses should have trusted that God would protect him. Instead, Moses reminds the people of his privileged relationship and tries to work the miracle in a more active manner than God had commanded. As a result, Moses loses the promised land.

Psalms and Deuteronomy

The books of Psalms and Deuteronomy are two texts in the Old Testament whose explicit purpose presents as liturgical. Deuteronomy is a collection of the last three sermons of Moses for the generation who would settle the promised land. The book is a retelling of the story of Israel from Abraham forward, hence the Greek title in the Septuagint, "Deutero"-nomy, or "second law." With its sermonic setting, Deuteronomy fits well in the context of covenant renewal or revival. When Jesus quotes from the Torah in the Gospels, his favorite source is Deuteronomy. Likely the homiletical arrangement of Deuteronomy suited Jesus's sermons.

Some see the book as the culmination of the Torah story, and others read the book of Deuteronomy as an introduction to the material that comes after it. The result is that the book serves as an excellent transition.

Deuteronomic Theology

Bernard of Clairvaux understood faith as a growth process in the life of a Christian.[14] There were three levels one could attain on earth:
1. Love Self for Self
2. Love God for Self
3. Love God for God

The highest level of faith one could attain on earth would be the ability to love God for God's sake, or disinterested piety. This level of faith was illustrated by Abraham in the sacrifice of Isaac in Gen 22. Just below disinterested piety is when an individual loves God only for self. In other words, faith and love are motivated by self-interest. Obedience to God's commands might be connected to the promise of earthly or eternal reward. It is a higher level of faith than only loving self, but it is not as selfless as the ability to love God even when it costs.

Deuteronomy most often expresses faith at this second level. The book focuses on a retributive faith that emphasizes reward for obedience and punishment for disobedience. While the idea occurs in other texts in the Old Testament, the numerous references in Deuteronomy give this theological perspective the name "Deuteronomic theology." A clear example of this is found in Deut 6:14-18:

> Do not go after other gods from the gods of the people who are around you. Because the God who is with you—the God Yahweh—is jealous. The anger of Yahweh, your God, would be kindled against you and would destroy you from the face of the earth. Do not try Yahweh your God as you did at Massah. You must surely keep the commandments, decrees, and statutes which Yahweh, your God, commanded. Do what is

---

14. St. Bernard of Clairvaux (1090–1153), *On Loving God*.

right and good in the eyes of Yahweh, so that God may do good for you.
So you may come into and inherit the fair land which Yahweh swore to
your ancestors.

The Old Testament is a complex text that tells stories of individuals
in a variety of stages of life and faith. Just as Ps 150 illustrates disinterested piety, several psalms illustrate Deuteronomic theology. Psalm 1 is an
obvious example:

> Blessed is the one who does not follow the counsel of the wicked
> or stand in the pathway of sinners
> or sit in the assembly of the haughty.
> But their delight is in the Torah of Yahweh!
> And they meditate on God's Torah—day and night.
> And they will be like a tree planted by streams of water
> which give their fruit in season. Its leaves never wither.
> Everything they do will succeed! (vv. 1-3)

Psalm 1 has historically been interpreted as promising the righteous ones
that they will find security and prosperity when they meditate on God's
instruction. When the righteous are rewarded for obedience, the corollary
of this theology is that the wicked are punished. Psalm 1 continues,

> Not so with the wicked.
> Rather they are worthless chaff, which is blown by the wind.
> Because of this, the wicked cannot stand in the judgment
> or sinners in the congregation of the righteous.
> But Yahweh knows the pathway of the righteous,
> but the pathway of the wicked goes to destruction. (vv. 4-6)

The Deuteronomic theology in this text and elsewhere could be referring to a follower of God in an early stage of faith. At the beginning of a
faith journey, individuals are often concerned with how a faith commitment affects them. Is their eternity assured? Do they receive material gifts?
Will God get them out of their current dilemma? Passages that follow
Deuteronomic theology might be meant for individuals early in a faith
walk. It would be like a parent instructing a child: "Clean your room if
you want your allowance. If you don't, you will be punished." The parent's
hope is that the child will learn the value of cleaning their room without
the promise of reward or threat of punishment. Likewise, the hope is that

the follower of God with this retributive faith will grow to the point where obedience to God's Torah comes without the promise of reward.

The book of Jeremiah provides several excellent examples of individuals interacting with God on two different faith levels. On the one hand, God seems incredulous that though Israel was promised rewards for obedience after leaving Egypt, they refused to show obedience. In Jeremiah 7, God says,

> I only commanded them this thing saying, "Obey and I will be your God, and you will be my people. Walk in the way I commanded you so that you will know true goodness! But they did not hear and bend their ears, and they walk in their own stubborn plans and destructive minds. And they looked backward rather than forward. (vv. 23-24)

God seems to marvel at the fact that Israel will not even clean their room for an allowance. Yet God's call to Jeremiah is not a call to blessing but a call to suffering. Jeremiah's obedience does not bring earthly blessing. It results in his imprisonment, beatings, scorn, and, tradition says, a martyr's death. Jeremiah preaches a theology to Israel that is not at work in his own life because his faith is more mature. Where Israel refused to show a retributive faith, or Deuteronomic theology, Jeremiah's life was showing disinterested piety.

The psalms quickly reveal that life does not always work according to simple formulas. While Deuteronomic theology may be a fine place to start faith, when life's experience doesn't match up to the psalmist's understanding of theology, that inspires songs as well. In Ps 44, the psalmist attempts to make sense of suffering even though the people have been faithful:

> All this has come upon us,
> but we have not forgotten you or violated your covenant.
> Our minds have not turned away,
> nor have we stepped away from your path.
> Still you have crushed us in land of jackals
> and covered us in deep darkness. (vv. 17-19)

Additionally, Scriptures like Ps 88, Job, and Ecclesiastes wrestle with the how to connect faith and reward in this life.

Conclusion

The entire book of Deuteronomy serves as Moses's "St. Crispin's Day" speech as he encourages the younger generation before they take the promised land. As Moses's speeches reach their climax in Deut 30, the people are again challenged to choose God. Only following God's instruction will lead to life:

> See, I have placed before you today life and goodness or death and destruction. I am commanding you today to love Yahweh your God, to walk in his way, and to keep his commandments and statutes and justice, then you will live and multiply and Yahweh your God will bless you in the land which you coming to possess. But if your mind wanders and you do not obey, and you are lured away and bow down to other gods and serve them, then I declare to you today, you will surely be destroyed, and you will not extend your time in the land you are crossing over the Jordan to enter and possess. (Deut 30:15-18)

Moses finishes his last speech in Deuteronomy by speaking a blessing over each tribe in Israel. For the first time in the Torah, Deut 33 introduces Moses as "man of God." In an interesting parallel, the superscription of Ps 90 also remembers Moses as "man of God." Additionally, in the first words of the psalm of Moses, Ps 90:1, God is celebrated as a refuge for the people: "O Sovereign, you have been our dwelling place from generation to generation." This verse echoes Moses's last words to tribes of Israel in Deut 33:27a: "The ancient God is a dwelling place, underneath eternal arms." Moses's first word to the people in exile in Ps 90 is the same as Moses's last word to the people seeking a home from the wilderness: "Wherever you might be, God is your dwelling place."

The wilderness story comes to an end in the plains of Moab with Moses's death. Moses dies at "three generations old."[15] Though Moses was older, the Bible makes clear that he was not infirmed in any way. His eyes were not impaired, and he could still father children (Deut 34:7). Moses's mission was simply over. His death and burial as handled by God alone. With Moses's death, all the leadership that led Israel out of Egypt was dead. Joshua and Caleb alone were left to see the promise of land realized.

---

15. Forty years was a way to say "one generation" in ancient Israel. When the text says that Moses was 120 years old, one could legitimately translate that as "three generations." In other words, Moses was a grandfather at his death.

QUESTIONS FOR FURTHER DISCUSSION

1. Syncretism is the most pervasive and insidious sin humans commit. It is also one of the easiest! Ancient Israel combined the worship of Yahweh with worship of fertility gods of the day. What are the contemporary "gods" whose worship is combined with the worship of God?

2. In both the golden calf story and the flood narrative, God "repents" and "changes his mind." If "God never changes," how do you read these passages?

3. The English translation of the Bible's report of the exact number of ancient Hebrews to leave Egypt causes trouble for readers of the text. Should it? Does the lack of firm answers about how to read the text affect the text's meaning? Why or why not?

4. The story of Moses shows that leadership has privileges and responsibilities. While God protects Moses from the leadership challenges of his own family, God also judges Moses and keeps him out of the promised land for one, seemingly minor mistake. What are the implications for contemporary leaders when thinking about these lessons?

5. Most people have lived long enough to recognize that "Deuteronomic theology" has exceptions in this life. Many, however, simply push off the blessings that come from obedience to the afterlife. Unfortunately, ancient Israel did not have the developed belief in the afterlife seen later in the text. How does one reconcile the texts that promise earthly blessing for obedience and the texts (like Jeremiah and Job) that throw those promises into question?

Chapter 7

SETTLEMENT

> *I just want to do God's will. And he's allowed me to go to the mountain. And I've looked over, and I've seen the promised land! I may not get there with you, but I want you to know tonight that we as a people will get to the promised land.*
> —Martin Luther King, Jr.

SETTLEMENT IN THE PSALMS

The period when Israel appeared in the land of Canaan is broadly referred to as "Settlement." This includes the thirteenth century BCE through the period of the Judges to the beginning of the United Monarchy, roughly 1000 BCE. The biblical books that are primarily associated with this period, Joshua and Judges, reveal a complicated and often contrasting narrative. Both books do share the most violent narratives in the biblical text.

The psalms contain a few direct references to the settlement period. Most of the references to the "land of Israel," however, focus on the land in the context of the return from exile or in an eschatological connection to an eschatological ideal. This should not be too surprising since many of the psalms were composed, and the shape of the book of Psalms itself was finalized post exile. In that period, "land" would symbolize God's provision and deliverance from the difficulties facing the people.

"Land" is, in fact, used as a metaphor in a variety of ways in the psalms. Psalm 25 provides an image of land as an example of God's forgiveness and human commitment to Torah:

> For the sake of your reputation, Yahweh,
> forgive my iniquity because it is excessive.
> Who fears Yahweh?
> One who teaches in the way God will choose.
> That soul will lodge in goodness.
> That soul's descendants will inherit the earth (vv. 11-13)

Ps 119 alludes to settlement as a metaphor for celebration of obedience to Torah. The word for "portion" is associated with the division of the land in Joshua.[1] The psalm uses that association to connect the land and Torah obedience.

> Yahweh is my portion.
> I promise to keep your words.
> I will seek your face with all my thoughts.
> Be gracious to me as you have promised. (Ps 119:57-58)

The book of Joshua also uses the word "heritage" in reference to the land.[2] Psalm 119 uses that association with settlement as a remembrance of God's deliverance from personal difficulty:

> The wicked laid a snare for me,
> but I did not wander about from your precepts.
> Your decrees are my inheritance forever.
> They are the joy of my mind. (vv. 110-111)

The psalms themselves do not explicitly celebrate the violent culture associated with the settlement period, though they do allude to and presume some of this violent tradition. Throughout the psalms, one finds strong, military images of Yahweh. While the graphic detail of violence found in Joshua and Judges is omitted, the psalms seem familiar with that tradition, and it can be seen in the way the psalmists talk about the texts.

While the primary narrative sources for the settlement period are Joshua and Judges, the battle for the land starts earlier in the biblical narrative. The book of Numbers records battles on the eastern side of the Jordan River prior to the entrance into the land. While some psalms discuss settlement in general terms, the battles on the eastern shore of the Jordan are the ones the psalms prefer to reference directly.

Violence in the Old Testament

Joshua and Judges use different genres to tell the story of the conquest. These genres result in often contrasting perspectives on how Israel came into the land. The book of Joshua, told using the genre of conquest literature, portrays the settlement as a swift, comprehensive, and mostly successful

---

1. See Joshua 15:13; 18:7; 19:9.

2. See Joshua 11:23; 14:3.

military campaign accomplished by a single generation. Judges uses the slightly different genre of narrative history and tells the story of an incomplete initial conquest. Judges shows conquest as a slower process filled with graphic stories of successes and failures over multiple generations. Both books, however, contain graphic depictions of violence ostensibly commanded and sanctioned by God.

Christians have struggled since the early days of the church to reconcile the violence in the Hebrew Bible with the loving message of Jesus. The early church heretic Marcion felt that the Yahweh of the Old Testament was distinct from the God of the New Testament and father of Jesus. He believed the legalistic, militaristic Yahweh of the Old Testament was bloodthirsty, and the loving, merciful father of Jesus in the New Testament emphasized grace.[3] While the early church officially rejected Marcion's theology, his perspective is latent within the church even today as individuals try to read the Old Testament narratives in light of the message of Jesus.

> *Cautions of Metaphor*
>
> The Old Testament uses many metaphors to talk about the divine. God is called "shepherd" (e.g., Ps 23:1), "king" (e.g., Ps 95:3), "father" (e.g., Ps 68:5), even the "sun" (e.g., Ps 84:11).
>
> While metaphors can aid in communication of ideas, they are limited. To say "God is father" is to say God is like an earthly father but at the same time also unlike an earthly father. This applies to any of the metaphors used for God. Metaphors are culturally dependent and speak to the culture.
>
> God consistently meets humanity where humanity is, and during the history of the biblical text, humanity was thoroughly patriarchal and terribly violent. As a result, many of the metaphors used to describe the divine are patriarchal and some are violent. Perhaps the more fascinating development is how an occasional alternative metaphor slipped into that patriarchal and militaristic society. Along with king, father, and military general, God is occasionally portrayed as a mother bird protecting her chicks (e.g., Ps 57:1) or as a mother nursing her child (e.g., Isa 66:13).

The narrative stories of violence in the Hebrew Bible are difficult to reconcile with the New Testament. What may be more surprising, however, is that Israel celebrated and sang about a militaristic God in the psalms.

---

3. James D. G. Dunn, "'The Apostle of the Heretics': Paul, Valentinus, and Marcion," in *Paul and Gnosis*, vol. 9 of Pauline Studies, ed. S. Porter (Boston: Brill, 2016), 105–18.

The title for God, "Yahweh Sabaoth" or, in this translation, "Supreme Commander Yahweh," was a powerful military confession. This title implies that Yahweh is a general with armies at the ready. This title is celebrated throughout the Old Testament and found numerous places within the psalms. For example,

> The nations roar, and kingdoms shake.
> God speaks and the earth melts.
> Supreme Commander Yahweh is with us.
> The God of Jacob is our stronghold.
> Go and see the works of Yahweh,
> you who set devastation in the earth! (Ps 46:6-8)

God is celebrated as the warrior-king who delivers Israel from their enemies: "Who is this 'King of Glory'?" (Ps 24:10). Supreme Commander Yahweh is the king of glory!

Even Jerusalem, ostensibly the "city of peace," is celebrated as a manifestation of God's military prowess. The security of God's headquarters reflects God's power. It shames and terrifies other kingdoms of the world. In Ps 48,

> God is within [Jerusalem's] citadels
> and is known to be a stronghold.
> When the kings looked,
> God was revealed, and they ran away together.
> When they saw,
> they were astounded, panicked, and fled.
> Trembling took hold of them,
> an agony like someone giving birth.
> Like an east wind
> that shatters the ships of Tarshish.
> As we have heard,
> so we have seen in the city of Supreme Commander Yahweh,
> in the city of our God of gods, established forever! (vv. 3-8)

It does not take long in the Old Testament texts before Marcion's understanding of a violent Yahweh makes sense. Do these texts celebrating a God whose military might terrifies the nations truly reflect the same God who challenges the people to "love their enemies" and "pray for those who persecute them" in Matthew 5:44? The short answer is "Yes." Recognizing the connection, however, can be difficult for a contemporary reader. As is often the case, help comes from being sensitive to the original occasion of the ancient text.

Ancient Military Context

As already seen in Exodus, the world of the ancient Israelites was violent. While Egyptian power was a present reality for Israel throughout its existence, two other powerful empires challenged Israel during the period of the Israelite monarchy. The Assyrians and the Babylonians were international superpowers with strong economies and militaries. The Assyrian empire effectively weaponized terror in warfare, and the Babylonians followed their example centuries later. These empires were not satisfied simply to fight battles and win. As they spread their empires, each of them would creatively and thoroughly humiliate conquered cities. The greater a city's resistance, the more severe the punishment and humiliation.

When the Assyrians successfully conquered a city, some individuals were beheaded. Assyria even preserved images of soldiers playing games with the disembodied heads of victims. Some of their victims were flayed and their skin hung on the city pillars or taken to other cities as a warning. The army often displayed tortured, dismembered, disemboweled captives around a burned city. Some men were impaled on stakes, and the Assyrians mastered impaling individuals without damaging vital organs. As a result, individuals suffered for hours as they died. The leadership of a city was publicly shamed for daring to challenge the Assyrians. Occasionally, captives were led into captivity nude.

The Assyrians' cruelty was designed to punish disobedience and deter further challenges from other cities. They proudly displayed these events in graphic detail on carved stone reliefs that lined the walls of their palaces and civic buildings. Whenever individuals visited an Assyrian king to pay homage, they walked down hallways with graphic images preserving the cruelty of Assyrian military practice. The images served as a warning of the consequences of challenging the king's authority.[4]

When the psalms sing of God as "Supreme Commander Yahweh," it is within this context of military power. This title is a confession of Yahweh's power in the world. Though other nations and armies seemed more powerful than Israel, Israel confesses that Yahweh is the one who controls

---

4. Albert Kirk Grayson, *Assyrian Rulers of the Early First Millennium BC: I (1114–859 BC) Royal Inscriptions of Mesopotamia*, vol. 2 of Assyrian Periods (Toronto: University of Toronto Press, 1991).

and humbles the world. To sing of "Supreme Commander Yahweh" is to make a statement of faith that the God whose character is justice is in control of a violent world. Yahweh's powerful military command brings an end to battle. Other nations may start wars, but Yahweh puts an end to them all:

> The one who ends wars to the ends of the earth.
> God will break the bow, shatter the spear, and burn the shield in fire.
> Be still and know that I, myself, am God,
> exalted in the nations and exalted in the earth.
> Supreme Commander Yahweh is with us.
> The God of Jacob is our stronghold. (Ps 46:9-11)

To confess Yahweh as commander in the psalms is also a liturgical answer to the Assyrian liturgies and theology of war. The Assyrian decisions to go to war, actions in war, and their celebrations following battle were steeped in religious observance and formal ritual. The king was thought of as the "viceroy" of the god Ashur. The king would employ diviners to ensure the god's support in battle. Prayers and rituals were performed to protect the king and army during battle, and the thanksgiving celebrations following victories often contained expressions of piety.[5]

When two nations battled in the ancient Near East, the assumption was that their representative gods were fighting as well. The winners felt they had evidence that their gods were more powerful. A massive empire with a seemingly unstoppable army would suggest to any ancient Near Eastern citizen that the Assyrian gods were the strongest in the world. In fact, when the Assyrian king's representative, the Rabshakeh, came to Jerusalem to encourage the city's surrender, he made that point in 2 Kings 18:

> Until I come and take you to a land like your land. A land of grain and wine—a land of bread and vineyards—a land of olive oil and honey—so you will live and not die, do not listen to Hezekiah because he misleads you saying, "Yahweh will rescue us!" Truly, have any of the gods of any nation ever rescued a single person from the hand of the king of Assyria? Where are the gods of Hamath? Or Arpad? Where are the gods of Sepharvaim? Hena? Or Ivvah? Did any god rescue Samaria from my

---

5. Sarah Melville, "The Role of Rituals in Warfare during the Neo-Assyrian Period," *Religion Compass* 10 (September 2016): 219–29.

hand? Who, among all the gods of all the countries, has ever rescued their land from my hand? But Yahweh will rescue Jerusalem?! (vv. 32-35)

The psalms explicitly counter this message. The most powerful being in the cosmos is not Ashur or Marduk or the king of Assyria. Supreme Commander Yahweh who resides the holy citadels of Jerusalem is the one who causes wars to cease.

God's Battle Tactics

The portrayal of Yahweh as a military commander, however, goes farther than simply providing a countercultural message to the hyper-militarized culture of the ancient Near East. The biblical text makes clear that Yahweh's battles are fought differently from Assyria's. In Deuteronomy, Moses tells the people how the conquering of the promised land will be conducted:

> When you come to a city to fight against it, reach out to it and offer peace. And if they answer your terms of peace and open the city to you, all the people you find in it will be task-workers and slaves for you. But if they do not accept your terms of peace, bringing war against you, then lay siege to the city. And when Yahweh, your God, gives the city over to you, you must kill all the males with a sword. However, the women, children, cattle, and everything else in the city you may plunder as spoil for yourself. You may consume the spoils of your enemies which Yahweh, your God, gave to you. This is how you deal with all the cities that are very far from you which are not towns of these nations you currently see. As for the cities of these people that Yahweh your God is giving you as an inheritance, no breathing thing should survive. Instead, you must utterly annihilate them—Hittites, Amorites, Canaanites, Perizzites, Hivites, and Jebusites—as Yahweh your God commanded you. So that they will not teach you to do all the abominable things they do. (Deut 20:10-18)

Much like the Assyrians, if certain towns were willing to live at peace with Israel, they were allowed to continue. If, however, they were unwilling to recognize Yahweh's sovereignty and decided to go to war, Israel was commanded to destroy them—though in the context of the warfare of Assyria, Yahweh's commands deviate sharply from their practice.

The command to annihilate all the living things in the towns as enemies of Yahweh is difficult to read as merciful in most any contemporary setting. In its ancient occasion, however, the reader would immediately notice the omission of any order to shame, torture, or make examples of the inhabitants from Yahweh's commands. The disrespectful enemies of Yahweh are not flayed, disemboweled, or impaled alive on sticks. They are not castrated or raped. While the Assyrian king thought of himself as the most powerful military force on the planet and tormented anyone who disagreed, Supreme Commander Yahweh treats divine enemies differently. God conquers without torture or shame. While it is difficult for a contemporary reader to reconcile these passages with the commands of Christ, from the ancient perspective and compared to the militaries of the day, Yahweh's actions would be understood as merciful—even weak.

Remembering that the books of Joshua and Judges likely came into their final form during the Babylonian exile helps modern readers hear the texts better. After experiencing the losses and cruelty of the Babylonians firsthand, the mercy of Yahweh must have been more obvious to the exiles.

Genre of Conquest

A contemporary reader would be tempted to read the book of Joshua in the same way they might read contemporary histories. In reality, the genre of Joshua is different even from the book of Judges. While Judges is written as a narrative history, the book of Joshua is told in the genre of an ancient Near Eastern military conquest narrative. In the same way that the authors of the biblical text wrote creation narratives in the genre of other ancient Near Eastern epics, the authors of Joshua told the story of the conquest in a style that reflected their understanding of conquest stories of their own time. In other words, Israel told these stories the same way cultures around them told these stories. Though it is an understandable bias, a contemporary reader should not expect communities who lived three thousand years ago to tell stories the same way contemporary communities tell stories.

The genre of conquest narrative has several characteristics:

1. The gods are celebrated as powerful.
2. Individuals are aided and strengthened by the gods in battle, sometimes in supernatural ways.
3. Hyperbole is often employed to emphasize the impressive degree of victory.
4. The enemy is driven to terror by the powerful military victory.

Several examples exist in the ancient Near Eastern texts. Thutmose III was a fifteenth century BCE militaristic Egyptian pharaoh. During his numerous military campaigns into Palestine, Thutmose claimed the god Amon gave him the victory. Thutmose III's record of the victories is organized in a manner similar to Joshua. James Hoffmeier illustrates some of the similarities between the narratives of Thutmose III's first campaign and Joshua's attack on Jericho:[6]

Annals of Thutmose III	Joshua 1–6
Divine commission to march to Palestine	Divine commission to conquer and assurance of victory
Thutmose calls for a war counsel and receives an intelligence report	Joshua dispatches spies to bring an intelligence report regarding Jericho
The march through the Aruna pass	The march through the Jordan River
Setting up camp and preparing for war	Setting up camp and preparing for holy war
The battle and siege of Megiddo	The siege of Megiddo
The surrender of Megiddo and presentation of tribute to Thutmose	The fall of Jericho and spoils of war dedicated to Yahweh

Even the celebrations after the battles resonate with one another. After his victories, Thutmose's record says, "Then the entire army rejoiced and gave praise to Amon because of the victory which he had given to him on this day. They lauded his majesty and extoled his victories."[7] After Israel's eventual victory at Ai, the people celebrate and renew their covenant with Yahweh:

> Then Joshua built an altar to Yahweh, the God of Israel on Mt. Ebal as Moses, servant of Yahweh, had command the sons of Israel. As written in the scroll of the Torah of Moses, "an altar of uncut stones which no one had shaped with iron." And they offered on it burnt offerings to Yahweh and sacrificed peace offerings. (Josh 8:30-31)

In addition to organizational similarities, the text of Joshua has stylistic similarities as well. Near Eastern military accounts occasionally engaged in hyperbole as part of the genre. The hyperbole in a poetic text like Psalms is often easier for a contemporary reader to process than the narrative texts.

---

6. James K. Hoffmeier, "The Structure of Joshua 1–11 and the Annals of Thutmose III," in *Faith, Tradition, and History: Old Testament Historiography in Its Near Eastern Context* (Winona Lake: Eisenbrauns, 1994), 174.

7. "The Asiatic Campaigns of Thut-mose III," *ANET*, 237.

In Ps 18:32-34, the psalmist also celebrates God's provision for the psalmist in battle:

> The God who arms me with strength,
> and who makes my way perfect—
> making my feet like the deer's,
> and giving me the ability to stand on the heights.
> Training my hands for battle
> so that my arm could bend a bow of bronze.

Most contemporary readers would recognize that this affirmation of God's divine equipping is a stylized celebration. Few would advocate that God gave this psalmist deer feet. Most contemporary readers recognize that this military preparation is stylized hyperbole.

In the same way that the poetic genre can contain this kind of exaggeration, the genre of Near Eastern conquest can as well. For example, when Ramses III defeated an invasion of "Sea Peoples" in the thirteenth century BCE, he said,

> Those who came forward together on the sea, the full flame was in front of them at the river mouth, while a stockade of lances surrounded them on the shore. They were dragged in, enclosed, and prostrated on the beach, killed, and made into heaps from tail to head. Their ships and their goods were as if fallen into the water. I have made the lands turn back from even mentioning Egypt; for when they pronounce my name in the land then they are burned up . . . for I am on the ways of the plans of the Lord, my August, Divine father, the Lord of the gods.[8]

Ramses celebrates the complete destruction of the Sea Peoples. Their seed is no more, and if they mention the land of Egypt, they burst into flame. The Sea Peoples' destruction, however, was not quite as complete as one might assume from reading this text. One of the Sea People groups, the Philistines, went on to settle along the coast of Palestine and cause numerous issues for Israel in the biblical narrative. This kind of exaggeration, however, is typical of this genre, and one can even see it in the book of Joshua: "The King Horam of Gezer went up to help Lachish, but Joshua struck him and his people until no survivors remained" (Josh 10:33). After reading about the total destruction of the king of Gezer and his people in Josh 10:33 and

---

8. "The War Against the Peoples of the Sea," *ANET*, 262–63.

12:12, the reader finds this in Josh 16:10: "They did not dispossess the Canaanites living in Gezer. So the Canaanites live in the midst of Ephraim until this day, and they do forced labor as slaves."

While a contemporary reader might desire a precise and detailed "after action report," the ancient narrative tells the story with different goals in mind. In a conquest narrative, the purpose is not to give the details of the story in a manner that would satisfy a contemporary reader. The goal is to use the story to make claims about the power of the military leader. In the case of the book of Joshua, the military leader is Yahweh. This kind of agenda in storytelling is common. When Sennacherib invaded Judah at the end of the eighth century BCE, the Assyrian records tell a story emphasizing Judah's defeat: "I laid waste the large district of Judah and made the overbearing and proud Hezekiah, its king, bow in submission."[9]

In many ways, the Assyrian account resonates well with much of the biblical account in 2 Kings 19. Many of Judah's fortified cities were destroyed, but Jerusalem was left standing, and Hezekiah remained on the throne. In neighboring Sidon, Sennacherib removed the sitting king and installed his own puppet-king to discourage further rebellion. Why Sennacherib did not do this in Jerusalem is not addressed in the Assyrian records. The biblical text tells the story of a miraculous deliverance by Yahweh in response to Hezekiah's repentance. Sennacherib naturally omits any mention of a plague or indeed any detail that would compromise his narrative as supreme leader of the vast Assyrian empire. The military stories are not about chronicling an objective historical record. They are about establishing the character of the king.

The creation stories are not so much about creation as they are about God. In the same way, the conquest stories are not so much about conquest as they are about God. The Bible is using the story of the conquest to make claims about God, and to hear these stories well, one needs to be sensitive to the genre of conquest narratives.

SETTLEMENT

While the traditions of the settlement were likely much older, the books of Joshua through 2 Kings came together in Babylonian exile when Israel trying to answer the questions, "Who are we?" and "How did we get here?" Like the book of Joshua, the psalms, which also got edited in the exilic period, focus on Yahweh's work in the settlement period, not Israel's

---

9. "Sennacherib," *ANET*, 288.

initiative. Psalm 44 specifically discusses the conquest and disregards any human contribution to victory:

> We have heard with our ears, O God.
> Our ancestors told us the deeds
> you performed in the days of old.
> You, with your hand, dispossessed the nations,
> but you planted them.
> You afflicted others,
> but you sent them out.
> Because they did not possess the land with their own sword.
> Their own right arm did not deliver them.
> But rather it was your hands, your arm,
> the light of your face,
> because you were pleased with them. (vv. 1-3)

Indeed, this perspective resonates well with the notion of the "holy war" in Joshua. No one in Israel could profit from the spoils of battle because Yahweh was the one fighting. Yahweh, therefore, received the spoils. Psalm 136 has a similar perspective:

> The one who struck down great kings because God's committed love is forever
> The one who killed noble kings because God's committed love is forever
> Sihon, king of the Amorites, because God's committed love is forever
> Og, king of Bashan, because God's committed love is forever—
> God gave the land for their inheritance because God's committed love is forever—
> An inheritance to Israel, God's servant, because God's committed love is forever. (vv. 17-22)

The phrase "committed love" is translating the word used to highlight Yahweh's enduring commitment to the covenant. In the context of exile, that commitment would be in the minds of the people of Israel.

Though the battle of Jericho receives more liturgical attention in Western worship music when thinking about the conquest, in the psalms, it is Sihon and Og who are remembered when Israel's settlement is celebrated to remember God's covenant commitment. These two kings are also mentioned in Ps 135:

> To Sihon, king of the Amorites, and to Og, King of Bashan, to all the kingdoms of Canaan
> God gave their land as an inheritance—
> an inheritance to Israel, God's people. (vv. 11-12)

Even faithful readers of the Bible might not remember the story of Og and Sihon. They were among the first kings to fall as Israel took land on the eastern side of the Jordan River while Moses was still in leading Israel. Sihon met his fate early in Numbers 21: "But Sihon would not allow Israel to pass through his territory. Sihon gathered all his people together, and went out against Israel to the wilderness; he came to Jahaz, and fought against Israel. Israel put him to the sword, and took possession of his land from the Arnon to the Jabbok" (vv. 23-24). Og met a similar fate soon after:

> They turned and went up the road to Bashan, and Og, the king of Bashan, went out to meet them, and all his people, to fight with them at Edrei. And Yahweh said to Moses, do not be afraid of him because I have given him into your hand—all of his people and his land. I did to him like I did to King Sihon of the Amorites, who was ruling in Heshbon. They defeated him and his children and all his people. No one remained. So they took possession of his land. (vv. 33-35)

It is a fascinating and curious choice that with the numerous military victories in Joshua to single out for praise, the psalmists choose Og and Sihon from the book of Numbers (twice!). Perhaps these battles might be important because they were the first battles Israel engaged in. Perhaps these kings had status to the early readers of the text that contemporary readers miss. In Phoenician inscriptions, "Og" is a renowned hero, a patron hero of the underworld. Perhaps this legendary status is what motivates the psalm's celebration of God's victory over him. This might also explain why Deut 3 felt compelled to mention the size of Og's bed.[10]

Deuteronomistic History

Biblical scholar Martin Noth first noted the similar theological vision shared by Joshua, Judges, 1 and 2 Samuel, and 1 and 2 Kings.[11] When stories are told in these books, they emphasize how obedience brought success and

---

10. Zvi Ron, "The Bed of Og," *JBQ* 40 (Jan–Mar 2012): 29–34.

11. In English translation, Martin Noth, *The Deuteronomistic History* (2nd ed., JSOTSup 15; Sheffield: Sheffield Academic Press, 1991).

disobedience brought punishment to the characters. Since the emphasis on retributive justice in these books resonated closely with the book of Deuteronomy, Noth called these books the "Deuteronomistic History." While these books give a reader some insights into Israel's early history, they likely received their final edit during the exile, and the specific stories were preserved to provide answers for the people's exilic context. (The authors never hide that they write with a specific theological agenda and refer readers to other sources for more information. Readers are directed to "Book of Jashar" [2 Sam 1:18], the "Books of the Acts of Solomon" [1 Kgs 11:41], or the "Books of the Annals of the Kings of Israel" [1 Kgs 14:9], among others, for additional information.

One can see this retributive justice emphasis at work earlier in the Deuteronomistic History. When Israel does what Yahweh commands in Joshua 6, they succeed at Jericho. When someone among them is disobedient, they fail at Ai in Joshua 7. The stories continue that emphasis through 2 Kings. The psalms reflect the theological outlook of these stories as well. In Ps 25:12-14 the psalmist writes,

> Who fears Yahweh?
> One who teaches in the way God will choose.
> That soul will lodge in goodness.
> That soul's descendants will inherit the earth
> Yahweh gives counsel to God's friends.
> God's covenant is known to them.

Much like the stories in Joshua, the psalms emphasize that Yahweh is the one who fights for Israel like in Pss 78 and 80:

God brought [Israel] to the holy hill,
to this mountain that God's right hand acquired.
God drove out the nations before them.
And divided their inheritance for them,
and settled the tribes of Israel in their tents. (Ps 78:54-55)

You [Yahweh] brought a vine out of Egypt. You drove out nations and then planted it! (Ps 80:8)

While other nations assumed their god assisted them in battle, the psalms remember Yahweh as the active fighter. Israel was a passive recipient, receiving the blessings Yahweh promises:

> God, when you went out before your people,
> when you marched through the desert
> The land shook and the heavens poured down before the God of Sinai—
> before God, the God of Israel.
> You showered down abundant rain, O God,
> You established your inheritance when it had grown weary.
> Your flock resided in it.
> In your goodness, you provided for the afflicted, O God.
> The Sovereign God gives the command,
> the one bearing the news is a large army!
> The rulers of armies flee—they run away!
> And the house of the shepherd divides the spoils.
> Though they rest between the sheepfolds,
> they have the wings of a dove, gilded in silver and its pinions of green and gold.
> When the Almighty scattered the kings there,
> it snowed on Zalmon. (Ps 68:7-14)

Psalm 68 does not tell the story of a well-armed people ready to battle the Canaanites. Israel is a parched, languishing group upon whom Yahweh rained blessings. Psalm 68:9 remembers the taking of the land as an example of God's protection of the divine heritage (not Israel's!).

> ### The Cherem
>
> God's active role in the conquest explains the rules of the *cherem* as well. The word means "consecrate" or "annihilate" because both are happening in the story. Because Yahweh does the fighting, Yahweh receives the spoils of war. The rules of the *cherem* are those shown from Deuteronomy 20. Israel should not profit from God's efforts. Precious metals go to the tabernacle treasury. Whatever can be burned is burned. Anything that breathes is killed. Israel cannot financially benefit from the work that God is doing. Israel can have no material wealth, no animals. No wives can be taken from the conquered people, and no slaves can be made of the men. In this way, victims of the *cherem* are "consecrated to God" and "annihilated" at the same time.

JUDGES

Where Joshua's story is fast and complete, the Judges narrative shows a settlement that was slower and incomplete. Cities destroyed in Joshua are standing and in Canaanite control in Judges.

The stories in Judges are some of the most graphic and disturbing in the entire Old Testament. The people show a cycle of sin and repentance that can be thought of as the "Deuteronomic cycle."

1. Israel sinned.
2. God allowed an enemy to conquer them.
3. Israel (eventually) repented.
4. God raised a judge (military leader).
5. The judge delivered Israel.
6. After the judge's death, Israel sinned, restarting the cycle.

The Deuteronomic cycle is clearly expressed in Ps 106:

> The anger of Yahweh burned against the people,
> and God came to abhor this [people,]
> God's divine inheritance.
> God gave them into the hand of the nations.
> The ones they hated ruled over them.
> Their enemies oppressed them,
> and they were subdued under their hands.
> Many times God delivered them.
> But they rebelled in their plans and degraded themselves in their iniquity.

But God saw them in their distress,
upon hearing their cry
for their sake, God remembered the covenant,
and showed compassion, according to the abundance of God's committed love.
God caused them to be pitied by all their captives. (vv. 40-46)

> ### What Is a "Judge"?
> The English translation of the Hebrew word *shophet* as "judge" is problematic. The term is used so commonly that it would be difficult to fight against it. Unfortunately, so much is culturally associated with the term that it can cloud the *shophet*'s ancient role. The *shophet*'s, or "judge's," primary responsibility was a military one. God would specially equip an individual in a time of need to deal with a crisis Israel faced. While the judge might arbitrate some legal disputes, it was the judge's job to "establish justice" in ancient Israel. The greatest injustice the judges faced was the oppression of Israel. Liberation and justice were part of the same story.

Psalms does not allude to many of the narratives of individual judges in the book of Judges. By the time the book was edited together, the people had begun to transition from an emphasis on human leadership to divine leadership. No military heroes are venerated in Psalms. The psalmists do not pray for God to raise a judge. The psalmists repeatedly pray that God will rise in the role of judge. The prayer is that God will bring justice and liberation. In Psalms, God is filling the role of judge as seen in the text of Judges and entering into a specific historical occasion to provide liberation: "Rise up, Yahweh, do not let humans prevail. Let the nations be judged before you" (Ps 9:19). And in two postexilic psalms, Pss 82 and 94:

> Rise up, O God, bring just judgements to the earth because all the nations are your inheritance. (Ps 82:8)

> Rise up, true judge of the earth! Return to the proud their wages! (Ps 94:2)

God's judgments are also associated with Yahweh's role as "supreme king," as in Ps 96:10: "Say among the nations, 'Yahweh reigns! The world is established and never shakes! God will judge people with fairness.'"

The psalms do allude to the battle of Deborah in Judges 4 and the battle of Gideon in Judg 6–8 in Ps 83:9: "Do to them as you did to Midian, as to Sisera and Jabin at the Wadi Kishon." Interestingly, the psalm does not mention either judge by name but only the enemies they faced. Gideon's omission is interesting since he is typically read as a faithful servant of Yahweh with a long, successful story. The Gideon story even begins with a "type scene" of a call experience and culminates in the people attempting to make him king. He is certainly a character that the psalms could reference without concern. Deborah's omission might be more surprising since she wrote a psalm herself! Deborah acquitted herself as an insightful and faithful military leader and prophet in Judg 4 and an excellent musician in Judg 5 with her psalm celebrating the Israelite victory at the Wadi Kishon. Psalm 83 also does not mention Jael, the Canaanite woman who successfully dispensed with Sisera to win the day for Israel as the ultimate hero of the Deborah story.

The psalm's focus on the enemies likely reflects the author's transition away from human heroes and the renewed focus on Yahweh as hero in Israel. The enemy's emphasis is also in keeping with the rest of the psalm, which deals with those who, like the enemies of the judges, plot Israel's destruction:

> Behold, your enemies are roaring,
> and the ones who hate you raise their heads.
> They conspire against your people,
> and plot against your treasured ones. (Ps 83:2-3)

Like much of Psalms, the psalmist's concern here is not with human leadership but with God's power to liberate Israel from their oppressors.

Religion of Canaan

Israel's sin during the settlement period sets the stage for the rest of the history of Israel. The biblical narrative emphasizes that Canaanite religion was a constant problem for Israel. Israel's attempt to live with the Canaanites led to rampant syncretism of Israelite and Canaanite religion. In Ps 106:34-39, the psalmist writes,

> They did not annihilate
> all the peoples like Yahweh told them.
> But they mixed with the nations,

and they learned from their deeds.
They served their idols,
which became a snare to them.
They sacrificed their sons and their daughters to demons.
They poured out innocent blood,
the blood of their sons and daughters
whom they sacrificed to the idols of Canaan.
The land was polluted with blood
They were unclean in their actions
and prostituted themselves with their deeds.

One aspect of Canaanite religion that receives regular condemnation is idolatry. In Gen 1, the Bible makes clear that humanity is the only acceptable "image of God" permitted in the world. The prohibition of idolatry is the second commandment. The emptiness of the idolatrous practice is specifically called out in Ps 115:3-8:

Our God is in the heavens.
All that God delights to do, God does.
Their idols are silver and gold,
products of human hands.
They have mouths, but they do not speak.
They have eyes, but they cannot see.
They have ears, but they cannot hear.
They have noses, but they cannot smell.
They have hands, but they cannot feel.
They have feet, but they cannot walk.
They cannot even clear their throat.
Exactly like the ones who made them will be,
and all who put their trust in them.

This combination led to Israel even resorting to child sacrifice in honor of Yahweh. This and other disapproved aspects of Canaanite religion are highlighted. Within a fertility religion, the sacrifice of an example of fertility, a child, would be a high offering. Israel's association with Canaanite fertility religion apparently led them to adopt the practice.

The book of Judges narrates one specific occurrence of human sacrifice in Judges 11. The judge Jephthah offers his daughter as an offering to Yahweh in exchange for victory over the Ammonites.

> ### *Canaanite Religion and Ras Shamra*
>
> For years, much of what was known about Canaanite religion came from the biblical text. In the early twentieth century, however, an ancient city known as "Ugarit" was uncovered at the modern site of Ras Shamra in Syria.† This city had a huge number of ancient texts, including Canaanite worship texts. The site gave a more complete understanding of Canaanite religion and new insights and contexts for biblical stories.
>
> Canaanite religion was fertility based. It was cyclical, connected to the seasons. Each year, Baal, the storm god, would be killed by the god of death in April, when the rains stopped. Each year, Baal would then be resurrected in October when the rains returned. Fertility was crucial in the ancient world. Individuals needed fertility for their crops and animals for food each year, and they needed fertility for themselves to aid in farming and provide for themselves in their old age. In the hopes to secure this fertility, Canaanite religion had the participant engage in sympathetic magic. The idea was that a worshiper performed an act on a small scale to induce the gods to act on a large scale.‡ The worshipers would engage in cultic prostitution and provide offerings of fertility, like crops, animals, or even children, in the hopes that the gods would bring fertility to the land. Canaanite religion seemed to hold the secret to the land's fertility, and it was a problem for Israel until after the exile.
>
> † Nicolas Wyatt, "Religious Texts from Ugarit: The Worlds of Ilimilku and His Colleagues," *Biblical Seminar*, vol. 53 (Sheffield, England: Sheffield Academic Press, 1998).
>
> ‡ A voodoo doll would be a form of sympathetic magic: torment a small representation of a person in the hopes that the actual person is tormented.

What would make Jephthah think this would please Yahweh? The clue is in his parentage: "Now Jephthah from Gilead was a mighty warrior. He was the son of a prostitute. Gilead was the father of Jephthah" (11:1). When the biblical text uses the term "prostitute," it is often a cultic prostitute whose responsibility was to work in local Canaanite shrines. Jephthah was the likely product of an Israelite man and a Canaanite prostitute. He was literally the incarnation of syncretism. When he thought of the worship of Yahweh, he did so from that context.

CONCLUSION

Each time the Deuteronomic cycle repeats, it seems to get worse. The great hero Gideon's son tries to claim kingship. Jephthah offers a human sacrifice to Yahweh. By the end of the story, Israel no longer looks any different from the nations. In fact, in Judg 19, in what may be the most difficult passage of Scripture in the Bible, the people of the town of Gibeah in the tribe of Benjamin fail to show hospitality to a man from the tribe of Ephraim. Their rejection of a fellow Israelite is deliberately told in a manner to evoke the hospitality violations of Sodom in Gen 19. This act results in an Israelite civil war and the near destruction of the tribe of Benjamin.

Notably absent from that brief survey of the history of Israel is any mention of God. While Yahweh plays a prominent role in the settlement story of Joshua, it seems Yahweh plays a diminishing role in the story of Judges. In the book of Joshua, the people commit to the words of Torah and Moses. The book regularly reports that the people were obedient, "just as Moses, the servant of Yahweh had commanded them . . . ."

In Judges, the people of Israel have an emergency religion. There is no commitment to Torah or acknowledgment of the need to live as God's example in the world. They simply live as they choose, and when their actions bring about oppression, they pray for God to deliver them. By the end of the story, Israel lacks leadership and covenant loyalty and looks identical to the other nations. So the settlement period in Israel is complicated. The books of Joshua and Judges tell the same story in two ways. Much like the canonical need for both Genesis 1 and Genesis 2, in broad terms, the books of Joshua and Judges could be summed up by saying, "Look what happens when the people trust in Yahweh" in Joshua and "Look what happens when they don't" in Judges.

Prior to the exile, Israel seems to hope that strong leadership like the rest of the nations have might answer their problems. Indeed, the last verse in the book of Judges seems to locate Israel's problem in the lack of kingship: "In those days, Israel had no king. Everyone did what seemed right to them" (Judg 21:25).

The psalms, however, from the reality of exile and with the value of hindsight, deal with this issue by removing human leadership from the story completely. The focus of the psalms is Yahweh's judgment of the earth. Only Yahweh's leadership can provide the hope that Israel needs.

Questions for Further Discussion

1. Does understanding the violence of Joshua's story of the conquest and its stylistic connection to other Near Eastern conquest narratives help or hurt interpreting that text from a faith perspective?

2. Christians confess that Jesus is God and God is Jesus. While they believe that has always been true, the truth of it was not explicitly made known to humanity until the first Christmas. In light of that confession, how can readers avoid either the Marcionite heresy of believing God was different in the Old Testament or ignoring the Old Testament altogether?

3. Does the fact that the violent stories of settlement were written down while the people were in captivity in exile affect how they are read?

4. The Bible confesses it is writing history with a specific agenda (a common method of historiography in the ancient world). In several places it encourages the reader to read other sources if they want to fill in the historical gaps. In contrast, after the Enlightenment, contemporary readers have liked to believe there is such a thing as "objective" history. Since the biblical authors don't tell their history the way contemporary historians do, what does that mean for the contemporary reader?

5. Considering the diverse responsibilities of a *shophet* in ancient Israel, is there a better contemporary word for the role than "judge"?

Kingship

> ... kingship was a bit like a grand piano—you could put a cover over it, but you could still see what shape it was underneath.
>
> —Terry Pratchett, *The Fifth Elephant*

The Psalms and Kings

The settlement period ends with Israel in the land, but unfortunately, that achievement does not result in the celebration one might hope. The settlement narrative finishes with a descending spiral of moral problems, which culminates in a civil war and the near destruction of the tribe of Benjamin. By the end of the book of Judges, Israel cannot be distinguished from Sodom, and in an effort to strengthen their national identity, the people of Israel ignore the warnings of Samuel and God and appoint a king.

Much of the written history in the Old Testament reflects on the period of the monarchy. In Psalms, the monarchy includes both a celebration of human kingship and a celebration of the kingship of Yahweh. With the book's traditional association with Israel's most famous king, David, it is not surprising that "kingship" is a dominant theme in the psalms. As mentioned, God's kingship is the central theme of the psalms for many scholars.[1] The monarchies in Israel and Judah provide the historical context for the majority of the prophetic texts in the Hebrew canon, which include the texts of 1 and 2 Samuel and 1 and 2 Kings. The stories begin with the united monarchy under Saul, tell of the heights of monarchic power under David and Solomon, and recount the stories of the divided monarchy with the northern kingdom of Israel and the southern kingdom of Judah. These texts reflect on events from the late tenth century BCE to the exile of both in 722 BCE and 587 BCE. The Hebrew text even includes a "retelling" of some of the stories of monarchy in Judah in the books of 1 and 2 Chronicles.

---

1. James L. Mays, *The Lord Reigns* (Louisville: Westminster/John Knox, 1994). For Mays, Yahweh's kingship is the key to understanding the rest of the book of Psalms.

Though many psalms reflect the period of divided monarchy, the book contains few explicit references to that historical period. More commonly, the psalms focus on the united monarchy, specifically the Davidic kingship with occasional references to "his descendants." The loss of the rule of the Davidic line during the Babylonian exile is also the focus of many psalms.

> ### Two Kingdoms
>
> When Rehoboam, the son of Solomon, vowed to continue the oppressive policies of his father Solomon (1 Kings 12), the northern tribes of Israel rejected the Davidic monarchy and decided to form their own country under Jeroboam. Rehoboam continued to rule the tribes of Judah and Benjamin. For approximately two hundred years, the two kingdoms lived side by side. The northern kingdom, called "Israel," existed from the split in the late tenth century until it was destroyed by the Assyrians in 722 BCE. The southern kingdom, called "Judah," was able to endure until the Babylonians destroyed it in 587 BCE. Each kingdom claimed Yahweh as their God, and each had their own religious sites with their own cultic practices. In Israel, Jeroboam constructed two temples at the northernmost and southernmost borders of the kingdom as places for Yahweh worship. Unfortunately, these sites were locations of a syncretistic faith, using golden calves to represent Yahweh.
>
> Though the Hebrew Bible is primarily the preservation of the documents of the southern kingdom of Judah, it is reasonable to assume that some of the northern kingdom's sacred texts found their way into the Bible. When the northern kingdom fell to the Assyrians in 722 BCE, refugees from the north fled south and took their holy books with them. The "Elohistic Psalter" (Pss 42–84) has long been theorized to represent texts with a northern origin.[†] These psalms prefer the name "Elohim" over "Yahweh" when referring to the divine, which might reflect a regional preference. The precise origin of the individual texts, however, has been lost to history.
>
> [†] Martin Buss, "The Psalms of Asaph and Korah," *JBL* 82 (1963): 382–92; Gary Rendsburg, *Linguistic Evidence for the Northern Origin of Selected Psalms* (SBLDiss 43; Atlanta: Scholars Press, 1990), 51–60.

Divine Kingship in Psalms

The most important monarch in the Hebrew text is Yahweh. God's kingship is explicitly celebrated in a collection at the center of the book of Psalms known as the "Enthronement Psalms" (Pss 93, 95–99). These psalms are marked by their frequent use the phrase "Yahweh reigns." This phrase first occurs after God's miraculous deliverance at the sea in Exodus: "Yahweh reigns forever!" (Exod 15:18). The supreme king over Israel proved supreme power by conquering the king of Egypt. While a contemporary reader might not immediately associate deliverance from Egypt with monarchy, it was Israel's first response to God's mighty act. Indeed, divine monarchy had numerous shadings that might elude a contemporary reader.

Creation

In Ps 93, God demonstrates kingship by subjugating the chaos waters:

> Yahweh reigns! God is robed in majesty. Yahweh is robed in a belt of strength! Indeed, God established the world. It will never shake. (v. 1)
> . . .
> Above the sound of many waters, mightier than the waves of the sea. Yawheh is mighty on high! (v. 4)

As already mentioned, creation and kingship are intertwined metaphors in the ancient Near Eastern perspective. The Babylonian creation epic, the *Enuma Elish*, provides an alternate vision of the creation of the cosmos. Like the royal celebration of Yahweh in Gen 1, the *Enuma Elish* seeks to establish Marduk as king over the universe. Psalm 93 reflects the blending of the themes of creation and kingship by reminding the reader of Yahweh's royal position and of Yahweh's majesty over the tumultuous waters.

Judgment

The ancient Near Eastern concept of kingship is often directly connected to judgments. In ancient Egypt, the consistency of the sun's movements suggested steadfast justice and an eternal judge. The pharaoh was the son and image-bearer of the sun-god, "Ra," and was considered the ultimate judge. Likewise, the prologue to the Code of Hammurabi says, "the king who has made the four quarters of the world subservient. . . . When Marduk commissioned me to guide the people aright, to direct the land, I established law and justice in the langue of the land, thereby promoting the welfare of the people."[2]

Law, justice, and the general welfare are the responsibilities of the king, and the Bible reflects this perspective. God's kingship is connected with fair judgments in Ps 96:10: "Say among the nations, Yahweh reigns! The world

---

2. "The Code of Hammurabi," *ANET*, 165.

is established and never shakes! God will judge people with fairness." And in Ps 9:

> Because you have made my cause just.
> You sat on the throne giving righteous and just judgments. (v. 5)
> . . .
> Yahweh sits enthroned forever,
> and has established that throne for justice.
> God judges the world with righteousness.
> God gives fair verdicts to the world. (vv. 7-8)

This concern for fair judgments was a focus of the people of Israel when they asked Samuel for a king in 1 Sam 8:5: "[The elders of Israel] said to Samuel, 'Look you are old and your sons don't follow in your ways. Now appoint a king over us to govern like all the nations have.'" And in 1 Sam 8:19: "But the people refused to listen to Samuel, and they said, 'That will not be the way it is when the king will rule over us. But we will be like all the nations. Our king will offer justice and go out before us to fight our battles.'"

The royal responsibility to judge fairly suggests that even texts that do not contain explicit kingship references but emphasize "God's judgment" and "God as judge," like Ps 94, presume God's kingship:[3]

> A God of vengeance, O Yahweh,
> O God of vengeance shine out!
> Rise up, true judge of the earth!
> Return to the proud their wages! (vv. 1-2)

Order

As seen in the book of Judges, the ability of the leader to provide order and security as a warrior was part of the expectation of leadership. Kingship brought that expectation as well. In Ps 47:2-3, God's kingship is presented in direct parallel to national security:

> For Yahweh, the highest, is one to be feared.
> A great king over all the earth.

---

3. Psalms that appeal to God as judge or God's judgments or justice without an explicit kingship reference include Pss 7, 10, 18, 19, 26, 33, 35, 36, 37, 43, 48, 50, 51, 58, 67, 72, 82, 89, 94, 103, 105, 111, 119, 140, 143, 146, 147, 149.

> God subdued people under us
> and nations under our feet.

The celebration of Yahweh as king over "all the nations" carries the association of security and order. Israel has nothing to fear since God is in control.

> Yahweh reigns over the nations.
> God sits on a holy throne!
> The princes of the peoples gather as the people of the God of Abraham
> because the shields of the earth belong to God. God is truly exalted. (Ps 47:8-9)

In each of these cases, Yahweh is not threatened by opposition and is the ultimate sovereign over all the nations.[4]

A contemporary reader may miss the countercultural nature of affirming God as king over all the nations. A byproduct of an interconnected globe is global perspectives on deities. In the ancient Near East, however, most deities were believed to have local areas of influence. Egypt had gods. Assyria had gods. Israel had Yahweh. The spheres of influence for specific deities might have been narrow.

To assert that Yahweh reigned over the world subjugates the rest of the world's gods under Yahweh's authority. This is seen in Psalm 82:1: "God stands in the divine assembly. In the midst of the gods, God brings just rulings." This elevates the responsibility of God to the whole of creation. Yahweh is responsible for all of the cosmos, not just Israel.

Righteousness

While kings often have a reputation for selfish and capricious behavior, God's kingship is connected to righteousness and uprightness of heart:

> Yahweh reigns! Let the earth rejoice! Let all the beaches rejoice!
> . . .
> If you love Yahweh, hate destruction!
> God guards the lives of the faithful.
> God rescues them from the hand of the wicked.
> Light is sown for the righteous
> and joy for the right mind! (Ps 97:1; 10-11)

---

4. See also Pss 96:10; 98:4-6; 99:1.

God's judgments often proceed from Yahweh's righteousness: "Clouds and darkness surround God. Righteousness and justice are the foundation of God's throne" (Ps 97:2) and "The mighty king loves justice! You have established fairness. You have made justice and righteousness in Jacob" (Ps 99:4).

In Ps 119:142, God's righteousness is even understood in parallel with Torah: "Your righteousness is eternal righteousness. Your Torah is truth." This likely should not be surprising as often as righteousness is associated with justice and how often justice is associated with Torah.

Torah

The final Enthronement Psalm celebrates Yahweh's kingship by remembering the giving of God's statutes and decrees:

> Moses and Aaron were among God's priests.
> Samuel was among those who called on God's name.
> They all called to Yahweh, and God answered them.
> In a pillar of cloud God spoke to them.
> They kept God's statutes and the decrees given to them. (Ps 99:6-7)

This association of Torah as "God's judgments" is also seen in Ps 119. While Yahweh's kingship is not explicitly referenced in Ps 119, the psalm connects the celebration of God's Torah instruction with numerous references to "God's judgments":[5] "I will praise you with a right mind when I learn your righteous justice" (Ps 119:7) and "Be pleased with the offerings of my mouth, Yahweh! Teach me your justice" (v. 108).

The concept of divine kingship seems to be a stained-glass window, with panes of creation, judgment, righteousness, order, and Torah shining throughout the text. Affirming that God's instruction leads to the best life, God's judgments are fair, or that God is creator makes a royal claim about Yahweh. Once this is recognized, the theme of kingship that is already acknowledged as a dominant theme in the book of Psalms is more pervasive than it appears on the surface.

---

5. Psalm 119 has numerous references where "judgments" is used to refer to Torah: Ps 119:7, 13, 20, 30, 39, 43, 52, 62, 75, 91, 102, 106, 108, 120, 121, 132, 137, 149, 156, 160, 164, 175.

Human Kingship in Psalms

Like divine kingship, human kingship is also celebrated throughout Psalms.[6] From the beginning of the psalms, the reader is reminded that human kingship proceeds directly from Yahweh's kingship:

> The one who sits in heaven laughs,
> the Sovereign mocks them.
> Then God will speak to them in anger,
> and terrify them in divine fury.
> "I myself have anointed my king on Zion,
> my holy mountain."
> I will recount the decree of Yahweh; God said to me,
> "You are my son. Today I have borne you.
> Ask of me and I will give you the nations as an inheritance,
> and the ends of the earth will be your possession." (Ps 2:4-8)

Unlike in Egypt, where the human king was in fact the incarnation of the god, or in Assyria, where the king was born from the gods, Yahweh's relationship to the human king did not begin until the king sat on the throne. Rather than a biological destiny (though biological language is used), human kingship in Israel seems more adoptive. That line gets further blurred, however, in Ps 89:

> [The king], himself, will call me
> "My father, you are my rock and my deliverance."
> Also, I, myself, will make him firstborn,
> the highest of the kings of the earth. (vv. 26-27)

These verses in Ps 89 do not state that the king has been biologically fathered but that Yahweh's relationship with the king is closer than a contemporary reader might assume. As seen in the chapter on the ancestors, the designation of an heir was a cultural reality. The human king is understood as a designated heir to God.

The psalms celebrate events in the life of a human king. Psalm 45 was likely used in celebration of royal weddings:

> Hear, daughter, look and lean your ear
> and forget your people and your father's house.

---

6. E.g., Pss 2, 18, 21, 45, 72, 101, and 110.

> The king will desire your beauty.
> Since he is your master, bow down to him.
> Daughter of Tyre,
> rich people will beg from you with offerings.
> The princess is all glorious on the inside and outside,
> her clothes are lined with gold!
> In embroidered clothes, she is led to the king.
> Maidens of honor follow,
> and her companions are brought after her.
> They are led with joy.
> In gladness they are brought in the palace of the king. (vv. 10-15)

Psalm 101 might have been used in coronations, perhaps recited by the king as a type of oath of office:

> I will regard the trustworthy of the earth! They can dwell with me.
> The ones walking in a blameless way, they can minister to me.
> People who act treacherously will not sit in the middle of my house!
> I will not regard people who speak lies before me!
> Each morning I will destroy all the wicked in the land.
> I will cut off all the workers of iniquity from the city of Yahweh. (vv. 6-8)

Psalm 101 and Ps 72 illustrate an important requirement of human kingship in Israel. Because the human king's authority proceeds directly from divine kingship, the human king needs to reflect the same priorities of Yahweh: justice, mercy, and righteousness. If the human king is thought of as an adopted heir of God's kingship, then he must embody Torah. The blessing of the king in Ps 72 clearly illustrates the king's responsibilities:

> Because [the king] delivers the needy in their call.
> And the afflicted who have no help.
> He takes pity on the weak and the needy.
> He delivers the soul of the one in want.
> From oppression and from violence he redeems their souls.
> Their blood is precious in God's sight. (vv. 12-14)

The Bible does not evaluate kings in Israel and Judah by military power, economic prosperity, or skilled diplomacy. Kings are evaluated by how well their concerns reflect Yahweh's concerns. This expectation should not come

KINGSHIP

as a surprise to the human kings. According to Deuteronomy, the king was required to regularly read the Torah (from the copy he made!):

> When he begins to sit on the throne of his kingdom, he must make a copy of this Torah on a scroll from the one before the Levitical priests. And it shall remain with him and he shall read it every day of his life so that he will learn to fear Yahweh, his God—to keep and to do all the words of this Torah and the statutes—to not exalt his mind over his fellow citizens, or turn aside from the commandments to the right or left—so that he might increase his days in his kingdom, he and his children, in the midst of Israel. (Deut 17:18-20)

Unfortunately, instead of advocating for the concerns of Yahweh and Torah, kingship in Israel looked a lot like kingship in the rest of the world. Kings advocated their own agendas to their own destructive ends.

Royal Failures

While the psalms are generally positive about human kingship, the loss of the monarchy in the exile and the kings' disobedience figure into the psalms as well: "You have abhorred the covenant of your servant. You profaned his crown in the dirt" (Ps 89:39). Even passages that seem positive regarding human kingship might indicate a deeper problem with monarchy than a first reading suggests. Psalm 20 is a psalm of David that asks God for a blessing in a manner that reflects deeper struggle:

> Some trust in chariots and some in horses,
> but we, ourselves, trust in the name of Yahweh, our God.
> They will bow down and they will fall,
> but we will rise and be restored.
> Yahweh will deliver the king.
> God will answer us whenever we call. (vv. 7-9)

This psalm is a caution that while some place their pride in the trappings of kingship (20:7), Yahweh is supreme king in Israel. If that reading is correct, Ps 20 knows that human kingship can go badly.

Much like Psalms, the rest of the Old Testament is supportive of the kingship of Yahweh but divided on the kingship of humans. The lack of king in Israel is highlighted four times in the last five chapters of Judges.[7]

---

7. Judg 17:6; 18:1; 19:1; 21:25.

The last verse in Judges implies that Israel would benefit from kingship to add some control to Israel's decision-making: "In those days, Israel had no king. Everyone did what seemed right to them" (Judg 21:25).

In the story of 1 Samuel, however, the motivation for moving from a loose confederation of tribes to a monarchy was more pragmatic than ethical. In 1 Samuel 8, following a difficult military exchange with the Philistines, the people demand that Samuel, the last judge, appoint a king "like all the other nations have" (1 Sam 8:5, 20). The people were not concerned with the king's ability to model faithful adherence to Torah or represent Yahweh well. They wanted a strong military leader so they could be like the other nations. Not even Yahweh's warnings of the king's policies could dissuade the people. Samuel warned them that moving to monarchy would result in:

1. Forced military service
2. An established military industrial complex
3. Conscripted labor
4. Seized property

The complaint that the king would "conscript your sons" (1 Sam 8:11) and "take your daughters to be cooks, bakers, and perfumists" (1 Sam 8:13) is reminiscent of the city of Uruk's complaints regarding Gilgamesh:

> Did not Aruru bring forth this strong wild ox? He has no equal. . . . Gilgamesh leaves not the son to his father; Day and night is his arrogance. Is this the shepherd of Uruk? . . . Gilgamesh leaves not the maid to her mother, the warrior's daughter, the noble's spouse.[8]

Yahweh assures Samuel that this attitude was a rejection of divine leadership and consistent with Israel's behavior to this point:

> And Yahweh said to Samuel, "Do everything the people ask. It's not you they have rejected. They have rejected me as king over them. Just as they have done since I brought them from the land of Egypt till today. They have rejected me and served other gods. This, they are also doing to you. Now, obey them—but you must certainly warn them and tell them about the judgments of the king who will rule over them." (1 Sam 8:7-9)

---

8. "The Epic of Gilgamesh," *ANET*, 74.

The people of Israel were using the kingship as a magic talisman that would fix their problems in the same way they tried to use the ark of the covenant a few chapters earlier (1 Sam 4–5).

Human kingship, however, does not appear to be a problem in and of itself. In fact, some biblical texts have a positive evaluation of kingship. In first 1 Sam 9, the writer says,

> And Yahweh told Samuel, one day before Saul came, saying, "At this time tomorrow, I will send you a man from the tribe of Benjamin. You will anoint him to be a leader over my people Israel, and he will save my people from the hand of the Philistines. Because I have seen my people and their cries have reached me." (vv. 15-16)

The messages of God in 1 Samuel 9 and 10 echo the callings of other great heroes in the biblical narrative. Despite the initial negative reaction by Yahweh and Samuel, both offer their blessing on Saul and the position of kingship: "And Samuel took a vial of oil and poured it upon his head. Samuel kissed him and he said, 'Are you not anointed by Yahweh to lead God's inheritance?'" (1 Sam 10:1). Saul even prophesies with the prophets of Gibeah. This prophet-king would seem to be on solid footing to begin his reign.

Unfortunately, Saul quickly becomes a wholly tragic figure. In Psalms, Saul is remembered only for his attempts on David's life. Saul's name appears in several psalm superscriptions, but in each case, the psalm is connected to his persecution of David.[9] For example, the superscription of Ps 18 says, "For the music director, [a psalm] of Yahweh's servant, of David who spoke to Yahweh the words of this song on the day Yahweh delivered him from the hand of his enemy and from the hand of Saul." It likely does not help the perception of Saul that his name is a homophone with the Hebrew word for "grave." In most translations of 2 Sam 12:7, God assures David that he was rescued from the "hand of Saul." The same phrase in Ps 49:15 is translated the "hand of Sheol" or "hand of the grave." This wordplay might affect how a reader of Hebrew reads Ps 18:5 after Saul's explicit challenge of David in the superscription: "The ropes of Sheol [Saul?] entangled me. The snares of death came upon me." The psalms make clear that Saul is the oppressor and enemy of David and perhaps even the personification of the grave.

---

9. Pss 18, 52, 54, 57, and 59.

> ### Saul: First King or Last Judge
>
> Officially, the era of the judges comes to an end with Samuel, transitioning to the united monarchy. While it is true that Saul is the first king of Israel, in many ways Saul looked more like a judge than a king. It was David who united the tribes behind a new capital in Jerusalem and established a ruling dynasty that lasted more than four hundred years.
>
> Saul, by contrast, rose to power in answer to a military situation, much like a judge. His rule was confirmed after a military victory (not something normally associated with kings). He had no dynastic succession. The "spirit of Yahweh" came on Saul and left, much like the charismatic leadership of the judges period.†
>
> Saul's tragic rule seems to know no limits. Even the number of years of his rule has been lost to history. Literally, the Hebrew text says, "Saul was . . . years old when he began to rule; and he ruled . . . and two years over Israel." Though a king in title, he might be better understood as the last of the judges. The early chapters of 1 Samuel provide a complicated understanding of kingship in general and a tragic characterization of Saul in particular.
>
> † In this case, "charismatic" means "specially gifted by God." Compare the actions of the "spirit of Yahweh" in Judges 3:10, 6:34, 9:23, 11:29, 13:25, 14:19, 15:14, and 15:19 with its actions in 1 Sam 10:10, 11:6, and 16:14-16.

DAVID

One cannot overemphasize the significance of David in the Hebrew Bible. David is celebrated throughout the biblical text. Though David may be the second king in Israel's history, he is the one who truly establishes the united monarchy, centralizing royal power in Jerusalem and earning the support of all the people. The praise begins in 1 Samuel when Saul is told he will be replaced by "one after God's own heart" (1 Sam 13:14). The reigns of the kings of the later southern kingdom of Judah are measured against David (most often unfavorably). Micah 5 looks forward to a Messiah from Bethlehem (David's hometown). Ezekiel sees David himself ruling over a resurrected nation in Ezekiel 37. Jesus is regularly referred to as "son of David."[10] The final reference to David comes in the climax in the last chapter of Revelation where Jesus celebrates his identity: "I, Jesus, have sent my angel to you to testify these things for the churches. I, myself, am

---

10. Matt 1:1; 9:27; 12:23; 15:22; 20:30-31; 21:9, 15; 22:42; Mark 10:47-48; 12:35; Luke 1:32; 3:31; 18:38.

the origin of and the descendent of David—the bright, morning star" (Rev 22:16).

The veneration of David may be at its pinnacle in the psalms. Indeed, later Jewish tradition associated the entire book of Psalms with David.[11] Even the non-Davidic psalms were understood as having a Davidic voice since many of the singers, like Asaph, Heman, and Ethan, had Davidic connections.[12] The Septuagint copy of the Psalms celebrates David to an even greater degree than the Hebrew text by titling thirteen untitled psalms in the Hebrew manuscripts with Davidic superscriptions in the Greek.

Though most of the Davidic references occur in the superscriptions of the psalms, the references are not dispersed evenly throughout the Psalter. David finds himself in the position of "singer" more commonly in the first half of Psalms and as the object of the "song" in the latter half of the book. While nearly half of the psalms (seventy-three) have a Davidic superscription, only seventeen occur after Ps 70. Of the eleven mentions of David in the body of a psalm, only one occurs before Ps 72 (Ps 18:50). This phenomenon is likely connected to the canonical shaping of the book of Psalms.

The favor of Yahweh on the Davidic kingship is clear when David is the object of the song. Consider Ps 18:50: "Giving God's king great victories and showing committed love to the anointed, to David and his descendants forever." Or the celebration of Yahweh's commitment to David in Ps 132:11: "Yahweh swore a trustworthy oath to David which will never be turned away from: 'I will set the fruit of your body on your throne.'"

The frequency of Davidic references and celebration of David in the psalm texts should not lead one to believe that the psalms portray an easy life for this favored king. The reverse seems to be true. Many of the psalms with Davidic superscriptions would be classified as laments. Often when David is the object of the psalm, the psalmist remembers David's struggles: "Where is the committed love from the beginning, O Sovereign, which you swore to David by your own faithfulness?" (Ps 89:49) and "The one who delivers kings, the one who rescues God's servant David from the sword of destruction: (Ps 144:10).

---

11. The Midrash Tehillim says that where Moses gave five books of Torah, David gave five books of Psalms.

12. 1 Chr 6:18, 24, 29; 15:17; 19:1.

A Hard Kingship

With the focus on David and his later veneration as a model king, one might expect David to be celebrated in the psalms and narrative material as a paragon. In truth, however, neither the psalms nor the narrative material idealizes David's decision-making or rule. In the psalms, this is perhaps best seen in the longer superscriptions. These psalms' superscriptions offer a historical occasion for their reading, and they make clear that David's life is not idyllic.

Ps 3	A Psalm of David, when he fled from his son Absalom.
Ps 18d	. . . A Psalm of David the servant of Yahweh, who addressed the words of this song to Yahweh on the day when Yahweh delivered him from the hand of all his enemies, and from the hand of Saul.
Ps 34	Of David, when he feigned madness before Abimelech, so that he drove him out, and he went away.
Ps 38	A psalm of David, imploring God's remembrance
Ps 51	. . . a psalm of David, written after Nathan the prophet confronted him after David's affair with Bathsheba.
Ps 52	. . . A Maskil of David, when Doeg the Edomite came to Saul and said to him, "David has come to the house of Ahimelech."
Ps 54	. . . A Maskil of David, when the Ziphites went and told Saul, "David is in hiding among us."
Ps 56	. . . A Miktam, when the Philistines seized him in Gath.
Ps 57	. . . Of David. A Miktam, when he fled from Saul, in the cave.
Ps 59	. . . Of David. A Miktam, when Saul ordered his house to be watched in order to kill him.
Ps 60	. . . A Miktam of David; for instruction; when he struggled with Aram-naharaim and with Aram-zobah, and when Joab on his return killed twelve thousand Edomites in the Valley of Salt.
Ps 63	A Psalm of David, when he was in the Wilderness of Judah.
Ps 70	A Psalm of David, imploring God's remembrance.
Ps 142	A Maskil of David. When he was in the cave. A Prayer.

The psalms remember David's frequent hiding from Saul, his adultery with Bathsheba, and the nearly successful coup d'etat attempt by his son Absalom.

The narrative material supports the psalm reading. In fact, the "Court History of David" is the name given the material from 2 Samuel 9 to 1 Kings 2. This narrative provides an exposé of the inner workings of the Davidic monarchy and the struggle for succession. Also called the "Succession Narrative," it contains stories of adultery, rape, fratricide, and poor decision-making that affect David's household. Like the stories of Abraham and Moses, the biblical narrative of David has no desire to offer propaganda and hide the indiscretions of its "heroes." The psalms are consistent in this desire. Even in David's celebration, his failings are acknowledged.

Davidic Covenant

Prior to things falling apart in David's reign following the Bathsheba incident, David receives a special honor and a promise from Yahweh. David desired to build a temple in Jerusalem as a "house" for Yahweh. God responds by forbidding David to build a temple but instead promises to build David a "house":

> During that time I commanded judges to be over my people Israel. I will give rest to you from all your enemies. And Yahweh declares to that Yahweh will make a house for you! . . . My committed love will not wander off from you as it turned away from Saul whom I turned away from before you. You can trust that your house and your kingdom will last forever. Your throne will be established forever. (2 Sam 7:11, 15-16)

This eternal and unconditional promise of divine favor is celebrated throughout the psalms. Psalms 18 and 21 specifically reference the Davidic covenant.

> Giving his king great victories
> and showing committed love to his anointed,
> to David and his descendants forever. (Ps 18:50)

> You put your blessing on him forever.
> You make him rejoice in the joy of your presence.
> Because the king trusts in Yahweh,
> and he will never move from the committed love of the most high (Ps 21:6-7)

God's promise that David's kingship would last forever led to the popular belief that a descendent from David's line would always sit on the throne in Jerusalem. With this unconditional promise from God and Yahweh's temple located in Jerusalem, the people of Judah believed the city could never be destroyed. For a time, the people seemed to be right. Though the northern kingdom of Israel was destroyed by the Assyrians and the nation of Judah had its share of close calls,[13] Jerusalem remained standing, and the king remained on the throne.

The prophets tried to fight this idolatrous interpretation of the Davidic covenant, reminding the people that God should not be mocked and a reckoning for their behavior would come. Jeremiah's temple sermon in Jeremiah 7 directly addresses the idolatry of the temple and warns that destruction would come.

> Thus Supreme Commander Yahweh, God of Israel, says, "Seek true goodness in the way you are living and the things you are doing, then I will dwell with you in this place." Do not trust in these lying words saying, "The temple of Yahweh—the temple of Yahweh—the temple of Yahweh is here!" . . . Therefore, thus the Sovereign Yahweh says, "Behold, my anger and my wrath will be poured out upon this place—upon humans and animals—even trees of the field and crops—it will burn and not be extinguished." (Jer 7:3-4, 20)

God provides a graphic object lesson for those who misunderstood the Davidic promise. The people of Judah recognized that with the impending Babylonian invasion, it might not be the right time to expand their settlements, but they would be safe provided they stayed in Jerusalem.

> God said to me, "Human being, these are the people who devise iniquity and counsel destruction in this city. They say, 'It's not close to the time to build houses. The city is a pot, and we are meat.' Therefore prophesy against them, human being. Prophesy!" (Ezek 11:2-4)

While a metal pot keeps meat safe, Yahweh says that Jerusalem will not keep the wicked safe. A reckoning is coming in the form of the Babylonian exile.

---

13. In 701 BCE, the Assyrian king Sennacherib destroyed all of Hezekiah's fortified cities and surrounded Jerusalem. Second Kings makes clear that were it not for Hezekiah's repentance and God's divine intercession, the kingdom of Judah would have been destroyed.

Solomon

The succession of David was told with drama and uncertainty, and the kingship finally rested on a child David had with Bathsheba. Only two psalms contain a mention of Solomon in the superscription. The first, Ps 72, comes at the end of Book II following the majority of the Davidic psalms in the book. With the strong Davidic voice at the beginning of the Psalter, some scholars have read the editorial placement of this psalm as a "passing of the baton" or transition to the next generation and an affirmation of the Davidic covenant.[14]

As with most superscriptions, it is difficult to determine if the psalm is sung "for" Solomon or "by" Solomon. The benediction of the psalm citing the end of the "prayers of David" might imply that this psalm should be read as a prayer for David's son by David himself. The psalm certainly illustrates a king's rule in the best possible light:

> O God, give your justice to the king,
> and your righteousness to a king's son.
> May he judge your people in righteousness,
> and your afflicted with justice.
> Let the mountains give flourishing lives to the people,
> and the hills bring righteousness.
> May he justly rule for the afflicted of the people.
> May he give deliverance to the children of the needy,
> and crush the oppressor. (Ps 72:1-4)

The concern in Ps 72 is for Torah, as was envisioned for the king in Deut 17.

Solomon's other song, Ps 127, reminds the reader of Solomon's association with wisdom traditions. Tradition has associated three canonical and several non-canonical wisdom books with Solomon. Though Ps 127 is among the "Song of Ascents" collection, this pilgrimage song that may have been sung on the way to Jerusalem seems like a collection of proverbs:

> Unless Yahweh builds a house, the builders labor in vain.
> Unless Yahweh guards the city, the guards keep watch in vain.
> It is vain for you to rise early and to delay resting,
> eating the food of painful toil.

---

14. Gerald Wilson, "Use of Royal Psalms at the 'Seams' of the Hebrew Psalter," *JSOT* 11 (1986): 88–89.

> So God gives sleep to God's beloved.
> Behold, children are an inheritance of Yahweh.
> The fruit of the womb is a reward. (Ps 127:1-3)

It is unsurprising that a psalm of ascents would allude to temple or that a psalm of Solomon would invoke memories of David. One thing, however, that is accomplished by framing Solomon in terms of David is that the psalms can gloss over or obscure the more difficult aspects of Solomon's life. Certainly, in the biblical evaluation, Solomon provides textbook examples of poor leadership.

Solomon's reign is not discussed in the psalms. His evaluation in the narrative, however, is not positive. The summary of his reign may seem positive when evaluated by the standards of successful kingship in the ancient Near East.

> The weight of the gold that Solomon received in one year was six hundred and sixty-six talents. . . . Solomon gathered chariots and horses. He had 1400 chariots and 12,000 horses. And he stationed them in his chariot cities and with the king in Jerusalem. The king made silver as common in Jerusalem as stones, and he made cedar as numerous as sycamores in the Shephelah. (1 Kgs 10:14, 26-27)
>
> . . .
>
> King Solomon loved many foreign women besides the daughter of Pharaoh—Moabites, Ammonites, Edomites, Sidonians, and Hittites. (1 Kgs 11:1)

When compared to the words Deuteronomy used to warn about bad kings, though, Solomon's reign seems far less positive:

> Also, he must not acquire numerous horses for himself. He must not return the people to Egypt so that he might acquire more horses. Yahweh has said to you, "You must never return that way again." He must not acquire many wives who would cause his mind to depart. And he must not acquire large amounts of silver and gold for himself. (Deut 17:16-17)

The text in Deuteronomy seems a clear warning against exactly the kind of king Solomon was. The author of 1 Kings, wrestling with Babylonian exile, included these specific details of Solomon's reign to invoke Deuteronomy in the mind of the reader and to help explain the events that led to the nation's eventual exile.

Solomon's shrewd administrative acumen did much to expand the wealth and international status of Israel. His wisdom, however, was not applied to the faithful representation of Yahweh and the administration of Torah. Solomon was more concerned with improving the status of Solomon. With Solomon's forced labor for his building projects, he looks more like Pharaoh than a faithful king of Israel.

Conclusion

The psalms echo the call of Deuteronomy: the king's responsibility is to Torah. This commitment and responsibility to Torah is seen in Ps 72, where the psalmist prays that the king's rule be long and celebrated because of his commitment to the marginalized:

> Because he delivers the needy in their call.
> And the afflicted who have no help.
> He takes pity on the weak and the needy.
> He delivers the soul of the one in want.
> From oppression and from violence he redeems their souls.
> Their blood is precious in God's sight. (vv. 12-14)

In Ps 101, David prays to study God's ways of justice and live them out. As already seen, the commitment to the marginalized is a key element of Torah, and the king's enforcement of Torah is important in the king's evaluation.

> I have carefully considered your blameless way.
> When will it come to me?
> I have conducted myself with a blameless mind in my house.
> I have not put any worthless thing before my eyes.
> I hate devious actions.
> They are not a part of me. (vv. 2-3)

Samuel had warned the people what kings would be like in 1 Sam 8:11-12:

> And he said, "Here are a king's judgments when he rules over you. He will take your sons and put them in his chariots or on his horses to run in front of his chariots. He will appoint commanders of thousands and

commanders of fifty. And they will surely plow his ground and reap his harvest. They will make his instruments of war and all his chariots."

These decisions do not come as much of a surprise. One normally associates kingship with absolute power and privilege. Yahweh, however, expected Israel to have a different attitude toward kingship. The king was not to be exempt from Torah. In fact, Deuteronomy commands that the Torah be copied and read in the king's presence. Monarchy did not afford the king special privilege. On the contrary, monarchy was simply another means by which Torah could be brought to the world. If the king did not honor that calling, the king's legacy would not continue.

Questions for Further Discussion

1. How is the concept of "kingship" that is generally understood at odds with the biblical concept of "kingship"?

2. God seems to be against human kingship in 1 Samuel, yet several texts in the Deuteronomic History and Psalms show God celebrating human kingship. Jesus tells Pontius Pilate that his kingdom is not of this world, yet God told Moses in Deut 17 that human kings must conform themselves to Torah. In light of all this, how does God feel about kingship? Does God have a favored form of human government?

3. What does the Bible's evaluation for what makes a "good king" and what makes a "bad king" have to say about contemporary evaluations of leadership? Of wealth? Of corporate power?

4. The Succession Narrative shows that David's reign was not a peaceful one. Why is David held as the standard for kingship? Should he be?

5. Samuel warned the people how exploitive a king would be, yet the people insisted that, even so, they wanted a king like everyone else. Why? What is behind this desperate submission to peer pressure?

Prophets

> *I'm the enemy of treason—the enemy of strife / I'm the enemy of the unlived meaningless life / I ain't no false prophet—I just know what I know / I go where only the lonely can go . . .*
> —Bob Dylan, "False Prophet,"
> *Rough and Rowdy Ways*

Psalms and Prophets

When kings began to believe their own press and rule in the manner that seemed right to them, prophets began to appear in increasing number to offer counter testimony. In contrast to a priest's primary responsibility to ensure that the people were acceptable before God, the prophet's primary responsibility was to bring the word of God to the people. That word was often spoken directly in the face of the royal establishment, though it would be an oversimplification to argue that the prophet had only one constituency. In addition to advocating for God's way to the people, the prophet often found a need to intercede for the people directly to God. Prophets found themselves standing in the gap between the divine and humanity—a lonely and frustrating place.

Many of the songs of the Psalter were first collected and used in temple liturgy by the priests. The priestly establishment, however, was often directly supervised—at times, it might be fair to say "controlled"—by the monarchy in Jerusalem. A royal palace was part of the temple complex in Jerusalem from its initial construction and throughout its history. The royal proximity to the priests could help explain why kingship language is common in Psalms and why that language is not limited to the "kingship of God." Since the kings were so often the target of God's—and therefore the prophet's—displeasure, one might not expect many challenging prophetic messages in Psalms. Additionally, since the psalms themselves are first "words *to* God," one might expect prophetic speech to be hard to find in the book since prophetic speech is by definition "words *from* God."

So it comes as no surprise that the most common word for "prophet" only occurs three times in the book of Psalms, once in a superscription and once each in the body of two individual psalms. The different contexts of each of these individual occurrences, however, offers insight into the nature of prophetic speech.

Speaking Truth to Power

The first occurrence of the word "prophet" comes in the superscription of the well-known Psalm 51. This superscription provides a glimpse of perhaps the most difficult job responsibility of the prophet: speaking truth to power. The superscription informs the reader that the narrative context of this psalm is "When the prophet Nathan came to David, after he had sex with Bathsheba." Within the narrative of 2 Samuel, the story of David's rape of Bathsheba is a mistake that his kingship never recovered from. Following this sin, David and his house faced numerous challenges: the murder of Uriah by David, the rape of David's daughter Tamar by her half-brother Amnon, the murder of Amnon by Tamar's brother Absalom, the insurrection of Absalom, and the murder of Absalom by David's loyal general Joab.

In 2 Samuel 12, God calls Nathan to confront the king for committing what is at its heart the most common sin kings fell victim to: using position and power for personal desire rather than using it for the good of the people. The prophet Nathan was likely a "court prophet" with easy access to the king. Court prophets were professional prophets in other parts of the ancient Near East, and Israel likely had a similar job description. Court prophets were on the government payroll and served as special advisors to the king.[1] Confronting a king about an issue like David's sin, however, was an excellent way for a royal advisor to become an "imprisoned royal advisor" or even a "dead royal advisor."

In the 2 Samuel text, Nathan accepts this calling and approaches the issue with wisdom and diplomacy. As a result, David acknowledges his mistake and repents. Unfortunately, Nathan's story is an outlier. Far more often, prophets were ignored, beaten, arrested, or killed—or some combination of all four—by kings who did not take correction as well as David. In 1 Kings 26, King Ahab of the northern kingdom imprisons the prophet

---

1. Archaeologists found a large cache of cuneiform documents at the ancient Near Eastern site of Mari that date several centuries before the biblical text. These documents show an office for professional "prophets." See Martti Nissinen, *Prophets and Prophecy in the Ancient Near East* (Atlanta: Society of Biblical Literature, 2003).

Micaiah ben Imlah for "never prophesying anything favorable about me, but only disaster" (v. 18). In 2 Chronicles 24 under the reign of King Jehoash of Judah (late ninth century BCE), the prophet Zechariah ben Jehoiada met an even unhappier end:

> The spirit of God clothed Zechariah son of Jehoida, the priest. He stood in front of the people, and he said to them, "Thus says God, 'Why do you pass over the commands of Yahweh? It will not make you prosperous. You have rejected Yahweh, and so Yahweh will reject you.'" So they bound him, and according to the command of the king, they stoned him in the court of the house of the Lord. (vv. 20-21)

This common prophetic mission—"Tell the Person Who Holds the Power of Life and Death over You They Are Wrong"—explains why the "prophetic call type scene" always featured an "objection to the call." No one who was called to be a prophet ever wanted to be a prophet. The callings of Micaiah, Nathan, and Zechariah son of Jehoiada provide examples as to why.

Type Scenes

Type scenes are stories with shared narrative structure. Several "type scenes" are used in the Bible. The "Finding of a Wife" type scene was common in the ancestors and later. Prophetic calls also follow a familiar formula:

1. Theophany—God or God's representative appears.
2. Introductory Word—The prophet is greeted and encouraged not to fear.
3. Commission—The prophet is told the mission.
4. Objection—The prophet objects to the mission.
5. Reassurance—God provides reassurance or counterargument to the objection.
6. Sign—A sign is offered as evidence for faith.

In type scenes, all the elements need not exist, but typically enough exist to tell the story. A specific prophetic call may not have all the elements listed here; however, the "Objection" is common enough to feel like a universal element. No one who understood the job of a prophet ever *wanted* the job of a prophet.

Other prophets in the biblical text may have been court prophets like Nathan who had the courage to speak uncomfortable truth to power. In fact, it is suggested that the prophet Isaiah fits this model as well. While many the prophets around the ancient Near East were on the government payroll, the majority of biblical prophets seem to come from outside political and religious leadership, which might explain why they meet so much resistance. With few exceptions, the court prophets were more commonly the "false prophets" who would simply affirm anything the king wanted.

One common feature of true prophetic preaching is its willingness to challenge leadership and tradition. The prophets of the Bible never let Yahweh be domesticated within a fixed theological understanding. Whenever kings tried, Yahweh would take the opposing side! In one of the most scandalous passages of the Bible, Jeremiah suggests that Yahweh is not on the side of the king of Judah. The king of Judah identified himself as the descendant of David, the leader of the chosen people whom God brought out of Egypt, and next-door neighbor to God's house in Jerusalem. Jeremiah made clear that this pedigree didn't matter because the militaristic, polytheistic king of Babylon, Nebuchadnezzar, was actually the servant of Yahweh and not Marduk, the god of Babylon.

> Therefore, Supreme Commander Yahweh says, "because you have not obeyed my words, see now, I am sending all the tribes of the north, declares Yahweh, and my servant, the King of Babylon—Nebuchadrezzar. I will bring them against this land and against its inhabitants and against all these nations around it, and I will make them a horror and an object of hissing scorn—an eternal desolation. (Jer 25:8-9)

Because the people of God had failed to live like the people of God, the prophet says God has changed sides! Judgment of Judah will come at the hands of Babylon. It is easy to understand why most prophets never lived to retirement.

A message this challenging was hard for anyone to accept. Even the prophet Habakkuk struggled to make sense of how "God on the side of the bad guys" was just:

> Are you not from old, Yahweh, my God, my Holy one? We will not die!
> Yahweh, you have set them for judgment?!
> O Rock, you have established them to rebuke us?! (Hab 1:12)

God's answer to Habakkuk would not satisfy most people:

> Behold the proud.
> Their soul is not right within them.
> But the righteous will live by their faith. (Hab 2:4)

God's message was that eventually Babylon would be judged, but until then, the righteous person was simply going to have to trust God. God's ways were challenging, even for the faithful.

Politics was not the only target of this kind of reframing. The prophets also broadened theological ideas when they got too narrow. The "Day of Yahweh," or the Day of the Lord, was a somewhat eschatological expectation that existed in the people's consciousness throughout Israel's history. People believed that the Day of Yahweh was the day when Yahweh would appear and destroy all of God's enemies. It was a simple matter of the transitive property for people to say, "That's the day God destroys the divine enemies. We are the people of God. It must be the day God destroys *our* enemies."

The prophets took this accepted theological truth and turned it upside down:

> Woe to the ones who desire the Day of Yahweh!
> What do you think the Day of Yahweh will be for you?
> It's a day of darkness, not light.
> As if someone was fleeing from a lion and met a bear,
> and came to a house and rested their hand upon the wall,
> then got bitten by a snake.
> Don't you know, the day of Yahweh is darkness and not light—
> gloom with no brightness. (Amos 5:18-20)

Amos confronted the people with an unsettling reality. The Day of Yahweh well may be the day when God destroys all the enemies of the divine. Unfortunately for Israel, they have made themselves enemies of the divine. This kind of scandalous prophetic preaching created existential crises for the people, so it was often met with violence against the prophet.

Speaking a Word for "Now," Not "Then"

The second explicit mention of the word "prophet" in the psalms occurs in Ps 74, and this occurrence helps correct a popular misunderstanding about biblical prophets. In the contemporary cultural understanding, "prophets" function more like fortune tellers. Eccentric prophets provide vague and imprecise forecasts about a distant future that have hints of a message that people decades or centuries later can interpret and decode for their context. This type of prophet, however, stands in stark contrast to the prophetic preaching of the Bible. A biblical prophet preached to their immediate audience, and their message was rarely difficult to understand. In fact, people clearly understood what the prophets meant by their preaching, and the prophets suffered for it.

Ps 74 is a communal lament that mourns the destruction of the temple and the reality of exile for the people of Judah. Verse 9 shows the psalmist longing for a prophet, not to offer lottery numbers or warn of centuries-later catastrophes but to provide a message for the present:

> We don't see our banners.
> There is no longer a prophet,
> and no one is given to know how long this lasts.
> How long, O God?
> How long will the foe mock,
> and the enemy despise your name?
> Forever? (vv. 9-10)

The community needed an answer to the question "how long?"—how long God was going to wait to deliver them, how long their prayer would go unanswered, how long their enemy would seem victorious. To answer that question, they needed a prophet who could provide God's answer.

The psalmist understood the role of the prophet and the immediacy of their preaching. Most prophetic oracles in the Old Testament focused on the present, but when the prophet did preach about the future, it sounded more like "before this year is out . . . ," "before my son turns two . . . ," or "before my son turns twelve . . . " than it did "in one thousand years . . . ." A biblical prophet spoke words to people standing in front of them much like a contemporary preacher shapes a message for the congregation in front of them. Imagine how odd it would sound for someone to preach a message that had no relevance to the listener but was targeted for the listener's great-great-great-great-grandchildren!

Biblical prophets' predictions and messages about the future had relevance for the prophets' contemporary audience. The prophet consistently confronted multiple realities at the same time. The prophet's preaching responded to "What now is" and "What now could be" and "What the future will be."

> ### "But What about Jesus?"
>
> Whenever a Christian talks about prophetic speech in the Old Testament, invariably the discussion turns toward Jesus. Historically, Christian apologetics have connected the interpretation of the prophetic texts in the Old Testament to a prediction of the Messiah in the New Testament. The Septuagint was the Bible of the early church, and it translated the Hebrew word for "anointed" into the Greek word for "anointed," anglicized as "Christ." A prophetic text's reference to the coming "anointed one" provided the New Testament authors Scriptures to quote in support of "Jesus the Messiah," or Jesus Christ.
>
> However, even the messianic predictions of the Old Testament were framed within the prophet's own lifetime. Mic 5:2-5a is often quoted during Christmas since Matt 2:6 uses it in the discussion of Jesus's birth:
>
>> But you Bethlehem, I will make you fruitful. Though you are small among the clans of Judah, from you will emerge one who will rule over Israel—someone whose origins are from the distant past, ancient days. So, I will give them up, until that time when the one in labor gives birth, and the rest of his brothers return to reunite with the children of Israel. He will stand and shepherd by the might of Yahweh, in the majesty of the name of Yahweh his God. And they will live because he is great. This one will be peace . . . .
>
> When reading the full oracle, one sees the prophet was expecting the coming Messiah, born in Bethlehem, to provide deliverance from the Assyrian empire, the principal threat to Judah's existence in Micah's lifetime:
>
>> . . . when Assyria comes against our land. And when they tread through our palaces. We will raise up against them seven shepherds, even eight rulers of people. They will rule the land of Assyria with a sword and the land of Nimrod in its gates. They will rescue us from the Assyrians when they come in our land and tread within our border. (Mic 5:5b-6)
>
> When the New Testament writers quote from Old Testament texts years later, they reflect interpretive conventions of the first century that did not regard the original contexts as important to making an argument. This is why the book of James uses "Abraham believed God, and it was reckoned to him as righteousness" to show justification by works, and Paul uses the same verse to show justification by grace. Neither is wrong, but their use of Scripture is different from contemporary readers' use. As a result, the ancient prophet was inspired to offer a message relevant for the ancient audience, unaware that small parts of that same message might have application for New Testament authors centuries later.

When biblical prophets spoke about the end that God envisioned for the earth, these eschatological prophecies had application to their time. Seeing the future God envisions was intended to inspire behavioral change in the people around the prophet. The prophet hoped that seeing "what will be" would change "what is" into "what could be." If the prophet spoke about a future that would occur within the hearer's lifetime or about the reality of the end of time—the implications of which should affect the way the hearer lives now—every prophetic word had contemporary application.

Fortunately, this concern for the immediate future allowed a prophet's predictions to be evaluated rather quickly, and a prophet's trustworthiness could be known soon after the words were spoken. The quick evaluation is fortunate because Israel did not have any other approved system to evaluate whether a prophetic word was true—beyond whether that prophetic word occurred.[2] A true prediction meant the prophet was a true prophet. A false prediction meant the prophet was a false prophet. Deuteronomy 18 explains this standard:

> And if you wonder, "How can we know a word which is not spoken by Yahweh?" Whatever a prophet speaks in the name of Yahweh—if it does not happen or the word does not come true, then Yahweh did not speak. In pride, the prophet has spoken it. Do not be afraid of it. (vv. 21-22)

Of course, "whether the thing takes place" comes too late if someone is trying to evaluate whether they should listen to a prophet. To overcome that difficulty, occasionally prophets provided "signs" for difficult prophetic words. Signs can offer focus for God's word or actions. In the case of prophetic speech, signs illustrate God's words or actions and confirm that the prophet is offering a true word of the Lord. When one sees the sign, one knows the spoken word is true.

In 2 Kings 20:8-10, Hezekiah wants to believe Isaiah when he promises God will heal him, but he also wants confirmation. God offers him an astronomical sign to confirm Isaiah's word. Hezekiah is also the recipient of what might be the most unusual and effective sign in the biblical text when the prophet Isaiah preaches naked for three years as a sign that Hezekiah should not rebel against the king of Assyria, like Egypt and Ethiopia had:

---

2. Other cultures often used divination to evaluate the truthfulness of prophetic oracles. In their estimation, divination was the objective, scientific test for the prophetic word.

> At that time the word of Yahweh spoke to Isaiah, son of Amoz, saying, "Go, take off the sackcloth from your waist and your shoes from your feet," and he did so, walking naked and barefoot. Yahweh said, "As my servant Isaiah has walked three years naked and barefoot as a sign and wonder against Egypt and Ethiopia, so the king of Assyria will lead the Egyptian captives and the Ethiopian prisoners—young and old—naked and barefoot, with bare butts showing Egypt's shameful nakedness. (Isa 20:2-4)

As the prophet Isaiah revealed, prophetic preaching was not limited to words. It was embodied by the lives of the prophets as well. "Sermon illustrations" were reflected in their lives: Jeremiah wore a yoke while preaching (Jer 28); Hosea was called to marry a prostitute (Hos 1); and Ezekiel ate a scroll and played war, among other creative actions (Ezek 2–7). Prophetic preaching went far beyond what was spoken.

SPEAKING A WORD, ONLY TO BE HEARD LATER

The third explicit mention of prophets in Psalms has already been discussed. In Ps 105:15, the word "prophet" is associated with Abraham, Isaac, and Jacob. The word is used in parallel with a word normally associated with kings, "mashiach [messiah]" or "anointed." This reference is odd since the patriarchs are not traditionally thought of as "prophets" or "messiahs" in the narratives about them, although God calls Abraham a prophet in Gen 20 when ordering Abimelech to return Sarah to Abraham: "Now return the wife of the man because he is a prophet, and he will pray that you will live. But if you don't return her, know that you will certainly die—you and everyone connected with you" (Gen 20:7). While God seems to know Abraham's prophetic status, the people don't catch up till the psalms. This does illustrate another feature of prophets: their calling was often only recognized much later.

During Jeremiah's life, his messages were ignored and reviled. He was beaten, imprisoned, and threatened with death. The majority of his contemporary prophets—certainly including those on the government payroll—were unsurprisingly on the side of the king, and in the short term, they likely did quite well for themselves. It was only after the destruction of Jerusalem and the reality of exile when Jeremiah's warnings were proven true that people could no longer deny he was the true prophet and his contemporaries were not.

> ### *How Does the Divine Speak to Prophets?*
>
> In the ancient Near East, people were aware of several different types of prophetic phenomena. Sometimes the gods took the initiative and spoke to the prophet in visions or in dreams. If the gods were silent, their concerns could be sought out in more supernatural ways by professionals who employed techniques like necromancy and divination. While those two methods of seeking a divine word are explicitly forbidden by the biblical text, the God of Israel has the freedom to act any way Yahweh wants to act, and God provides a word to King Saul at the end of his life through a necromancer at Endor in 1 Sam 28. Biblical tradition also permitted "casting lots" to seek divine will. While that might seem dangerously close to "divination" to the modern mind, to the ancient believer who did not understand any separation between "natural" and "supernatural," casting lots was an objective and divinely sanctioned method to receive confirmation from God when one did not want to leave a decision to chance.
>
> In most ancient Near Eastern tradition, the act of divination was seen as an objective evaluation of the prophetic word. Dreams and visions were not understood as infallible or absolute commands of the gods. After a prophet spoke a word of prophecy for the king, prophets would often submit a hair and clothing sample to accompany the prophetic word.[†] The king would then seek to have that prophetic word verified by the act of divination. If the divination confirmed the prophetic word, all was well. If the divination contradicted the prophet, then the prophet was identified and appropriately punished for misrepresenting the gods and enticing the king.
>
> [†] For examples, see Martti Nissinen, *"Prophets and Temples," Ancient Prophecy: Near Eastern, Biblical, and Greek Perspectives* (Oxford Academic, 2017), 211–13.

Prophetic Speech Embodied in the Psalms

Though there is a scarcity of explicit prophetic mentions in Psalms, one should not infer that prophetic speech is absent. While prophetic speech in Psalms is not introduced with the traditional "Thus says Yahweh" or a prophet's name, the psalmist's prayers often reflect prophetic concerns. Additionally, much like the words spoken by the prophets, in the psalms, God's direct speech is seen on occasion. Like the prophetic word was embodied in the life of the prophet, prophetic speech is often embodied in the language of the psalms.

The Psalter's prophetic voice resembles the prophetic voice elsewhere in the Hebrew Bible. Its messages fall into the same two categories as traditional prophetic speech: eschatological visions and prophetic warnings.

Eschatological oracles focus on end of the age when God's ultimate reality finally manifests in this world. Prophetic warnings, which are the majority of the prophetic speech, offer contemporary evaluations and warnings concerning the behavior of Israel.

"What Could Be": The Hope of Eschatological Prophecy

Eschatology is concerned with the "last things." The word means "the study of the end." When people think about the end of the world, they usually think in terms that sound like the conversation at the end of the movie *Ghostbusters* (1984): "Fire and brimstone coming down from the sky! Rivers and seas boiling! . . . Forty years of darkness! Earthquakes, volcanoes . . . . The dead rising from the grave . . . . Human sacrifice, dogs and cats living together—MASS HYSTERIA!"

While those images are not uncommon in "apocalyptic" narratives (apart from the cohabitating dogs and cats), they are not necessarily representative for eschatological texts. Apocalyptic texts are eschatological, but eschatological texts are not necessarily apocalyptic. Indeed, many eschatological texts are beautiful, hope-filled oracles, envisioning what could be if the world committed itself to the divine.

Psalm 96 is an example of an eschatological (but not apocalyptic) text, as it looks forward with great anticipation to the end of days when Yahweh finally will be worshiped by all the families of all the peoples of the earth, and all the nations will finally confess Yahweh as king.

> Give glory to Yahweh! All the families of the earth!
> Give glory and strength to Yahweh!
> Give to Yahweh the glory of God's name!
> Bring an offering and come into the divine courtyard!
> Worship Yahweh with holy beauty!
> Tremble before God, all the earth!
> Say among the nations, "Yahweh reigns!
> The world is established and never shakes!
> God will judge people with fairness." (vv. 7-10)

It is an optimistic end shared by the oracle in Micah 4:1-4 and its parallel in Isaiah 2:2-5:

> In the future, the mountain of Yahweh's house will be established as the most important of the mountains. It will be lifted up above the hills, and

people will stream to it. Many nations will come and say, "Come, let us ascend Yahweh's Mountain and go to the God of Jacob's house so that God might show us the divine way, and that we might walk the divine path because the Torah will come out of Zion, and the word of Yahweh from Jerusalem. And God will judge between many people and make decisions for strong and distant nations, and they will crush their swords and shape them into plowshares, their spears into pruning hooks. Never again will nation lift up a sword against nation. Never again will they learn war. But people will sit under their own vine and under their own fig tree. No one will cause them any fear because the mouth of Supreme Commander Yahweh has spoken. Though all peoples, each follow in the name of their god, we—we will follow in the name of Yahweh our God forever! (Mic 4:1-4)

The promise of eternal peace becoming real on the earth is shared in other psalms as well:

Go and see the works of Yahweh,
who set devastation in the earth!
The one who ends wars to the ends of the earth.
God will break the bow, shatter the spear, and burn the shield in fire.
Be still and know that I, myself, am God,
exalted in the nations and exalted in the earth.
Supreme Commander Yahweh is with us.
The God of Jacob is our stronghold. (Ps 46:8-1)

God's defense of Israel provides ultimate protection and security. Indeed, God's protection is so sure, the gates of the city can be opened. In a world where siege warfare was an ever-present reality, "open gates" powerfully symbolize trust and security.

On that day, this song will surely be sung in the land of Judah,
"We have a strong city. Deliverance is set up like walls and ramparts.
Open the gates so a righteous nation can come in—one that can be trusted.
You keep the steady mind in peace. In peace because they trust in you.
Trust in Yahweh forever because in Yahweh—Yahweh—you find an everlasting rock." (Isa 26:1-4)

The eschatological victory of God comes with God enthroned as king over all the nations:

> Yahweh reigns over the nations.
> God sits on a holy throne!
> The princes of the peoples gather as the people of the God of Abraham
> because the shields of the earth belong to God.
> God is truly exalted. (Ps 47:8-9)

Even psalms classified as laments express moments of trust and hope with eschatological prophetic elements that sound like prophetic oracles, as in Ps 22:27-31:

> All the ends of the earth will remember and return to Yahweh.
> And all the families of the nations will worship before him.
> Because dominion belongs to Yahweh.
> God rules the nations.
> The prosperous ones in the earth shall eat and bow down to God—
> all those who are going down to the dust and can't keep themselves alive.
> Their descendants will serve God.
> Generations will tell stories of the Almighty.
> They will come and tell of God's righteousness forever,
> to the next generation because of what God has done.

While some oracles look forward to the ultimate and ideal future when all the promises of God have been realized for all the world, sometimes the end, for prophet and the prophetic psalmist, is distant but not quite as far off as the end of time. Some "eschatological" oracles look forward to a nearer—though still some time off—future when the people of God will find promised hope in their life of struggle. The Day of Yahweh oracle seen in Amos is an example of this kind of oracle. These oracles often care less about the rest of the world (except to bring judgment on the wicked in it) and more about a time when the people of God will be restored and no longer make the mistakes they have historically made.

> Praise Yahweh! How good it is to sing praises of our God.
> Because God is gracious, praise is fitting!
> Yahweh builds up Jerusalem.
> God gathers the outcasts of Israel.
> The one who heals the broken mind
> and binds their wounds.
> The one who counts the stars
> and names them all!
> Great is our Sovereign in abundant strength!

> There is no way to quantify God's understanding!
> Yahweh relieves the humble,
> and casts the wicked to the ground (Ps 147:1-6)

This type of "nearer eschatological" hope is analogous to that found at the end of several prophetic books. See, for example, the last words of Zephaniah:

> Look, I will deal with all your oppressors in that time, and I will deliver the lame and I will gather the outcast, and I will make their shame into praise and renown in all the earth. In that time, I will lead you and I will gather you. I will give you fame and praise in all the peoples of the earth, when I restore your captivity before your eyes, says Yahweh. (Zeph 3:19-20)

Indeed, the restoration of the people is one nearer eschatological hope that is shared across the prophets and the psalms.

> Therefore, the Sovereign Yahweh says this, Now I will return Jacob from captivity and I will have compassion on the whole house of Israel. I will show loyalty to my holy name. The shame of all their unfaithful acts which they practiced against me will be forgiven. They will live securely in their land, and nothing will make them afraid. (Ezek 39:25-26)

The confident declaration of the psalmist in Psalm 10 looking forward to judgment on the wicked and restoration to the outcast sounds much like the hope the prophet Joel looked forward to. Compare them:

> Break the arm of the wicked and the destructive.
> Seek out their wickedness until you find none.
> Yahweh is king forever!
> The nations are destroyed from their land.
> Yahweh, you have heard the desires of the afflicted,
> so you have strengthened their resolve by inclining your ear.
> To do justice to the fatherless and the oppressed.
> So that no one on earth might terrorize them again. (Ps 10:15-18)

> Egypt will be a desolation. Edom will be a desolate desert wilderness. Because of the violence done to the children of Judah. They shed innocent blood in their land. But Judah will dwell forever, and Jerusalem

from generation to generation. I will clean their blood that I have not cleansed, and Yahweh will reside in Zion. (Joel 3:19-21)

Since many of these oracles focus on the consequences of exile, the restoration of Jerusalem is a common focus. The city's restoration symbolizes the hope and peace that will come to all the people. Much like Ps 147 and the prophet Joel, the prophet Ezekiel also envisions an eschatological hope expressed in a restored city of Jerusalem.

> I will make a flourishing covenant with them. It will be an eternal covenant. I will establish them and multiply them. I will set my sanctuary in their midst forever. And it will be a dwelling among them. I will be their God. They will be my people. Then the nations will know that I—myself—Yahweh—sanctify Israel, when my sanctuary is in their midst forever. (Ezek 37:26-28)

In the book of Ezekiel, the restoration and transformation of the city will be so dramatic that it will result in a name change. The city will no longer be named Jerusalem, or "City of Peace." But in the final verse of the book, in Ezekiel 48:35b, we find ". . . the name of the city from that time on shall be, 'Yahweh is There.'"

Before Yahweh can dwell forever in this "new" Jerusalem, the people will have to be changed. The psalmist in Ps 18 celebrates God's preparation of Israel for ultimate victory with language that is similar to Micah. Compare them:

> For who is a God except Yahweh?
> And who is a rock but our God?
> The God who arms me with strength,
> and who makes my way perfect.
> Making my feet like the deer's,
> and giving me the ability to stand on the heights. (Ps 18:31-33)

> Who is a God like you? Who forgives iniquity and pardons rebellion for those who remain God's possession? Who does not maintain fierce anger forever but rather delights in showing committed love? God's compassion for us will return, and God will walk over our iniquities. You will hurl all our sins into the depths of the sea. Show faithfulness to Jacob, committed love to Abraham which you swore to our ancestors in ancient days. (Mic 7:18-20)

God's mercy and compassion are celebrated in the prophets and in the psalms as the psalmist looks forward to ultimate restoration of the people:

> Yahweh, you were favorable to your land.
> You restored the fortunes of Jacob.
> You forgave the iniquity of your people.
> You covered all their sins.
> You removed all your wrath,
> and you turned from your burning anger (Ps 85:1-3)

And in Amos 9:

> I will restore the people of Israel from captivity, and they shall rebuild the ruined cities, and dwell in them. They shall drink wine from the vineyards they plant. They will eat the produce of the gardens they work. I will plant them, and they will never be uprooted again from their land which I have given them, says Yahweh your God. (Amos 9:14-15)

The promised hope does not always have to be eschatological, or even "nearer eschatological." In fact, Ps 91 provides one of the examples of God directly speaking in the psalms and promising rescue in real time. While the rest of the psalm is in the third or second person, at the end, God speaks directly:

> I will deliver the one devoted to me.
> I will exalt the one who knows my name.
> When they call me I will answer them.
> I ,myself, will be with them in their distress.
> I will rescue and honor them
> I will satisfy them with long life,
> and I will show them my deliverance. (Ps 91:14-16)

Like Psalm 91, prophetic preaching ends in hope, and that hope often takes the form of the visions of what could be if the people of God would finally be the people God created them to be. The psalms share that vision of the "almost end" and "really the end," as well as the hope that is possible for the people who commit themselves to God. Unfortunately, "what could be" comes up against "what is," which brings us to the second, and more common, type of prophetic message: the word of prophetic challenge.

"What Is": Prophetic Challenge

In addition to the eschatological and the "nearer eschatological" oracles, the psalms also contain speech reminiscent of more typical "rebuke" prophetic preaching. Occasionally, there is overlap between the prophetic message and the psalms. Both share a strong rebuke of idolatry.

> The nations' idols are silver and gold,
> works of human hands.
> They have mouths but they do not speak.
> Eyes but they do not see.
> They have ears but they do not hear.
> Indeed there is not breath in their mouths.
> And the ones who make them will be just like them,
> and all the ones who trust in them. (Ps 135:15-18)

The references to idolatry in the prophets are too numerous to list comprehensively, but Isaiah does a nice job illustrating God's feelings on the issue:

> Everyone who makes idols is nothing.
> What they desire is worthless.
> Their witnesses can't see, and they can't know,
> and so they are put to shame.
> Who would form a god
> or cast an idol that proves worthless?
> Look, all its associates will be put to shame.
> Their craftsmen are humans!
> Let them assemble and stand.
> They will panic and be put to shame all together. (Isa 44:9-11)

This view is shared by Ps 97:6-7:

> The heavens proclaim God's righteousness,
> and all the peoples see God's glory.
> Let the servants of idols be put to shame,
> the ones who praise mere images. All the gods bow before God!

Two of the historical psalms (Pss 78 and 106) tell the same story the prophets tell. Idolatry was commonplace in Israel, even to the point of human sacrifice to false gods:

> They made God angry with their high places
> and jealous with their idols
> God heard and was angry.
> and utterly rejected Israel. (Ps 78:58-59)

> But they mixed with the nations,
> and they learned from their deeds.
> They served their idols,
> which became a snare to them.
> They sacrificed their sons
> and their daughters to demons.
> They poured out innocent blood,
> the blood of their sons and daughters
> whom they sacrificed to the idols of Canaan.
> The land was polluted with blood
> They were unclean in their actions
> and prostituted themselves with their deeds. (Ps 106:35-39)

> For they have committed adultery and blood is on their hands. They have committed adultery with their idols, and even their children whom they bore to me, they have offered up as food for them. Even more than this! They have done this to me. They have defiled my sanctuary on the same day they profaned my Sabbath! On the same day—slaughtering their children for their idols, and coming to my sanctuary to defile it. See! This is what they have done in the middle of my house! (Ezek 23:37-39)

Apart from shared topics, the psalms offer direct prophetic speech at times. Indeed, Psalm 50 sounds as though it was lifted from the prophets themselves. While the psalms might lack the rhetorical indicator "Thus says Yahweh," the reader cannot miss when the God has begun to sing rather than the psalmist (as in Ps 91:14-16). Psalm 50 provides an excellent example of challenging prophetic speech, delivered by God directly.

> Hear, my people, I will speak. Israel,
> I will warn against you.
> I am God, your God
> I am not condemning you because of your sacrifices
> or your burnt offerings which are continually before me.
> I don't need a bull from your house
> or a goat from your herds.

> Because all that lives in the forest,
> the cattle on a thousand hills, is mine.
> I know all the birds of the hills
> and the creeping things in the field are mine. (vv. 7-11)

The passage resonates well with the eighth-century prophetic messages of Amos to Israel:

> I hate—I thoroughly despise your sacred festivals!
> Even if you offered burnt and grain offerings, I will not accept them.
> I won't look at the peace offering of your best animals.
> Get your noisy songs away from me!
> I won't listen to the melodies of your harps.
> But justice will roll down as waters,
> and righteousness like strong stream! (Amos 5:21-24)

It also resonates with the message of Isaiah to Judah:

> "What do I care about your multitude of sacrifices?" says Yahweh. "I've had my fill of your burnt offerings of rams and the fat from steers. The blood of bulls or lambs or goats do not make me happy. . . . When you stretch out the palm of your hand, I will hide my eyes from you. Even if you offer a multitude of prayers, I will not listen. Your hands are full of blood. Wash yourselves! Cleanse yourselves! Turn aside from your destructive actions from in front of me. Stop being destructive! Learn true goodness. Seek justice. Bless the oppressed! Judge in favor of the orphan and contend for the widow!" (Isa 1:11, 15-17)

The Isaiah and the Amos text both feature a concept that is common to the prophets: the idea of justice. The issue of justice has come up in discussions of the Torah and in discussions of kingship. Because the king should rule with justice, injustice within the people of God seems to motivate most prophetic preaching. It also is a major feature of the psalms. Often, the psalms make the natural connection of the performance of justice to the Torah:

> The mouth of the righteous one murmurs wisdom.
> And their tongue speaks justice.
> The Torah of their God is in their minds,
> and their steps do not slip. (Ps 37:30-31)

Justice was the topic of the first of the two "Psalms of Solomon" in the Psalms:

> O God, give your justice to the king,
> and your righteousness to a king's son.
> May he judge your people in righteousness,
> and your afflicted with justice.
> Let the mountains give flourishing lives to the people,
> and the hills bring righteousness (Ps 72:1-3)

Even the royal influence that surrounded the psalms wasn't enough for the psalms to miss that the prophets were right. The kings were not ruling with justice. In Ps 146, a psalm likely written post exile after the psalmist had seen what consequences came from the choices of Israel and Judah's kings, the psalmist offers practical thoughts regarding political leadership:

> Do not trust in princes, in humans,
> who cannot bring deliverance.
> When their breath departs, they return to the ground
> on that day their plans perish.
> Blessed are those whose help is in the God of Jacob,
> whose hope is in Yahweh their God.
> The one who made heavens and the earth, the sea and all that is in them.
> The one who remains faithful forever.
> The one who make justice for the oppressed and gives food to the hungry.
> Yahweh releases the prisoners. (Ps 146:3-7)

No matter your position or connections—even if one is divine (cf. Ps 82!)—the standard for leadership is justice. In fact, after dismissing the human leaders in Ps 146, the psalm goes on to show what effective leadership looks like with a tone that sounds very much like the Isaiah passage that Jesus selected to summarize his calling in Luke 4. Compare the two:

> . . . releases the prisoners.
> Yahweh gives sight to the blind.
> Yahweh raises up the one who is bent.
> Yahweh loves the righteous.
> Yahweh protects the foreigner.
> God upholds the fatherless and the widow,
> and cripples the way of the wicked. (Ps 146:7b-9)

> The spirit of the God, Yahweh, is upon me because Yahweh has anointed me to bring good news to the oppressed and to heal the broken-hearted, to decree release for the captives and prisoners. To decree the year of the favor of Yahweh and the day of vengeance for our God. To comfort all who mourn . . . . Strangers stand and shepherd your flocks, the children of foreigners farm your land and dress your vines. And you yourselves, shall be called priests of Yahweh, and ministers of our God. You shall consume the strength of the nations and boast in their glory. . . . Because I, Yahweh, love justice. (Isa 61:1-2, 5-6, 8a; quoted by Jesus in Luke 4)

Justice is so pervasive in the psalms and the prophets that it would be impractical to quote all the examples of overlap.[3] But it seems clear that the "prophetic voice" of the psalms is far more common than one might expect. In fact, encountering verses out of context, it would be difficult to know where they came from, a psalm or a prophet?

> Who can adequately utter the deeds of Yahweh?
> Who can make known all that God has done which is praiseworthy?
> Blessed is the one who keeps justice!
> Who is doing righteousness all the time. (Ps 106:2-3)

A Passionate God

The God of the prophets is a deeply emotional God. Though people often seem more comfortable imagining a stolid and dispassionate God judicially accepting those ruled as innocent or dispassionately punishing those who are found guilty, this caricature bears little resemblance to the God of the Bible. In Genesis 1, humanity is created in the image of God, and human beings are complex emotional creatures. It shouldn't be surprising to learn that God is a complex emotional being as well. In Ps 95, God's direct speech expresses a range of emotions from imploring, frustration, and even loathing and anger by God's own admission.

> Today, if only you would listen to God's voice!
> Do not harden your thoughts as you did at Meribah,
> as on the day of Massah in the desert wilderness.
> When your ancestors tested me and asked me for proof,
> when they had seen my deeds!
> Forty years I felt a loathing for that generation,

---

3. The prophets use the word for "justice" nearly 145 times, from Isaiah to Malachi. The psalms have 65 occurrences of the word alone.

and said, "These people's minds wander about, and they do not know my ways!"
So I swore in my anger, they will not come to my rest!" (Ps 95:7b-11)

The prophets all express this deep "pathos" of God, but perhaps none show quite the range of Hosea. Hosea shows a God who expresses all the emotions of a wronged partner in a relationship. From the longing for happier times at the beginning of Hosea 11—

When Israel was a child, I loved him. And from Egypt, I called him to me.
The more I called to them, the more they walked from me. They sacrificed to the Baals and to idols and made offerings to idols.
Yet it was I—I taught them to walk, taking them in my arms.
But they didn't know that I healed them. I led them with cords of humanity, with bands of love. I eased the yoke from upon their neck and bent down to feed them. (Hos 11:1-4)

—to the destructive judgment that will come upon them in anger in the middle of the chapter—

But they will return to the land of Egypt,
and Assyria will rule them because they refuse to repent
The sword dances through their cities and finishes off their diviners.
It devours them because of their schemes
My people are hung up on turning away from me.
They call to the high God together,
but will never be exalted. (Hos 11:5-7)

—and finally to the regret and mercy God is willing to show because of the power of the divine love:

How can I give you up, Ephraim, or hand you over, Israel? How can I give you up, like Admah? Or make you like Zeboiim? I shake the thought from my mind and warm to the idea of tender compassion. I will not bring my burning wrath. I will not destroy Ephraim because I am God and not a human. I am the Holy One in your midst. I will not come in wrath. (Hos 11:8-9)

In only nine verses, truly God reveals the emotional roller coaster of breakups. While the psalms may not capture that extreme range, they do reflect a passionate God who hurts for the people's disobedience. Like Hosea, Psalm 81 provides direct speech from an emotional God who cycles between anger—

> But my people did not listen to my voice.
> Israel did not desire me.
> So I set them free to their own stubborn minds,
> to walk according to their own plans. (Ps 81:11-12)

and a deep longing for things to be better:

> If only my people would listen to me.
> If only Israel would walk in my ways.
> Then I would humble their enemies in a moment.
> And upon their foes, I would return my hand.
> The ones who hate Yahweh would submit before God,
> and their time will be over forever.
> I would feed Israel with the finest wheat,
> and I would satisfy them with honey from the rock. (Ps 81:13-16)

ORACLES AGAINST THE NATIONS

One feature of prophetic preaching that has a close analog in the book of Psalms is the "Oracle against the Nations." Prophetic preaching often interrupts oracles directed at Israel or Judah to take a moment to preach against the nations of the world, warning of the judgment that will come to them. Some psalms take up this preaching style referencing specific nations, and some psalms preach against generic "nations." The prophets seem to believe that there is enough revelation of God in this world that judgment against the nations is merited, and the psalms agree.

In Ps 9, the judgment comes against "all" the nations because of their sinfulness. The nations have failed to remember the poor and the needy.

> The nations have sunk in the pit they dug.
> They have captured their own foot in the net they hid
> Yahweh has made the divine character known.
> God has established justice.
> By the deeds of their hands, the wicked have been snared.
> The wicked will withdraw to the grave—
> all the nations who forget God.
> Because the needy will not be forgotten forever.

> The hope of the poor will not perish forever.
> Rise up, Yahweh, do not let humans prevail.
> Let the nations be judged before you.
> Yahweh, make them afraid,
> and let them know they are only human. (Ps 9:15-20)

Likewise, Ps 59 offers a word of judgment against the all the nations for their wicked plotting.

> You are Yahweh. Commanding God of Israel!
> Awaken to punish all the nations!
> Do not show mercy to any who treacherously plot iniquity!
> They return in the evening and howl like dogs,
> and they prowl around the city
> They are bellowing with their mouths,
> with a sword in their lips because they say, "who hears us?"
> You, Yahweh, you laugh at them.
> You mock all the nations. (Ps 59:5-8)

Ps 60 and its copy in Ps 108 provide more specific forecasts of destruction analogous to the prophets. Compare Ps 60 to an oracle against Moab in Isa 15:

> God spoke in the divine sanctuary:
> "With joy, I will divide up Shechem
> and I will measure the valley of Succoth."
> Gilead belongs to me.
> And Manasseh belongs to me.
> Ephraim is my helmet.
> Judah is my scepter.
> Moab is my washing pot.
> I will throw my shoe at Edom.
> I will shout over Philistia. (Ps 60:6-8)

> An oracle concerning Moab.
> Truly in the night it is devastated.
> Ar of Moab is ruined.
> Truly in the night it is devasted.
> Kir of Moab is undone.
> They went up to Bayith—to Debin—to the high places, to lament.
> Upon Nebo—upon Medeba—Moab wails!

Every head is bald.
Every beard is shaved.
In their streets, they wear sackcloth.
On their roofs and in their squares,
everyone wails,
and collapses in tears. (Isa 15:1-3)

The word against Moab continues through Isa 15 to the end of chapter 16.

Ps 83 provides an example of one of the specific contrasts between the psalms and the prophets, specifically, the use of the verb tense.

They conspire against your people,
and plot against your treasured ones.
They said, "Come let's destroy them from the nations
so that the name of Israel isn't remembered again."
Because they conspire with a unified mind,
and they have made a covenant against you,
the tents of Edom, and the Ishmaelites,
Mot and the Hagrites
Gebal and Ammon and Amalek,
Philistia with the inhabitants of Tyre.
Even Assyria has joined them
to give their arm to the children of Lot.
Do to them as you did to Midian,
as to Sissera and Jabin at the Wadi Kishon. (Ps 83:3-9)

In the psalm, the psalmist's song uses an imperative to ask God to bring justice upon the offending nations. The prophet's preaching shows that God has already decided to bring judgment on the wicked.

Two of the prophetic books act as self-contained "Oracles against the Nations." Obadiah remembers the destruction of Edom in a single chapter, making it the shortest book of the Hebrew canon. The book laments Edom's hubris, which brought its destruction, and reminds them of the karmic reality in verse 15: "Because the day of Yahweh is near for all the nations. As you have done, so it will be done to you. Your repayment will return on your own head." The tone of Obadiah is one of regret for Edom's behavior. The nation was thought of as a "brother" nation whose patriarch was Esau. Its cruelty is lamented.

This attitude contrasts with the book of Nahum, the other prophetic text that acts as a self-contained "Oracle against the Nations." Nahum remembers the destruction of Nineveh, the capital city of the cruel Assyrian empire, and while his message is the same as Obadiah's, his tone could only be described as jubilant. In fact, the book ends with a statement that everyone who hears the news of Assyria's fall is happy:

> There is no easing your hurt,
> for your wound is fatal.
> Whoever hears the report of you,
> will clap their hands about it
> because no one missed suffering
> from your unceasing destruction. (Nah 3:19)

And the text is not simply celebrating Nineveh's destruction but its humiliation:

> Behold, I am against you, declares Supreme Commander Yahweh,
> and I will lift off your skirts above your face,
> and I will let the nations see your nakedness,
> kingdoms will see your shame.
> I will throw detestable things at you.
> I will treat you with contempt,
> and I will make you a public spectacle,
> and everyone who sees you will run from you
> and say, "Nineveh is devastated, but who will mourn her?"
> There is nowhere I could seek comforters for you. (Nah 3:5-7)

While it is true that Nineveh performed these acts against others and they are simply suffering the way they caused others to suffer, the book of Nahum puts emotions in the mouth of God that can seem very different than the person that Christians see incarnate in Jesus. Although Nahum says these oracles are "Thus Yahweh says . . . ," they sound exactly like the emotions of a people who suffered at the hands of a cruel empire like in Ps 137:

> Remember, Yahweh, what the children of Edom said on Jerusalem's day—
> the ones saying, "Strip it down, strip it to the foundations!" against the city!
> Daughter of Babylon, the destroyer,
> Blessed is the one who fulfills

and repays you for your deeds to us.
Blessed is the one who grabs
and then shatters your child against the rocks. (vv. 7-9)

While it is possible to read this difficult book of Nahum like Ps 137, as an expression of human emotion of the "bad guys finally getting theirs," this doesn't make the book very "prophetic." The political and religious leadership do not appear to be challenged. Indeed, this message would not cause Nahum a problem to preach at all. For this patriotic message, he would be celebrated!

Perhaps the reader should adjust who the intended audience might be. What if Nahum is not about spiking the football in Nineveh's face but is rather directed at Judah? Indeed, it might be possible to think of all the Oracles against the Nations as intended for Judah and Israel rather than the "nations."

If that is the case, these oracles become prophetic cautions for God's people: "If Edom, Moab, Philistia, even Egypt, Assyria, and Babylon, couldn't get away with mocking God, what chance do you have?" Indeed, it seems that the prophet Amos is using his "Oracles against the Nations" passage in exactly this way. He opens the book calling attention to the failings of all the nations around Israel only to finish with Judah and Israel as similar, if not worse, examples of disobedience. Read this way, these oracles become warnings that Israel and Judah are not exempt from judgment. Indeed, by wearing God's name and failing to uphold God's Torah, Israel and Judah will find worse judgment than the pagan nations surrounding them.

Conclusion

It might be tempting to consider the prophetic message of Psalms as analogous to the psalms' coverage of the ancestor stories: the message is in what they don't say! The psalms, however, are far more prophetic than they first seem. Certainly, through the canonical process, but even in their canonical form, these "words to God" are "words from God" in direct ways. The psalms offer words of condemnation against what is, regret for the loss of what could be, and a celebration of what will be. The psalms offer judgment against the nations and explanations for the judgment against Israel and Judah. On occasion, God speaks directly in the psalms. "Bringing God's word to the people" is the classic definition of a prophet.

Questions for Further Discussion

1. Using the simple definition for prophet as "one who brings God's word to the people," who are contemporary prophets? How does their treatment by people of faith and the establishment correspond to the treatment of biblical prophets?

2. A deeply emotional God makes some people uncomfortable. Yet the emotional range that the prophets portray God as having is clear. Does belief in a "complex, emotional God" cause discomfort or comfort? Why?

3. If someone says they want their church "to be prophetic" in this world, what should they know from Scripture? Do they truly want their church to be prophetic?

4. Knowing how the story ends at the end of time was supposed to have an effect on how people lived in their time. Part of Israel's struggle was that they did not have a healthy theological understanding of how the story ended ("Woe to you that desire the Day of Yahweh . . ."). Is the contemporary theological understanding of the end of the story any better? What makes contemporary worship "noise" and "offensive" to God?

5. The prophets and the psalms have more than two hundred references to "God's justice." Does it feature as prominently in contemporary worship preaching and singing? Why or why not?

WISDOM

> *Talking to you is like making dumplings on a groundhog . . .*
> *you just waste your flour.*
> —John F. Wallace, grandfather

THE PSALMS AND WISDOM

My grandfather's formal education ended in the sixth grade, and he began to work in the coal mines not long after. A life of mining, subsistence farming, and raising four children in the hills of Eastern Kentucky, however, offered hard-earned wisdom that Papaw Wallace was always willing to share. That wisdom occasionally took the form of proverbs that he had collected over the years. Some proverbs were well known, like "you can't make a silk purse out of a sow's ear," and others, like this chapter's epigraph, originated with him. My brother and I still use his proverbs. Years later, my grandfather still teaches wisdom and still brings a smile.

People like my grandfather leave a mark on our lives with the wisdom they offer. Older mentors or family members offer counsel that comes from a broader perspective and provides instruction on how to live better. This kind of counsel reflects the Hebrew idea of "wisdom." The original Hebrew word translated as "wisdom," *hokmah* (הכמה), is associated with knowledge, but that knowledge goes beyond intellect. The word can be used to talk about the skills of smiths, carpenters, and craftsmen. In the Hebrew mind, wisdom is not simply gaining knowledge; it is learning how to live well.

The psalms and the wisdom literature share a philosophy of inspiration. While prophetic speech and Torah feature the phrase "thus says Yahweh" and present their words as spoken directly from the mouth of Yahweh, the psalms and the wisdom literature represent "indirect" revelation. Indirect revelation assumes that God's creation intentionally reflects God's will. Therefore, one can know something of God's will by observing creation diligently. Truth comes indirectly, mediated not by a prophet but by living in the world. More living means more opportunity for wisdom. For this reason, wisdom is associated with age. Grey hair is a "crown of glory" (Prov 16:31) and beautiful (Prov 20:29).

The wisdom material of the Bible, however, is divided over exactly how much truth indirect revelation can reveal. The book of Proverbs embraces and celebrates the truths that come from observing the world. Ecclesiastes and Job offer counter testimony—or at least caution—regarding precisely how much of the "truth" one learns from the world can be attributed to God's will. For the rules and principles found in Proverbs, exceptions are found in Job and Ecclesiastes.

This contrast provides two broad categories in which biblical wisdom is classified. "Practical" wisdom is the kind associated with my grandfather and the book of Proverbs. "Skeptical" or "philosophical" wisdom asks questions, expresses doubt and frustration, and is associated with my grandmother[1] and the books of Job and Ecclesiastes (Qoheleth). The canon preserves both perspectives: the answers and the questions. The wisdom material found in the psalms contains both perspectives as well. Some psalms advocate for the simple truths found in practical wisdom. Some psalms struggle to find meaning in a confusing world, like philosophical wisdom.

Practical Wisdom

While the book of Psalms is associated with David, several other names appear in the psalms' superscriptions. In the same way, Proverbs is traditionally associated with Solomon, and several other contributors are named. The book seems to be gathered in collections with introductory statements marking the beginning of each new section.

- Proverbs 1–9 are introduced as "Proverbs of Solomon, son of David, king of Israel."
- Proverbs 10–22:16 are also said to be the "Proverbs of Solomon."
- Proverbs 22:17–24:22 are called the "Sayings of the Wise," which bear remarkable similarity to an Egyptian wisdom document.
- Proverbs 25–29 are introduced as "Other proverbs of Solomon that the officials of King Hezekiah of Judah copied."
- Proverbs 30 contains the "Words of Agur son of Jakeh."

---

1. Papaw Wallace used to say of my grandmother, "If she didn't have enough to worry about this week, she'd go into next week to borrow something to worry about."

- Proverbs 31 finishes the book with the "words of King Lemuel, an oracle his mother taught him."

The final oracle in Proverbs 31 is striking because Israel never had a king named Lemuel. This wisdom not only originates from a woman (King Lemuel's mother) but also comes from a source outside Israel. This oracle is one of several examples that show Israel's sages believed "wisdom was wisdom" no matter its origin. They seemed happy to include foreign wisdom teachings that seemed relevant.

Most wisdom in the book of Proverbs is captured in simple thoughts that usually fit in one verse or even one part of a verse. Occasionally, however, thoughts can be more complex. Woman wisdom has a large section in the middle of book (Prov 8:1–9:6), and to end the book, King Lemuel's mother offers a complex and beautiful acrostic poem on the qualities of a "strong woman" (or perhaps how the qualities of woman wisdom can be lived out). Psalm 133 offers a wisdom teaching with slightly more detail than a traditional proverb. This three-verse Psalm of Ascent celebrates how good it is for family to live together well, taking two additional verses to celebrate the truth found in the first verse.

> Look how good and how pleasant
> when family reside together as one.
> Like good oil on the head,
> running down on the beard, on the beard of Aaron,
> which goes down over the collar of his garment.
> Like the dew of Hermon,
> which goes down upon the mountains of Zion
> because there Yahweh set a divine blessing, life forever.

Psalm 37 contains numerous examples of the pithy wisdom statements that could be confused for verses in Proverbs. Compare these couplets:

> Refrain from anger and forsake wrath!
> Do not worry, it only leads to destruction. (Ps 37:8)
> A quick-tempered person stirs up strife,
> but one slow to anger eases strife. (Prov 15:18)

> The meek will inherit the earth,
> and delight themselves in abundant flourishing lives. (Ps 37:11)

Because the upright will dwell in the land,
and the innocent will remain in it. (Prov 2:21)

Better is a little that the righteous person has
than the abundance of many wicked. (Ps 37:16)
Better to have little in righteousness
than a great harvest without justice. (Prov 16:8)

The wicked borrow, but do not make peace with them.
The righteous one shows compassion and gives generously. (Ps 37:21)
Someone with a generous eye will be blessed.
Strife and insults will cease. (Prov 22:9)

Behold, children are an inheritance of Yahweh.
The fruit of the womb is a reward. (Ps 127:3)
Grandchildren are a crown to the elderly,
and parents are beauty to their children. (Prov 17:6)

Unless Yahweh builds a house, the builders labor in vain.
Unless Yahweh guards the city, the guards keep watch in vain. (Ps 127:1)
The curse of Yahweh is on the house of the wicked.
But he blesses the home of the righteous. (Prov 3:33)

Brief examples of practical wisdom, giving instruction on how to find a good life, are not uncommon in the psalms.[2]

Psalm 1 as Practical Wisdom

For scholars who believe in the genre category of "wisdom psalm,"[3] Ps 1 is considered an excellent example of the genre. The themes of the psalm resonate with themes in the book of Proverbs: how to have a good life, the

---

2. In addition to Ps 37 and 127, one can find practical wisdom statements in Ps 112 and Ps 128, which shares a lot in common with Ps 1.

3. The existence of "wisdom psalms" is a contested issue in Psalms scholarship. Hermann Gunkel listed the category in his seminal work on Psalms (*Introduction to the Psalms: The Genres of the Religious Lyric of Israel* [4th ed., comp. Joachim Begrich, trans. Jim Nogalski; Mercer University Press, 1998]; translation of *Einleitun in die Psalmen: die Gattungen der religiösen Lyrik Israel*, 1933, 293–305). Subsequently, however, scholars have failed to reach a consensus on whether "wisdom psalm" is a type of psalm or whether some psalms simply express the wisdom features in service of other psalm genres like "Torah" or "kingship." James Crenshaw has been one of the louder voices challenging the existence of "wisdom psalms" (see his *The Psalms* [Grand Rapids: Eerdmans, 2001], 87–95).

outcomes of the righteous and the wicked, how the righteous should avoid association with the wicked, and behavior that will lead one to a happy life.

> Blessed is the one who does not follow the counsel of the wicked
> or stand in the pathway of sinners
> or sit in the assembly of the haughty.
> But their delight is in the Torah of Yahweh!
> And they meditate on God's Torah day and night.
> And they will be like a tree planted by streams of water
> which give their fruit in season.
> Its leaves never wither.
> Everything they do will succeed!
> Not so with the wicked.
> Rather they are worthless chaff,
> which is blown by the wind.
> Because of this, the wicked cannot stand in the judgment
> or sinners in the congregation of the righteous.
> But Yahweh knows the pathway of the righteous,
> but the pathway of the wicked goes to destruction. (vv. 1-6)

The echoes of these ideas are found throughout Proverbs:

> Blessed is the one who finds wisdom,
> the one who obtains understanding. (Prov 3:13)
> . . .
> Her ways are ways of pleasantness,
> and all her paths lead to flourishing.
> She is a tree of life to those who hold tightly to her.
> Those who hold her are blessed. (Prov 3:17-18)
>
> Do not enter the path of the wicked
> and do not walk in the way of destructive people. (Prov. 4:14)

The end of Ps 1 detailing the way of the wicked and the way of the righteous identifies this psalm as a wisdom text for many. The "two ways" is a common feature of Proverbs.

> Blessings are on the head of the righteous,
> but violence covers the mouth of the wicked.
> The memory of the righteous is a blessing,
> but the name of the wicked will rot. (Prov 10:6-7)

...
> The wage of the righteous is life.
> The produce of the wicked is sin. (Prov 10:16)

This doctrine of retribution is found in over one-fourth of the proverbs. Life works according to a simple formula: the righteous get good things, and the wicked get bad things. Psalm 1 reflects this theology and offers instruction on how to find success. The righteous should avoid the situations of the wicked, and things will go well. When the righteous meditate on God's Torah, they will be like a tree planted by a stream. The wicked, on the other hand, get blown away like dandelion fluff.

In addition to the pithy proverbial sayings found in Ps 37, the psalm also provides an excellent survey of the two ways:

> Do not be angry because of the destructive.
> Do not be jealous of the workers of iniquity.
> Because they will wither quickly like grass—
> they will fade like green grass.
> Trust in Yahweh and do good.
> Dwell in the land and be shepherds of faithfulness.
> Delight yourselves in Yahweh
> and God will answer your questions. (Ps 37:1-4)

Fear of Yahweh

In addition to the "two ways," a common theme in the book of Proverbs is the "fear of Yahweh."[4] As already discussed, this "fear" is more accurately a recognition of position than an emotion of terror. The theme is reflected in the psalms as well; in fact, Ps 111 sounds as though it came directly from the proverbs. Compare these two passages:

> The fear of Yahweh is the beginning of wisdom.
> Understanding comes to all who do good.
> God's praise stands forever. (Ps 111:10)

> The fear of Yahweh is the beginning of knowledge.
> Fools despise wisdom and discipline. (Prov 1:7)

---

4. Prov 1:7, 29; 2:5; 3:7; 8:13; 9:10; 10:27; 14:26-27; 15:16, 33; 16:6; 19:23; 22:4; 23:17; 29:25. In Prov 24:21, the reader is commanded to fear both Yahweh and the king.

One difference between Psalms and Proverbs on this issue, however, is that more commonly in Psalms, "fear of Yahweh" is connected to Torah. The great Torah psalm, Ps 119, has five references to "fearing" God, and as already seen, Ps 19 likens "fear of Yahweh" to Torah observance. Even through Ps 111 connects "fear of Yahweh" to wisdom in verse 10, it connects "fear of Yahweh" to the covenant a few verses before: "God will give food to the ones who fear the divine. The ones who remember the covenant forever" (Ps 111:5). This interchange is not surprising. Torah and wisdom are commonly associated with one another. Despite the different philosophies of revelation, Torah is often thought of as "God's Wisdom" in Jewish tradition. Psalm 1 reflects the natural overlap of the two. While it is used as an example of a "wisdom psalm," the psalm does not promise that meditating on *wisdom* leads to a "happy" or "blessed" life—meditating on Torah does. Even the "two ways" of the psalm connect wisdom with the Torah, since another name of the "two ways" is "Deuteronomic theology." Trying to separate what constitutes a "wisdom psalm" as compared to a "Torah psalm" is just one of the reasons scholars disagree over labeling a text a "wisdom psalm."

Sources of Wisdom

Since the basis for the revelation of the wisdom literature is simply observations from living in the world, the wise men in Israel used sources of wisdom beyond their own country. Israel is not the only group of people who lived in the world and made observations about life in it, and Israel's sages never hesitated to borrow from the traditions of the people around them.

Whenever the sages borrowed ideas, they always fixed the wisdom theologically. If the focus was on a foreign god, Israel would make the focus Yahweh, but the wisdom teachers would preserve the truth no matter where it came from. Two examples of this international borrowing are found in Proverbs. First, Prov 22:17–24:22 has sections that directly parallel the Instruction of Amen-em-opet,[5] an Egyptian wisdom document.

---

5. "The Instruction of Amen-Em-Opet," *ANET*, 421–25.

Proverbs	**Amen-Em-Opet**
22:20: Have I not written to you thirty excellent examples of counsel and knowledge?	(30) See thou, these thirty chapters; they inform, they instruct.
22:22: Do not exploit the poor because they are poor, and do not crush the afflicted in court.	(2) Guard thyself against robbing the oppressed and against overbearing the disabled.
22:24-25: Make no friends with those given to anger, and do not associate with hotheads, or you may learn their ways and entangle yourself in a snare.	(9) Do not associate to thyself the heated man, nor visit him for conversation . . . lest a terror carry thee off.
23:4-5: Do not make friends with an angry master or associate with a hothead. Lest you learn their ways, and your life is entangled in a snare.	(7) Cast not thy heart in pursuit of riches . . . if riches are brought to thee by robbery, they will not spend the night with thee . . . or they have made themselves wings like geese and are flown away to the heavens.
22:28: Do not move an ancient boundary marker which your ancestors placed.	(6) Do not carry off the landmark at the boundaries of the arable land . . .. nor encroach upon the boundaries of a widow."
23:10: Do not move an ancient landmark to encroach on the field of the fatherless.	

The second clear example of borrowing is more explicit—King Lemuel's mother's oracle in Proverbs 31. Lemuel's kingdom is unknown, though some translations assume the word commonly translated "oracle" in verse 1, "Massa," might refer to his city or land. Regardless, he and his mother are clearly non-Israelite and offer a complex and beautiful acrostic poem on the qualities of a "strong" woman, which is ironic since in 31:3, she warns him not to give his "strength" to woman, using the same word.

The strong woman envisioned by King Lemuel's mother is remarkably progressive for the ancient patriarchal society. She is bringing her husband good and not harm. She works in the textiles business (vv. 13, 19, 22, 24), brings food to the family (v. 14), works harder than the servants (v. 15), works in real estate and winemaking (v. 16), is generous (v 20), and is a capable teacher of wisdom. Such a woman would be more at home in Helen Reddy's 1972 hit "I'm a Woman" than in the patriarchal world of the ancient Near East. How did this text make it into the canon?

Occasionally, one finds glimpses in the biblical story that remind the reader that the patriarchal subjugation of women was a consequence of humanity's fallen state and not the vision that God had for humanity. Perhaps, like the "strong woman" named Ruth and the beautiful reciprocal love without subjugation found in Song of Songs, Proverbs 31 slipped through the patriarchal gatekeepers of the ancient world, though even then, the ideas needed to come from a foreign king—or his mother; however, no Israelite king would take ownership.

Rather than a progressive statement on women's rights, Prov 31 might be the culmination of the celebration of wisdom in the book of Proverbs. The oracle might offer what "Woman Wisdom" looks like personified. After all, the personification of Wisdom herself was said to be at creation:

> Yahweh possessed me at the beginning of his work,
> before his deeds from old.
> From ancient times, I was set up, from the beginning,
> even before the world existed.
> When there were no depths churning,
> and when there were no springs of deep water. (Prov 8:22-24)

In Proverbs 31, the "strong" woman is trusted by her husband. She does him good and not harm (vv. 11-12). She brings honor to her husband (v. 23). These are all rewards that come to the young man who seeks out Woman Wisdom. She sings,

> I will walk in the path of righteousness in the midst of the pathway of justice.
> To provide an inheritance to the ones who love me. They will have a full treasury! (Prov 8:20-21)
> . . .
> Blessed is the one who listens to me,
> watching at my gates every day,
> guarding my doorway (Prov 8:34)

So the foreign oracle of Prov 31 might offer examples of personified qualities of the wisdom of God—personified as a woman—or it might affirm the wisdom capabilities of women who were so often marginalized in the ancient world. Either interpretation is remarkably progressive in the ancient patriarchal society.

Contradictions in Wisdom

Absolute statements rarely hold true universally.[6] Rules always seem to have exceptions, and the wisdom literature knows this as well. The books of Job and Ecclesiastes offer exceptions to what can often be read as the absolute rules of Proverbs; however, Proverbs itself recognizes that sometimes a single proverb might not always be true. For example,

> Do not answer a fool according to their own foolishness,
> or you will make yourself a fool.
> Answer a fool according to their foolishness,
> or they will be wise in their eyes. (Prov 26:4-5)

Without an appreciation of the genre of wisdom literature and indirect revelation, this kind of contradiction within Scripture would be troubling. For hyper-literalistic readers of Scripture, Prov 26:4-5 offers a contrast that could shake faith. One must remember, however, that Proverbs is an example of the genre of wisdom literature. The special qualities of the genre need to be considered.

Proverbial traditions contradict one another because proverbial traditions always contradict one another. Even common American proverbs contradict one another. For example, it is said to "Look before you leap" but also that "He who hesitates is lost." Which choice is correct? Prudence or daring? It depends on the situation. Sometimes patience is needed before deciding, and sometimes an opportunity needs to be seized before it passes by. Real wisdom comes in knowing when to do one and when to do the other.

In the same way, Prov 26:4 warns that one can't let stupid people pull them into a fight. Prov 26:5 warns that sometimes stupid people need to be told they are stupid. The real wisdom comes in knowing when to apply which proverb. Prov 26:4-5 provides an important lesson. While the proverbs are written as absolute prohibitions and promises, in keeping with the style of wisdom traditions, they should not be applied as absolutes. Sometimes "the early bird gets the worm," but other times "the second mouse gets the cheese."

This caution is especially important when considering one of Proverbs' more popular passages, often used in parenting guides:

---

6. As seen in my reticence to use an absolute statement about absolute statements.

> Train a youth in the way they should go, then
> when they are old they will not wander from it. (Prov 22:6)

If one forgets this verse is in the genre of wisdom literature, it could lead to unhelpful, and even dangerous, interpretations. Certainly, as this verse implies, one can think of examples of good parents who raise good children. Good parents, however, can also be estranged from their children through no fault of their own. Even more confoundingly, sometimes one can find good children who come from terrible parents.

None of these counter examples "disproves" Scripture. One cannot read this Scripture as a guarantee or control over life's uncertainties or individual choices. In truth, Gen 3 provides a significant contradiction to this proverb, showing that even when provided with the perfect instruction, environment, and supervision, children will still eat from the tree of the knowledge of good and evil and get kicked out of the garden. Like the rest of proverbial wisdom, this proverb offers a general rule that provides the best odds for living a good life. To raise good children, one will have better results being a good parent than being a bad parent.

More broadly, while the book of Proverbs presents wisdom statements as absolute, even Proverbs notes exceptions. Though the book is famous for advocating the two ways, Prov 17:8 observes that sometimes the wicked prosper: "A bribe is like a magic stone to the eyes of a master, and will make one prosper in everything." And lest one believe that bribes are a good thing, the sage also offers thoughts on what category bribes fall in: "The wicked take and conceal a bribe to pervert the ways of justice" (Prov 17:23). So sometimes bribes work, but the wicked take them, and they pervert justice.

Psalm 37 offers the same generalized optimism as Proverbs for how the righteous will not be forsaken. The assurance is written, however, in a declarative statement that echoes the two ways earlier in the psalm: "I have been young and old, and I have not seen a righteous person forsaken or the children of them begging for bread" (v. 25). It seems to be a pretty simple equation. If someone is forsaken, they can't be righteous. If children are begging, their parents are clearly wicked: "Yahweh does not permit the righteous soul to go hungry but will thwart the craving of the wicked" (Prov 10:3).

Life in this world is complicated, however. One doesn't have to live long or read far in the psalms to discover that life does not always work according to the seeming simple formula of Ps 1 or the guarantees of Ps 37 and Prov 10. One does not have to read too far into the psalms to see that after this confident confession of God's regard for the righteous, the psalmists offer example after example of the righteous suffering and the wicked prospering. This frustration with the tension between the way things are and the way they should be is taken up by philosophical wisdom more explicitly.

Skeptical, or Philosophical, Wisdom

While it might be difficult to settle on exactly what constitutes a wisdom psalm in the convention of "practical wisdom," the psalms fit well within the tradition of skeptical or philosophical wisdom. Indeed, were skeptical wisdom the primary definition of the genre, one could say that "wisdom psalms" exist without any issue.

Skeptical or philosophical wisdom uses the same type of revelation as practical wisdom, indirectly observing the world. Unfortunately, rather than providing answers, the world has simply provided more questions. These wisdom texts question the truths the sages of the Proverbs have offered—at times quite directly.

The Hebrew title of the book of Ecclesiastes is "Qoheleth" (קהלת), named for the speaker in the text. The best contemporary translation of the word is likely "the Teacher." The book is associated with Solomon since the Teacher identifies himself as "the son of David, king in Jerusalem," though to be fair, every king of Judah would have called themselves "son of David, king in Jerusalem." One imagines that Solomon's wisdom reputation contributes to the traditional identification.

The Teacher reflects on life and is frustrated that they cannot reconcile how the world appears to work with the lessons they have been taught about how the world is supposed to work. Indeed, they conclude that the indirect revelation that offers the truth claims of Proverbs is ultimately "meaningless." Ecclesiastes sets the tone at the beginning: "'Complete futility,' says the Teacher. 'Complete futility, everything is futile'" (Eccl 1:2). For the Teacher, life is meaningless. No truth from observing the world can make sense of life, and ultimately, one has no control. The Teacher has observed life, just like the sages of Proverbs, and they have found no insights that can make life's brief existence on earth make sense: "What does someone gain from all their toil? A generation comes, and a generation goes, but the earth remains forever" (Eccl 1:3-4).

The transience of life is a shared issue with the psalms:

> My inner thoughts became heated.
> While I mused, a fire burned.
> Then I spoke with my tongue:
> Yahweh, help me understand my end
> and the measure of my days.
> What I know is how fleeting I am.
> Look, you have made my days just a few inches,
> and my lifetime as nothing in front of you.
> Surely all of humanity stands as nothing more than a breath. (Ps 39:4-6)

Even more frustrating than life not working the way they had been taught, more often, life worked in the opposite way of what they had been taught: "During all my futile days, I have seen the righteous perish in his righteousness, and I have seen the wicked live long in his destructiveness" (Eccl 7:15). The psalmist had similar frustrations:

> But for me, I was almost tripped,
> my feet almost stumbled.
> Because I was envious of the proud.
> I saw the flourishing life of the wicked.
> They have no struggle in their death
> and their bodies are well fed.
> They don't have the trouble other people have.
> They aren't plagued like others. (Ps 73:2-5)

Being "wicked" seems to work. The psalmist wonders what the point of being righteous is.

> I have kept my thoughts clean,
> and I have washed my hands in innocence for nothing.
> I am plagued every day. I am rebuked every morning. (Ps 73:13-14)

The Teacher's cynicism can make people of faith uncomfortable, but it would be unfair to say that the Teacher lacks faith. The Teacher believes in God but refuses to grant the premise that God's ways can be known from experience or carefully examining the world.

> I said to myself, "Look! I am greater and have acquired more wisdom than all who came before me in Jerusalem. Yes, my mind has had great experience and knowledge. 17 I have applied my mind to know wisdom

and to know foolishness and madness. I realized that all this is a chasing after the wind." (Eccl 1:16-17)

Ultimately, for the Teacher, the only meaning can be found in God:

> Sinners will commit a hundred acts of destruction and live long, but still, I myself know that it is better for the ones who fear God—because they stand in fear before God. But it will not go well for the wicked and they will not lengthen their days as a shadow, because they do not stand in fear before God. (Eccl 8:12-13)

Wickedness may seem to bring success. Righteousness may seem to bring nothing, but the Teacher knows that answers are not found in observing the world. They are found in the presence of God. In Ps 73, Asaph said the same as they tried to make sense of this world. After a crisis of faith, they ultimately found answers in the divine presence.

> When I tried to understand this,
> it was troubling to me.
> Until I came into the sanctuary of God,
> and I understood their destiny. (vv. 16-17)

In the sanctuary of the Lord, everything made sense.

> My mind was bitter and my emotions were pain.
> I was ignorant and without knowledge.
> I was like a beast is with you.
> But I am continually with you.
> You hold my right hand.
> You lead me in your plans.
> And afterwards, you receive me in glory.
> Who do I have in heaven?
> I don't desire anything on earth besides you.
> My body and mind may fail,
> but God is the bedrock of my thoughts forever. (Ps 73:21-26)

Questions of meaning occur throughout the Bible and throughout the psalms. In Ps 49, the psalmist does not hide the desire to offer wisdom to anyone who might listen, and at first, that wisdom seems like it will take the form of the practical wisdom of Proverbs:

> Hear this all you peoples!
> Give ear all you inhabitants of the world!
> All the rich and all the poor together!
> My mouth will speak wisdom
> and my mind will meditate on understanding.
> I will lean my ear to a proverb.
> I will solve a riddle to a harp. (vv. 1-4)

The story quickly changes, however. After confessing that God is the source of security that no wealth could provide, the psalmist drifts toward the Teacher's attitude:

> Because one can see the wise die, and
> the fool and the stupid all perish together,
> and leave their wealth to others.
> Their inward thought is that their house will last forever,
> a dwelling from generation to generation. They give lands their name.
> But humans cannot last by their own worth.
> They are like the animals that perish.
> This is their way, their folly,
> and that of those who come after who approve of their words
> like sheep appointed for Sheol.
> Death will be their shepherd and dominion over them.
> The righteous will dominate them in the morning,
> and from there, their form will decay in Sheol. (vv. 10-14)

The Teacher feels the same way about death:

> So I reflected on all of this. I committed my mind to all of this. The works of the righteous and the wise are in the hand of God—whether loved or hated—they can't know. Everything is ahead of them. 2 Everyone shares the same destiny: righteous and wicked, good, clean and unclean, ones who sacrifice and those who don't. The good are the same as the sinners. The one who takes an oath is the same as the one who fears an oath. 3 This is the futile reality for all who work under the sun, the same destiny comes to everyone. Besides this, everyone's mind is full of destructiveness. In their minds is madness all their lives, and after that, they die. (Eccl 9:1-3)

The psalmist found a bit more hope than the Teacher could find, however: "But God will redeem my soul from the hand of Sheol because God has received me" (Ps 49:15).

The psalmist did not exactly made sense of life but found hope in the simple idea, "Don't worry when things don't make sense. Death equalizes everything."

> Do not fear when someone becomes rich
> or when the wealth of their house increases
> Because when they die, they will not carry anything.
> None of their glory will go down with them.
> Though they might bless themselves while they are living,
> as you praise yourself when you do well.
> But they will join their ancestor's generations
> and never see light again (Ps 49:16-19)

In direct contrast to Proverbs, the Teacher wrestled with the lack of understanding that came when looking at the world. The formulas that the sages of proverbs used offered no truth in the Teacher's experience. Everything was complete futility.

> I returned to this thought, and I saw that under the sun, the race is not to the swift, and the battle is not to the strong. More than that, food doesn't come to the wise, neither do riches come to ones of understanding. Grace doesn't come to the knowledgeable, but time and random occurrence happens to them all. Because no one knows their appointed time. As a fish suddenly taken in a strong net goes to destruction. Like a bird taken in a trap. Like them both, humans are snared for a time of calamity when it falls upon them suddenly. (Eccl 9:11-12)

But this lack of understanding did not translate to a lack of faith. In fact, the conclusion of the matter for the Teacher was *only* faith, not because it because it guarantees success but because that is humanity's duty.

> The end of all this, once everything has been heard. Fear God and obey God's commandments because this is everything for humans. Because all that is done, all the hidden things, God will judge whether they are good or destructive. (Eccl 12:13-14)

Some regard this ending as a tonal shift from the rest of the book of Ecclesiastes, but the message of the book is consistent. God is sovereign. The world does not make sense. While righteous living may not offer any explanation or control over life now, righteous living will make sense in the presence of God.

Psalm 1 as Philosophical Wisdom

Psalm 1 is traditionally understood as a classic example of practical wisdom for all the reasons listed above. More might be going on in the psalm than first appears, however. The images of Ps 1 would be familiar to anyone who has read Jeremiah 17:

> Thus Yahweh says, "Cursed are those who trust in human beings and think mere flesh is strength. Their minds wander away from Yahweh." They will be like a shrub in the desert plain. They will not see when true goodness comes. They will dwell in the parched desert wilderness, a barren land where no one can live. Blessed are the ones who will trust in Yahweh, whose trust is in Yahweh. They will be like a tree planted by flowing waters, which sends out its roots to the stream. It has nothing to fear when the heat comes. Its leaves will be green. In the year of drought it will not be anxious, and it will never stop bearing fruit. (Jer 17:5-8)

Like in Ps 1, the ones who trust God in Jeremiah are flourishing trees amid despair and destruction. The context of Jeremiah, however, is judgment. God's anger is against those who have forsaken God. In that context, Jeremiah declares the wicked are parched bushes in the desert, but the righteous are flourishing trees planted by water.

On the surface, this oracle of Jeremiah seems to offer the same Deuteronomic theology as Ps 1. The reality for both could be more complicated. In the context of Jeremiah, this confession does not appear to be true. The wicked may have brought the destruction and suffer when the Babylonian armies conquer the land, but the righteous will suffer as well. This oracle of Jeremiah offers a word of encouragement to the righteous victims of the choices of the wicked: "In this time of drought, don't be anxious. Yahweh is your help."

The suffering of the righteous is not new. In more than half of the psalms, the righteous cry out to the Lord for help in a variety of dire circumstances. As the Teacher observed, life can be hard. The wicked seem to prosper. The righteous seem to suffer. Psalm 1 might seem to be a denial of that; however, the psalmist seems to be keenly aware of this struggle. Psalm 1:6 literally says, "Yahweh knows the way of the righteous." "Knowing" in the ancient Hebrew mind conveyed more than intellectual ability. The word implied deep connection. It could even serve as a euphemism for intimate relationships. To "know" something conveyed a deep understanding.

As seen, one of the most poignant places one can see the closeness of "God knowing" is found at the beginning of Exodus. After Moses flees Egypt and takes refuge in Midian, the text says:

> After a long time, the king of Egypt died. The children of Israel groaned from their slavery. They cried out to God for help from their slavery. God heard their groaning and remembered the covenant with Abraham and Isaac and Jacob. God saw the children of Israel, and God knew. (Exod 2:23-25)

God does not simply know *about* the suffering of the people. God hears, sees, and intimately knows Israel's pain. The knowledge of their struggle motivates God to remember the covenant and take action to deliver them. Indeed, after this expression of God's connection to Israel's suffering, the next event is the call of Moses where God's connection to Israel's pain is expressed again: "And Yahweh said, 'I have truly seen the affliction of my people who are in Egypt and I have heard their cries from the oppression of their taskmaster. I know their sorrows'" (Exod 3:7).

If both the context of the flourishing tree as the suffering of the exiles in Jer 17 and the context of God's close knowledge of the Egyptians' oppression of the ancient Hebrews inform the reading of Ps 1, then this psalm may not be a formulaic statement about blessing and punishment. Perhaps, like the righteous in Jer 17 being exiled from their homes and dragged to a foreign land, the psalmist of Ps 1 is also suffering and reflecting on how to respond.

Read this way, Ps 1 becomes a confession of faith. The psalm encourages those who are suffering with the assurance, "Take courage; God knows your way, just as God knew the suffering of ancient Israel." The righteous should continue to meditate on God's instruction. They should not leave God for other sinful "ways" and "counsels" that promise answers.

Read in this way, the psalm is not an outlier with the laments of the Psalter. Instead, it is at home in a text that takes up the suffering of the righteous regularly. Individual and communal laments make up nearly half of the hymnbook of ancient Israel.

Hope in Despair

No matter how hard life is, every lament in the psalms has a moment at the end of the psalm in which the psalmist expresses trust in Yahweh. Psalm 6 is a classic lament where the psalmist laments poor health. After despairing about their health, their grief, and their enemies, the tone changes in verse 8:

> Depart from me all you workers of iniquity
> because Yahweh has heard my weeping.
> Yahweh has heard my request for favor!
> Yahweh has accepted my prayer.
> All of my enemies will be ashamed and completely dismayed.
> They shall withdraw and be shamed in a moment. (vv. 8-10)

Every lament psalm contains a similar affirmation of trust. Only one psalm breaks the pattern—Psalm 88. No other psalmist sings with the despair of Ps 88. The last word of it is literally "darkness." Additionally, unlike other laments, the psalm does not contain a petition for God to do anything about the psalmist's suffering. Ps 88 does not contain a moment of "Heal me!" or "Be gracious to me!" or even "Hurt my enemies!" like one finds in other lament psalms. The psalmist makes only one request, and it comes at the beginning of the psalm:

> O Yahweh, God of my salvation.
> By day and by night I cry out directly to you
> Let my prayer come before you.
> Bend your ear to my piercing cry. (vv. 1-2)

Although the psalmist has come before God with requests before (daily, according to v. 9), this time the psalmist only has one request of God: "Listen to me." The psalmist wants God's attention so that the divine can hear the ways the psalmist's life is hard and, ultimately, how it is God's fault for their troubles.

> Because my soul is filled with destruction,
> and my life balances on the edge of the grave.
> I am regarded with the ones who go down into a pit.
> I am like someone with no help.
> Set apart among dead,

> like the slain who lie in sepulchers,
> whom you never remember again.
> They are cut off from your hand.
> You have put me in the depths of the pit,
> in depths of darkness. Ps 88:3-6)

The psalmist cannot understand why their faithfulness to God is being met with suffering and God's silence. "But I, I cry for help to you Yahweh. In the morning my prayer comes before you. Why, Yahweh, do you reject my soul? Why do you hide your face from me?"

God does not make sense. Life does not make sense. The despair of the psalmist in Ps 88 provides the perfect transition to reading the book of Job.

JOB: MASTERPIECE OF PHILOSOPHICAL WISDOM

Harold Kushner said in his book *Why Bad Things Happen to Good People* that in the same way every actor wants to play Hamlet, every Bible student wants to write a commentary on Job.[7] The point is hard to argue. The book of Job is remarkable. Its poetry is complex and beautiful. Its topic is timeless. Its truth is difficult to understand. Though widely studied, the book has generated little agreement on its purpose and message. The book is a work of genius from the Israelite community, which is ironic because it does not appear to be an Israelite story.

Job is from the unknown land of "Uz" and called the "greatest of all the people of the east." "East" of what remains unsaid. Distant "east" could be Babylon. A Babylonian story called "The Babylonian Theodicy"[8] is acrostic poem that takes the form of a dialogue of someone talking with their friends about suffering. A Sumerian Wisdom text titled "Man and His God" tells the story about a righteous man who, although faithful to the gods, suffers at their hand.[9] The book of Job is not a direct adaptation of either story, but the biblical narrative could have been inspired by either or both stories. As shown, ancient Israelite authors were aware of and borrowed freely from the literature of the world around them—particularly wisdom stories.

---

7. Harold S. Kushner, *When Bad Things Happen to Good People* (Anchor Books, 1981), 37. Ironically, Kushner was as good as his word and went on to write *The Book of Job: When Bad Things Happen to a Good Person*.

8. "The Babylonian Theodicy," *ANET*, 601–604.

9. "Man and His God," *ANET*, 589–91.

The story might also originate nearer to Israel. Job's friend Bildad comes from a city in Israel's neighbor Edom.[10] Edom had an association with wisdom,[11] so "the east" in Job might be more southeast. Job could be a traditional Edomite story; however, one should not dismiss the possibility that this remarkable story originated within the Israelite community itself.

Along with the location, the date of the book's composition is also debated. One thing scholars agree on is that the story itself is set in the time of the ancestors. The reader is not given many details of Job's life, but his moral character is clear. Job was blameless and "feared God and turned from evil." This detail is critical to reading the book of Job. From time to time, psalmists protest their innocence as a justification for God's blessing and deliverance. For example, "Judge me, Yahweh, because I have walked in blamelessness, and in Yahweh I have trusted without shaking. Examine me, Yahweh, test me. Try my emotions and my mind" (Ps 26:1-2); "Test my motivations. Visit me by night and try me and you will not find any scheming. I will never transgress with my mouth" (Ps 17:3). The reader of Job, however, has the advantage of knowing that in Job's case, he *is* blameless. The story establishes from the beginning that the events that befall Job are not a consequence of wicked behavior.

The two-chapter, prose beginning of the book tells of the undeserved suffering that befalls Job and provides the context for what comes next—thirty-nine chapters of complex and beautiful poetry trying to make sense of a senseless world. Contrary to many interpretations, however, the book of Job does not explain the nature of suffering in the world. Rather, Job's suffering is how "the Satan's" question in Job 1:9, "Does Job fear God for nothing?" finds an answer. The Satan argues that Job's motives for obedience cannot be known since God blesses Job's obedience. The Satan's goal is to use suffering to answer the question of Job's true motivations.

After losing his wealth and children in a single day, Job holds on to his faith. He grieves, but he worships God, saying "Naked I went out from my mother's womb, and naked I will return there. Yahweh has given and Yahweh has taken. Let the name of Yahweh be blessed" (Job 1:21). The Satan is wrong about Job's faith. Unfortunately, in Job 2 the Satan doubles down on his complaint to God; as a result, Job also loses his health. From that point in the story, Job's faithfulness remains an open question. For the

---

10. Eliphaz is from Teman, and Bildad and Zophar come from locations in Arabia.

11. Obadiah 8, Jeremiah 49:7, and the Apocrypha book of Baruch 3:22 associate "wisdom" with the country of Edom.

rest of the book, the reader is unsure if Job will "fear God for nothing" or curse God. After sitting in silence with his friends for a week, Job finally breaks the quiet with a desperate lament that, like Jeremiah's lament in Jer 20, curses the day he was born:[12] "Let that day be darkness! May God above not seek it, neither let light shine upon it" (3:4).

> ### "The Satan" vs. "Mr. Satan"
>
> A new character appears in the prologue to Job. "HaSatan" (lit., "the Satan") presents himself before Yahweh. Although no major Bible translation preserves it, two of the three passages in which the word "Satan" occurs in the Hebrew Bible include the article "the." In addition to the occurrences in Job, "the Satan" occurs in Zech 3, where the character challenges the high priest Joshua's worthiness to the office. In the remaining Old Testament occurrence, 1 Chr 21:1, "Satan" occurs without the definite article and seems to be used as a name more than a title. In 1 Chr, however, the actions of "Satan" tell the same story that occurs in 2 Sam 24. The difference is that in 2 Sam the Lord's anger motivates David's actions, and in 1 Chr "Satan" motivates David's actions. Throughout the Hebrew Bible (even in 1 Chr), the character of Satan is working for Yahweh: giving performance reviews in Job, offering a fitness evaluation in Zechariah, or serving as the personification of God's anger in 1 Chr.
>
> None of those roles would be exactly what the New Testament presents as a fully realized "Mr. Satan"—an evil character who interacts with Jesus in the temptations in the Gospels and who is cast down in Revelation. It seems clear the word is being used differently between the testaments. While the New Testament tells the story of the personification of all that stands against God in the world, the Hebrew Bible seems to have a position of "the Satan" or, literally, "the Accuser" that was occupied by one of the divine beings. This divine being's job was to test the motives of people. The best contemporary metaphor might be "prosecuting attorney." This character is testing the motives and determining the fitness of human beings. The problem in Job is that God's blessings to Job have prevented him from doing his job.
>
> While some like to think the book of Job is a contest between God and Satan, the book does not support that reading. "The Satan" leaves the story in chapter 2. In the book of Job, the contest is between God and Job, and both characters own that. Job calls God his "adversary," and God answers Job's charges at the end.

---

12. Never underestimate human ingenuity when it comes to circumventing rules. The Torah forbids cursing God (Lev 24:13-16) or your parents (Exod 21:17) on pain of death. By cursing your birthday, you can express your frustration and indict both God and your parents without fear of penalty.

Job's lament uses several allusions to God's creation in Gen 1 but in a negative way. Instead of "Let there be light," Job cries, "Let that day be darkness." Instead of the stars numbering the seasons in Gen 1, Job says:

> Let thick darkness take that night.
> Let it not be celebrated among the days of the year,
> and let it not be counted among the months.
> See now! Let that night be barren!
> Let no joyful cry come in it! (3:6-7)

If the anti-creation allusions were too subtle, Job makes them more explicit in verse 8: "Let those who can curse days curse it, those skilled at waking Levithan!" A personal complaint may seem an odd place to invoke a sea monster; however, in the Old Testament, the Leviathan is the personification of primordial chaos. Job's pain and despair are so great that he wants chaos to be stirred and God's ordered creation to unmake itself. In Jer 20, Jeremiah wishes he had never been born. In Job 3, Job wishes no one else had either.

In Ps 88, the psalmist does not explicitly align himself with the enemy of God's ordered creation like Job does—his expression of despair might be worse. The language he uses to describe his despair implies that God is the true agent of chaos in his life.

> Your wrath leans on me,
> and your waves oppress me. . . .
> Your wrath has swept over and against me.
> Your terrors are ending me.
> Every day they sound me like water,
> altogether surrounding me. (vv. 7, 16-17)

Ps 88 uses the language of raging waters to talk about the chaos of his life—a chaos that he accuses God of being responsible for.

One other point of connection exists for Ps 88 and Job as well; their friends are no help. Though at least the psalmist's friends don't pile on, they abandon him: "You have caused my loved ones and friends to shun me. My companion is darkness" (Ps 88:18). Job's friends are silent for a week, but they are uncomfortable after Job aligns himself with the enemy of God's good creation. After Job breaks the silence, the book has three cycles of long speeches, from chapter 3 to chapter 31, and Job and the friends alternate speaking. At first, the speeches might be read as trying to respond to the other's concerns, but by the end, they are talking past one another. Job's friends accuse Job of self-righteousness in his claims to be blameless. Job finds no help or comfort in his friends or their words:

> I am a joke to my friends.
> I, myself, called on God and God answered:
> "The just and blameless one is a joke." (Job 12:4)

> My friends scorn me to God while tears pour from my eyes. (16:20)

> All my closest friends abhor me. And these I have loved have turned against me. (19:19)

In fact, like the psalmist of Ps 88, all Job can see is darkness: "My face has become red with weeping. And darkness has come to my eyelids" (Job 16:16).

The reader has known since chapter 1 that Job is blameless and the suffering he experiences is not tied to any sin in his life. His friends are not a comfort because the reader knows his friends are wrong—which is ironic because Job's friends make good sense. Eliphaz reminds him that no one is truly innocent: "Can a human be righteous before God? Can they act in purity before their maker?" (4:17). And God works in mysterious ways, so Job should stay on God's side: "However, I myself would seek God—to God I would commit my cause" (5:8).

Bildad, unaware of the opening of the book, cannot bear that Job believes he is blameless. Obviously, God would never harm an innocent person, so Job must be guilty. Bildad asks, "Does God pervert justice? Does the Almighty pervert what is right?" (8:3).

Job's third friend Zophar goes further, pointing out that Job is obviously getting what he deserves. Zophar thinks Job should feel lucky his punishment is not worse:

> Should your many words not be answered?
> Should a blabbering person be seen as righteous?
> Should your boasting be met with silence?
> Should someone not shame you for your mockery?
> You say, "My teaching is pure"
> and "I am clean in Your sight!" ...
> But let God show you the secrets of wisdom because understanding is complex!

Know that God has even forgotten some of your iniquity! (11:2-4, 6)

Job and the reader, however, know that these punishments are not brought by guilt. This leads Job to the disturbing conclusions that God does pervert justice. Like the Teacher in Qoheleth, Job respects God's position but expresses frustration that God is not fair. In fact, following the indirect revelation of Proverbs has led Job to some disturbing conclusions about God and the world. Since he knows he is blameless and he is suffering, obviously God is feckless and capricious. The wicked prosper: "But the tents of bandits are at ease and those who provoke God, who carry their gods in their hands, live secure" (12:6).

The psalmist in Ps 73 had the same problem with the wicked:

> They have no struggle in their death
> and their bodies are well fed.
> They don't have the trouble other people have.
> They aren't plagued like others. (vv. 4-5)

The only conclusion one can draw is that justice is arbitrary:

> God leads counselors to shame and makes judges fools.
> God removes the sashes of kings and binds their waist with it.
> God leads away naked priests and overthrows the mighty
> God silences those who are trusted and takes away the discernment of elders.
> God pours contempt on noblemen and loosens the belt of the strong.
> (Job 12:17-21)

Job even rehearses what he would say to God if he could hold his nerve and not be overwhelmed by the divine presence:

> I would say to God, "Do not condemn me!
> Show me what issue you have against me!
> Is it good for you to oppress people?
> To despise the labor of your hands
> while you favor the acts of the wicked?" (10:2-3)

Unfortunately, Job knows that even though he is innocent, he cannot hope to contend with God:

> If it is an issue of strength, God is mighty!
> If it is an issue of justice, God will say, "Who can match me?"
> Though I am innocent, my own mouth would indict me.
> Though I am blameless, I would be shown to be perverse. (9:19-20)

Job desires a mediator who would not be intimidated by God and would be able to make the case for his innocence before the divine.

> Because God is not like I am,
> not like an ordinary a human that I could answer.
> There is no mediator between us
> who could put a hand on both of us. (9:32-33)

Finally, Job's suffering overwhelms his patience, and he demands that God appear before him and produce evidence to justify his punishment. Job's complaint has moved beyond Ps 88:14's "O Yahweh, why do you hide your face from me?" to "Yahweh, get your face down here and answer me!"

In Job's climatic speech in Job 31, he gives a complete recitation of his behavior, daring God to appear and prove him wrong. This challenge culminates in Job signing an indictment against God and demanding a written indictment from the Almighty listing what he is guilty of.

> Oh, that I had someone to hear me.
> Here is my signature. Let the Almighty answer me!
> As for an indictment by my opponent,
> if I had one, I'd wear it on my shoulder!
> I'd lift it up and affix it as a crown!
> But I can give a record of my steps,
> and I could approach my opponent like a prince! (31:35-37)

If God could produce a reason for the punishment, Job would wear it on his head, but Job is confident God cannot do it. Job's frustration may be what the psalmist in Ps 73:16 meant when they said, "My feet almost stumbled," to express what Job would consider understatement: "When I tried to understand this, it was troubling to me" (v. 16). One might expect God to appear to answer the charges that an insolent Job brought. But Job was right in Job 9:19: "Who can summon the divine?" God doesn't show up for another seven chapters.

The intervening chapters are filled with the speeches of Elihu, a previously unnamed fourth friend who appears from nowhere and tries (and fails) to rebuke everyone in the story. While many scholars assume the speeches of Elihu were added later to the book, narratively, Elihu's speeches provide some room between Job's summoning and the divine's appearing. God's sovereignty is preserved since a mere mortal's challenge cannot summon the divine.

God eventually appears in the manner that Job imagined in Job 9, "shaking the earth . . . commanding the sun . . . stretching the heavens and trampling the waves." God's opening words confirm everything that Job feared. God is too big to fight.

> Yahweh answered Job out of the storm, saying,
> "Who is this who obscures the divine plan, speaking words without knowledge?
> Brace yourself like a grownup. I will question you, and you will inform me." (Job 38:1-3)

God has a list of questions for Job before God gets to Job's questions, and all of God's questions emphasize the same point. God is God, and Job is not.

> Where were you during the founding of the earth?
> Tell me if you possess the knowledge.
> Who set its measurements, if you know,
> or who set the boundary line upon it?
> On what were its pedestals sunk,
> or who laid the corner stone?
> When the morning stars sang in a chorus
> and all the heavenly beings shouted for joy? (38:4-7)

God's questions even get snarky:

> Where can you find the dwelling of the light?
> Where is the place of the darkness?
> That you might take them to their borders.
> Do you know the path to their house?
> Surely you know that,
> because you were born then and are so old! (vv. 19-21)

To Job's credit, he understands he is losing this argument, and he tries to interrupt God and throw in the towel.

> Job answered Yahweh saying
> Behold, I am small account.
> What answer could I return?
> I put my hand over my mouth
> I have spoken once,
> but I cannot answer.
> Twice, but I will not do it again. (Job 40:3-5)

God, however, needs to answer Job's earliest challenge—the raising up of the water chaos dragon, Leviathan. For good measure, the Leviathan's land chaos counterpart, the Behemoth, is also addressed. If Job thought rousing Leviathan would scare of intimidate God, he was wrong. God wants to make Job's error clear:

> Can you pull in Leviathan with a fishhook? Or bridle it with a rope?
> Can you put a rope in its nose? Or pierce its cheek with a hook?
> Will it seek your favor a multitude of times if you speak to it tenderly?
> Will it commit to you to taken as your servant forever?
> Can you play with it like a bird? Or leash it for your young girls?
> Will traders barter over it? Will they divide it among the merchants?
> Can you fill its skin with harpoons or its head with fishing spears?
> Set your hands on it and you'll know war, and you'll never do it again!
> (41:1-8)

Far from the archenemy of God, Leviathan is a plaything. Jon D. Levenson calls the Leviathan in Job a "rubber-ducky for the divine."[13] Ps 104 finds a Leviathan that does not serve as God's enemy but as part of God's created order:

> This is the sea! Great, spacious, and wide!
> There are creeping things and so many living things one can't count!
> Small and Large!
> There, the ships will sail,
> and the Leviathan that you shaped plays in it!
> All of these look to you
> to be given to eat when it is time.
> You give food, and they gather it up!
> You open your hand, and they are filled with goodness! (Ps 104:25-28)

---

13. Jon D. Levenson, *Creation and the Persistence of Evil: The Jewish Drama of Divine Omnipotence* (San Francisco: Harper & Row, 1988), 57.

After God finishes bombarding Job with questions, Job yields.

> Then Job answered Yahweh:
> "I know that you can do all things,
> and no purpose of yours impossible.
> 'Who is this who hides the divine plan without knowledge?'
> For truly I spoke of what I did not understand, deeds too wonderful for me to know.
> 'Hear now, I myself will speak.
> I will ask you and you will inform me':
> For I had heard about you with my ears,
> but now my eyes have seen you!
> Therefore I reject my attitude,
> and I will comfort myself away from the dust and ashes." (Job 42:1-6)

Job acknowledges God's power (which he consistently acknowledged), and like the psalmist in Ps 73 and the Teacher in Ecclesiastes promised, Job is satisfied in the presence of God. Finally, in Job 42, the Satan is proven wrong. Job will fear God when God does not make sense.

> ### Job: A Lousy Theodicy
>
> Some call the book of Job a theodicy. Theodicies attempt to answer why an all-powerful, all-good God would allow suffering to exist. The question of the "problem of Evil" is still the number one question people have for the divine.
>
> If Job is an attempt to answer that question, it's an unsatisfying response that compromises God's goodness. Job comes to God, asking why he is suffering, and God responds with "You don't know how to be God. When you do, we can have this conversation." If Job is a theodicy, God seems condescending and cruel.
>
> Rather than answering the problem of evil, the book of Job is answering the Satan's question in Job 1:9. Job's suffering is a test to see if he will follow God when God does not make sense. Read this way, God's speeches don't address Job's *questions* but rather Job's *need*. God reminds Job exactly whom he is being asked to trust. When Job encounters and is reminded of God's power, he places his hand over his mouth and proves he will follow God no matter what.

God then chastises Job's friends. Their sound theology was wrong: "After Yahweh spoke these words to Job, Yahweh said to Eliphaz the Temanite,

'My anger burns against you and against your two friends because you have not spoken concerning me correctly, as my servant Job has'" (Job 42:7). When one considers how brash and insulting Job was toward God in his speeches, this statement from God might seem shocking. The lesson from Job and the lament psalms seems to be that God desires authentic communication. The praise of Ps 100 and the accusations of Ps 88 are both accepted prayer by God, and both are included in the hymnbook of Israel. For some, the restoration of Job is read as endorsement of the two ways. After all, Job is obedient and, subsequently, is blessed. The restoration of Job, however, might say more about God than Job. Job is restored to twice his former possessions. The double restoration corresponds to the amount in Exod 22:7 that a thief must pay in restitution to the one who lost their possessions. God using this number in Job's restoration may be an acknowledgment from God that Job was correct: what was taken from Job was taken wrongly.[14]

Conclusion

Recognizing the danger of agreeing with one of Job's friends, perhaps Zophar had a point when he said "wisdom is complex" (Job 11:6), and the psalms show the full range of that complexity. The psalmists, like Israel's sages, offer truth that comes from trying to live in the world—both the answers and the questions. As the Teacher said, "The last word, after everything has been heard, is fear God and keep the divine commandments" (Eccl 12:13). Perhaps, ultimately, that is what connects wisdom and Torah. As humanity lives and observes the world, whatever truth is found that helps one keep the commandments is wisdom. Sometimes that truth is found in the answers that come in the practical advice of Proverbs and Ps 37, and sometimes that truth is found in the questions that defy answers like in Job and Ps 88.

---

14. Some suggest that the speaker of the last half of what is traditionally identified as Job's speech in Job 42:2-6 might be God's words. Job 42:5-6 is God's apology to Job, which would make sense of 42:7: "after Yahweh had spoken these words to Job." See Troy W. Martin, "Concluding the Book of Job and YHWH: Reading Job from the End to the Beginning," *JBL* 137/2 (Summer 2018): 299–318.

QUESTIONS FOR FURTHER DISCUSSION

1. How does an understanding of the different nature of the inspiration of wisdom literature affect the way that genre is read as compared to the rest of the material in the canon?

2. Is Psalm 1 an instruction on "practical wisdom" or an encouragement of "skeptical wisdom"?

3. James Sanders said, "The canon is self-correcting." How does this statement work itself out in the wisdom literature?

4. Does the honesty of Job, Qoheleth, or the psalmist of Ps 88 challenge or encourage faith? What do these texts teach us about how to pray?

5. If, as argued in the chapter, the book of Job is a story about God and Job (not God and Satan or Satan and Job), what is the book about?

Exile

You told me to go back to the beginning! So I have. This is where I am, and this is where I will stay. I will not be moved.
—Inigo Montoya, in *The Princess Bride*

Psalms and the Exile

One cannot overestimate the significance of the exile on the life of Judah. The Babylonian exile was an ending and a beginning—the ending of the divided monarchy and the nation of Judah and the beginning of "Judaism" as it comes to be known. Many of the contemporary understandings of the Jewish faith have their origins in exile. The exile was the end of the vocations of kings and prophets and the beginning of a new vocation, "scribes" who would preserve and become experts in the Torah. The worship of idols ended, and the canonization process began. The exile is the undercurrent of the entire Old Testament, shaping its make-up. The choices about what ancient stories to preserve and how to tell them were shaped by the exilic experience. While many rightly consider the exodus story to be formative for Jewish identity, the story was preserved because an exilic people needed a "new exodus" to bring them out of captivity.

No one knows exactly what the "hymnbook of ancient Israel" might have looked like when the exile began. If the "books" of the Psalter are roughly indicative of compositional periods as previously suggested, then when Nebuchadnezzar first exiled the top strata of society to Babylon in 598 BCE, the exiles may have had a small collection of psalms from Books I and II (Pss 1–72). Many psalms wrestle with difficulty, and some psalms explicitly reflect exilic concerns. The psalms of Book III wrestle with a destroyed temple (as in Ps 74) and a lost king (as in Ps 89). Psalms from Books III–V (73–150) more explicitly reflect the theological struggles and the theological changes that occurred in exile. The psalms even name the perpetrators of exile whom they would like to see judgment come against, like Edom and Babylon in Ps 137.

That is not to say that one cannot find exile in earlier psalms. Exilic connections can also be subtler. In Ps 44, the psalmist laments,

> Yet, you have rejected and humiliated us.
> You have not accompanied our armies.
> You have made us withdraw from our foe,
> and the people we hate have plundered us!
> You have given us over as sheep to be eaten
> and scattered us among the nations. (vv. 9-11)

The psalm's exilic language is obvious, but what is less obvious is what exile it refers to. This psalm could have a later occasion and refer to the Babylonian exile of the sixth century BCE. It might also reflect a northern origin and refer to the Assyrian exile of the northern kingdom in 722 BCE. It also might refer to a different problem altogether. The exact process of canonization of Psalms is unknown, and one cannot be too definitive about compositional and editorial dates without the danger of overstatement. If Ps 44 and other parts of the "Elohistic Psalter" (Pss 42–84) are from the northern kingdom, this "scattering among the nations" in Ps 44 might refer to the Assyrian practice of taking a conquered people and settling them throughout their empire to prevent uprisings. It is a tragic situation when scholars are unable to use the topic to date a text because one cannot identify which identity-shaking destruction and imprisonment a text might be referring to!

Exilic suffering always brought hard questions for the divine as the psalmists tried to process the reality of exile:

> How long, Yahweh?
> Will you be angry forever?
> Will your jealous wrath burn like a fire?
> Pour your anger on the nations who do not know you
> and upon the kingdoms who do not call upon your name!
> Because they have devoured Jacob
> and made his pastures a desolation. (Ps 79:5-7)

> Supreme Commander Yahweh,
> how long will you rage against the prayers of your people?
> Have you not already fed them with tears for food?
> And caused them to drink a measure of their own weeping?

> You have made us an embarrassment to our neighbors,
> and our enemies mock us. (Ps 80:4-6)
>
> [O God,] will you be angry with us forever?
> Will you draw out your anger to future generations?
> Will you not return and revive us,
> so that your people might rejoice in you? (Ps 85:5-6)

Many of these exilic questions revolved around the loss. Specifically, how can the people process the loss of the three indispensable aspects of religious identity: the holy temple, the holy city, and a holy kingship? How can the people of God be the people of God without these manifestations of God's presence with the people?

THE TEMPLE, JERUSALEM, AND DAVID

Temple

Any time of difficulty or oppression felt like a rejection by God, but the loss of the temple heightened the feelings of abandonment. Ps 74 tries to process that rejection:

> O God, why do you permanently reject us?
> Why does your anger smoke against the sheep of your pasture?
> Remember your congregation which you acquired a long time ago,
> which you rescued as the tribe of your inheritance,
> and remember you resided on Mt. Zion.
> Lift your feet to the permanent ruins,
> to all the damage your enemies have done in the sanctuary.
> Your enemies roar in the midst of your place.
> They have set their banners. (vv. 1-4)

The temple's destruction was impossible to understand. The reasoning was straightforward. The temple represented the house of God—and not in a figurative way. God resided in the temple. Even if things looked dire, everyone was certain that God would never let anything happen to the divine residence.

The prophets had tried to warn the people not to be misled. Standing in the gates of the temple, Jeremiah warned people not to trust in slogans or mottos but to act with mercy toward immigrants and the powerless:

> Thus Supreme Commander Yahweh, God of Israel, says,
> "Seek true goodness in the way you are living
> and the things you are doing,
> then I will dwell with you in this place."
> Do not trust in these lying words saying,
> "The temple of Yahweh—The temple of Yahweh—The temple of Yahweh is here!" (Jer 7:3-4)

Yahweh made clear that the divine will not abide with anyone whose life is not defined by justice. Clever slogans and performative acts of worship will chase God away, and in a vision with apocalyptic imagery, Ezekiel saw exactly that. As a result of the people's lack of justice and mercy, God's glory left the temple:

> Then the glory of Yahweh went out from above the threshold of the house and stood above the cherubim. And the cherubim lifted up their wings, and they rose up from the earth before my eyes. When they went their wheels were beside them. And they stopped at the entrance to the Eastern gate of the Yahweh's house and the glory of the God of Israel was above them. (Ezek 10:18-19)

In other words, the building in Jerusalem that God formerly called home was now an ordinary building, and ordinary buildings can be destroyed. Even so, the psalmist was unsure how God could tolerate such an insult and appealed to God by reminding the divine of the dishonor and shame that should be felt in the treatment of the (former) holy dwelling place:

> They seemed like people swinging axes in a thicket of trees.
> And now, they are smashing the engravings,
> with hatchets and hammers together.
> They have set fire to your sanctuary.
> They have profaned the dwelling place of your name
> all the way to the ground.
> They said to themselves,
> "We will oppress them together."
> They burned all the meeting places in the land.
> We don't see our banners.
> There is no longer a prophet,
> and no one is given to know how long this lasts.
> How long, O God?
> How long will the foe mock

> and the enemy despise your name?
> Forever? (Ps 74:5-10)

> God, the nations have come into your inheritance!
> They have polluted your holy temple.
> They made Jerusalem a ruin! (Ps 79:1)

One significant theological development that came from exile was, in many ways, a return to the idea of a portable god. The powerful message of the tabernacle was that Yahweh would travel with the people wherever they might go. The temple in Jerusalem had created a fixed location and limited the vision the people had for the divine.

David

The loss of the temple would be hard enough. Add the loss of the Davidic monarchy, and the people of Judah faced another theological crisis that was impossible to understand. Like the temple, the Davidic covenant from 2 Sam 7 was an eternal manifestation of God's commitment to Israel. The exile meant that Judah had to reckon with an everlasting thing that no longer existed! God appeared to have broken an eternal and unconditional divine promise. How could an everlasting covenant come to an end? David's offspring were supposed to sit on the throne "forever." It was an eternal kingship. Now it was over. How could that make sense?

The last psalm of Book III, Ps 89, asks that very question. The psalm is structured like an inverted lament with the praise coming before the complaint. It begins by celebrating how one can always rely on God:

> I will sing of your committed love forever, Yahweh!
> From generation to generation, I will proclaim your faithfulness with my mouth.
> Because I have said your committed love is built up forever.
> Your faithfulness is as sure as the heavens

Seven times in vv. 1-37 (Ps 89:1, 2, 4, 28, 29, 36, 37), the word "forever" celebrates God's eternal faithfulness. The word is even used to explicitly emphasize God's eternal promise in the Davidic covenant, the dominant theme of the psalm.

> I have made a covenant with my chosen one.
> I have sworn to David my servant:
> "I will establish your descendants forever,
> and I will build your throne from generation to generation." (Ps 89:3-4)

Using absolute language with no provision for exception, the first half of the psalm remembers and celebrates God's promise of David's eternal kingship:

> Then you spoke in a vision to your faithful ones,
> and you said, "I have placed a helper over the mighty,
> I have exalted one, chosen over the people.
> I have found my servant David,
> with holy oil I have anointed him.
> My hand will support him,
> and I will certainly strengthen his descendants.
> The enemy will not fool him,
> and the children of iniquity will not oppress him.
> I will crush his foes before him,
> and I will strike down the ones who hate him.
> May faithfulness and my committed love be with him.
> and in my name his horn will be exalted. (vv. 19-24)

The relationship between God and David goes beyond patron/client. David, and by extension David's offspring, will look on God as a father figure:

> He, himself, will call me
> My father, you are my rock and my deliverance.
> Also, I, myself, will make him firstborn,
> the highest of the kings of the earth. (vv. 26-27)

The eternal nature of the Davidic covenant is non-negotiable. God said it would last forever.

> Forever, I will keep my committed love to him.
> My covenant with him is secure.
> I will establish his descendants and his throne forever,
> as long as the heavens endure. (vv. 28-29)

The first half of the psalm concludes by celebrating the inviolability of the divine word and covenant, reminding everyone, including the divine, that God's word can never be broken:

> I will never break from my committed love for him,
> and I will never lie about my faithfulness.
> I will not profane my covenant,
> and I will not alter what went out from my lips.
> Once and for all I have sworn by my holiness;
> I will not lie to David.
> His line will be forever.
> His throne will endure like the sun.
> It will be as permanent as the moon—
> a faithful testimony in the sky! (vv. 33-37)

Forever God is faithful. Forever God's word remains. Forever. Forever. Forever.

This language makes for inspiring lectionary readings and inspirational songs. In the context of the psalm, however, this confidence and faith is only the prelude to what the psalmist truly wants to address—a setup for what is coming in Ps 89:38 when the tone of the psalm changes dramatically. For the psalmist, "what is" makes no sense after considering what was promised. The psalmist accuses God of breaking an eternal covenant:

> But now, you have spurned,
> and you have rejected.
> You have become angry with your anointed.
> You have abhorred the covenant of your servant.
> You profaned his crown in the dirt.
> You have breached all of his walls.
> You have made his fortress a heap of ruins. (vv. 38-40)

After thirty-seven verses celebrating the eternal nature of God's promises, the psalmist tries to reconcile that truth to their life experience: "Where is the committed love from the beginning, O Sovereign? Which you swore to David by your own faithfulness?" (Ps 89:49).

The psalm ends with what might be the snarkiest benediction in the Bible. After celebrating the eternal commitment of God repeatedly in the beginning of the psalm and emphasizing how God's word lasts forever, only to then express why it was *not* forever, the psalmist closes the psalm with this: "May Yahweh be blessed forever. Amen and Amen" (v. 52). This "forever" might be an earnest blessing. Faced with questions and no answers, the psalmist might also be mocking God's apparent new definition of "forever."

Much like the loss of temple reminded the people of the God who wandered with the people in the desert wilderness, the loss of the Davidic monarchy allowed the people to look back to a time after crossing the sea, when God was first celebrated as king. The Davidic monarchy is still important, and messianic expectations develop. The kingship of Yahweh, however, is what answered the psalmist's question.

Jerusalem

Several psalms, like Ps 74 and Ps 89, process the reality of exile with specific references to what was lost. Often, however, "Jerusalem" and "Zion" serve as metonyms for all the loss exile brought. In other words, authors often summarize exilic destruction, including temple and kingship, by simply referencing the loss of "Jerusalem."

The loss of Jerusalem and Zion is the subject of what may be the darkest of the imprecatory psalms (or "cursing psalms"), Ps 137. The psalmist sings for vengeance to come against Babylon, desperately hoping to see the same cruelty befall Babylon that they themselves suffered:

> By the rivers of Babylon, there we sat,
> and indeed, we wept, when we remembered Zion.
> In the midst of willows,
> we hung our harps.
> Because there, those who held us captive asked us to write a song.
> Our tormentors asked us for joy:
> "Sing us a song of Zion."
> How can we sing the song of Yahweh sitting in a foreign land?
> If I should forget you, Jerusalem,
> let my right hand be forgotten.
> Let my tongue stick to my palate, if I don't remember it.
> If I don't hold Jerusalem above my greatest joy!
> Remember, Yahweh, the children of Edom on the Jerusalem's day—
> the ones saying, "Strip it down, strip it to the foundations!" Against the city!
> Daughter of Babylon, the destroyer,
> Blessed is the one who fulfills
> and repays you for your deeds to us.

> Blessed is the one who grabs
> and then shatters your child against the rocks. (Ps 137:1-9)

The Edomites found their way into a cursing psalm originally aimed at Babylon by aligning themselves with Babylon during the invasion. The Edomites' betrayal is remembered in several exilic discussions. Ezekiel warns that because the Edomites sought vengeance against Judah in the invasion, God would bring judgment against them:

> Thus Sovereign Yahweh says, "Because of the acts of Edom, taking excessive vengeance against the house of Judah, they are guilty of vengeance against them. Therefore, thus Sovereign Yahweh says, I will stretch out my hand against Edom and I will cut humans and animals from it. I will make it a waste. From Teman to Dedan they will fall by the sword. (Ezek 25:12-13)

While it is hard to imagine singing a worship song based on Ps 137, the psalm is included among the "hymnbook of ancient Israel." Additionally, Ps 137, like Ps 88, is a reminder that prayer and worship come from a place of authenticity in the biblical text. The singer is filled with anger, and that anger is prayer. Significantly, it is an honest anger that asks God to act, not to be the instrument of their own vengeance. The psalmist also is asking that Babylon suffer in the same way they made Judah suffer.

While the anger creeps out occasionally, more commonly the reaction to the exile is befuddled despair:

> On the day of my trouble, I seek my Sovereign.
> My hand was stretched out in the night and did not grow numb.
> Yet, my soul refuses to be comforted.
> I remember God and I roar.
> I meditate and my spirit is feeble.
> You hold my eyelids open,
> and I am so troubled I can't speak.
> I think of the ancient days, years gone by.
> I remember my song in the night.
> I meditate in my mind,
> and my spirit searches.
> Will my Sovereign reject forever?
> Will God never again show favor?
> Has God's committed love ceased forever?

Are God's words ended for generation after generation?
Has God forgotten grace?
Is God's compassion trapped in anger? (Ps 77:2-9)

The book of Lamentations more explicitly owns the just nature of the punishment that came upon Judah, but the rightness of God to act does little to comfort the despair of destruction.

> ### Ordered Grief
>
> Lamentations is a five-chapter book where each chapter is a discrete poem of its own. The first four chapters are acrostics. Chapter 3 has three lines for each Hebrew letter (accounting for its sixty-six verses).[†] The intense feelings expressed contrast with the discipline required to write a structured poem like an acrostic. The book is not an irrational or random expression of emotions. The author's grief has been ordered from "aleph" to "taw."[‡]
>
> Acrostics often convey wholeness, as in "everything, from A to Z." It may be that Lamentations' use of complex acrostics is meant to convey the totality of grief. The pain expressed covers the full expression of human experience. The grief is physical as well as spiritual.
>
> Interestingly, while Lamentations 5 does contain twenty-two verses, it is not an acrostic. Scholars have debated why this is the case, but it does make an interesting artistic statement. While sometimes grief can be ordered and rational, grief also defies structure and pattern. Both are normal and biblical expressions of the emotion.
>
> [†] The Hebrew alphabet has twenty-two letters.
> [‡] The first and last letters of the Hebrew alphabet.

While the book is traditionally attributed to Jeremiah, the author of Lamentations remains unknown. Clearly the author is someone who knows the reality of the pain of the city's destruction and former friends, like Edom, becoming enemies.

How lonely dwells the city that was once full of people.
The noble woman has become a widow.
The princess over the provinces has become a slave.
She weeps at night and the tears run down her cheeks.
There is no one to comfort her from all her lovers.
All her friends have betrayed her and now have become her enemies.
(Lam 1:1-2)

The author of Lamentations, though, agrees that Judah's punishment is deserved:

> Yahweh is right.
> I have rebelled against all God said.
> Hear now, all you people!
> See my suffering.
> My young women and young men have gone into captivity! (1:8)

Despite the deserved punishment, the author can't help wondering if God might have overreacted because as so often happens in war, those who suffer the most are the most vulnerable. At times, the punishment seems indiscriminate:

> Yahweh, look and consider this.
> Who have you ever acted this severely with?
> Should women have to resort to cannibalism and consume their own children?! Infants?!
> In the sanctuary of our Sovereign, should priests and prophets be murdered?
> Young and old lie dead on the ground and in the streets.
> Young women and young men have fallen by the sword.
> You murdered them in your anger.
> You slaughtered them without mercy. (Lam 2:20-21)

The book of Lamentations, like most laments, contains a word of hope. Unlike in most laments, however, that word of hope is in the middle of the book. In chapter 3, the author provides a remarkable statement of confidence and hope that darkness and despair won't endure:

> I continually remember this and despair.
> But this returns to my mind
> and then I have hope.
> Because Yahweh's committed love never ceases,
> because God's compassion never ends
> They are new in the morning.
> Great is God's faithfulness.
> Yahweh is my portion,
> I have said to myself. That's why I will hope in God.
> Yahweh is good to those who wait,
> to the soul who seeks God.

> Goodness and strength and patience
> come from the deliverance of Yahweh. (3:20-26)

The author puts their trust in knowing that they are not forgotten:

> Because our Sovereign will not reject us forever.
> Although God brings grief,
> God has an abundance of compassion.
> It is not God's way of thinking
> to cause harm or grief to humanity. (vv. 31-33)

The author was correct. The exile does come to an end several generations later, and Judah returns to the land changed for the experience.

Prophetic Encouragement

Though the psalmist and the author of Lamentation respond to the exile with shock, frustration, and even bitterness, the prophetic response to the exiles was far more encouraging, which is ironic since the prophetic warnings about exile had been direct and decidedly negative. Jeremiah 29 provides explicit and practical guidance from the divine on how to face the exile:

> These are the words of the letter that the prophet Jeremiah sent from Jerusalem to the remaining elders of the exiles and to the priests and to the prophets and to all the people who were exiled by Nebuchadnezzar from Jerusalem to Babylon. . . . Thus Supreme Commander Yahweh, God of Israel, says to all the exiles which I have exiled from Jerusalem to Babylon: "Build houses, and live in them. Plant gardens, and eat their produce. Marry and give birth to sons and daughters. Take wives for your sons, and give your daughters in marriage so that they may give birth to sons and daughters. Multiply there, do not decrease." (vv. 1, 4-6)

God's advice at first is not too surprising. While the false prophets who dominated the public consciousness promised the exile would be a short matter (once they acknowledged the exile was a reality), Jeremiah warned that the exiles should plan on unpacking. They should buy, not rent. They should plan on their kids and grandkids getting married in Babylon.

The last part of God's advice in Jer 29 might be surprising, however: "Seek the flourishing of this city where I have exiled you, and pray to

Yahweh for it. Because in its flourishing, you will flourish" (v. 7). One might expect God to give advice encouraging civil disobedience, akin to Gandhi and Martin Luther King Jr. Surely, Judah should try to bring down Babylon with sit-ins and peaceful resistance. Surely God cannot be serious that the exiles should seek Babylon's flourishing!

The key to understanding God's advice, however, is the word translated "flourishing". In other translations, the word is often translated as "welfare" or "good." The Hebrew word is *shalom* (שלום)—a word that means "wholeness" or "completeness." It is a word for the ideal created state of humanity. In other words, Judah is not being called to work to improve the economy of Babylon or help Babylon expand its territorial borders. Judah is called to do what Israel had always been called to do: be a light to the nations. Judah was expected to continue to live into the calling they had from the beginning and work for the *shalom* that comes from commitment to God's vision for life.

The exile came because Judah failed to live into that calling. They failed to model lives of meaning and purpose while occupying the land; and as a result, the people lost the land. The exile was not meant to be a "timeout" where Judah was sent to their room, and then in seventy years, they could return and be God's people again. The prophetic expectation was that while Judah may have failed to be the people of God with the land, they now were expected to be the people of God without the land. They did not get to pause being God's people to serve their time. They were called to work for Babylon's *shalom* just like they were always called to work for everyone's *shalom*. From 598 to 529 BCE, however, it would have to be done from exile.

The incentive for Judah to do this (beside God calling them to do it) was that in working for the *shalom* of others, Judah would find their *shalom*. This context better explains the meaning of Jeremiah's most marketable verse, Jer 29:11: "Because I surely know the purpose which I have planned for you, declares Yahweh. A purpose of flourishing, and not destruction—to give you a future and hope." This verse is not meant to show how to prosper materially. Neither does this verse simply spiritually bypass the reality of the horrors of exile. This verse reminds the exiles of God's plans from earlier in the chapter. The plan for the *shalom* of the people was revealed in verse 7: "During your long captivity, work for the *shalom* of others; that's where you will find your *shalom*."

POSTEXILIC RECONSTRUCTION

One does not emerge from the dark night of the soul the same way as one entered. Judah endured several significant theological changes as a result of the exile. Some theological changes simply meant a change in focus. Other changes were more existential.

Kingship

The answers to the hard questions of Ps 89 regarding the loss of Davidic kingship are addressed quickly in Ps 90 and Book IV. The superscription of Ps 90 identifies this psalm as "the Prayer of Moses, man of God." In trying to find an answer to the question of the failure of Davidic covenant and the reality of exile, the Psalter turns to an ancient authority.

Moses, the archetype for prophet in the Hebrew Bible, intercedes for an exiled people using language reminiscent of Exod 32 following the golden calf incident. Moses calls upon God:

> Turn, Yahweh! How long?
> Have compassion on your servants.
> Satisfy us in the morning with your committed love
> so that we might sing for joy and rejoice for all our days! (Ps 90:13-14)

Psalms 90–100, with vocabulary connections to Exodus and Deuteronomy,[1] show a renewed emphasis on Torah obedience and celebration of Yahweh as king. This renewed focus on the Mosaic covenant and God's kingship answers the loss of the Davidic covenant and Davidic kingship. God is king, not David. Torah should be the focus, not the Davidic covenant. The later psalms of Book IV and V have a less romanticized picture of the Davidic kingship. Psalm 132 even modifies the unconditional nature of the Davidic covenant to allow for punishment when David's progenies are disobedient by using the "if" at the beginning of verse 12:

> Yahweh swore a trustworthy oath to David
> which will never be turned away from:
> "I will set the fruit of your body on your throne.
> If your sons keep my covenant and decrees that I will teach them,

---

1. These connections are fully worked out in Robert E. Wallace, *The Narrative Effect of Book IV of the Hebrew Psalter* (New York: Peter Lang, 2007).

then also their sons will sit on your throne forever and forever . . . ."
(vv.11-12)

While the unquestioned sovereignty of God has been a theme throughout the psalms, Book IV emphasizes the point with a series of psalms that emphasize God as king and serve as a turning point in the "story" of the psalms.[2] David's return to the psalms in the later books (after the "prayers of David, son of Jesse" are ended in Ps 72), show a somewhat different attitude than the psalms earlier in the Psalter that celebrated Davidic kingship. Although David is celebrated in Ps 110, he is not exactly celebrated as "king": "Yahweh will promise and will not renege! 'You are a priest forever in the way of Melchizedek!'" (v. 4).

Even in this psalm that praises David, God's rule is what matters. Instead of David "breaking the nations with a rod of iron" as in Ps 2, God is doing the fighting and executing judgment in Ps 110:

> The Sovereign is at my right hand
> and will shatter kings in the day of anger!
> God will judge the nations and fill them with corpses,
> and God will shatter heads over the whole earth. (vv. 5-6)

Temple

While it is difficult to establish an exact timeline, many scholars attribute the beginning of the synagogue as the center of Jewish life to the period of the exile. One can see how that might happen. Without a temple, smaller, local gathering places provided a place to read Scripture, sing psalms, and teach Torah—as well as marry, bury, and perform the necessary tasks for living a religious life (absent sacrifice, which could only occur in the temple).

After several generations of life without a temple, one might imagine people could lose their sense of urgency in the rebuilding. As already noted, verses 18 and 19 of Ps 51 were likely added post exile to prevent people from developing the wrong idea about sacrifice. The scribes did not want people to think the temple was not important.

The prophets of the rebuilding, Haggai and Zechariah, both fought against the same apathy toward rebuilding God's house:

---

2. Pss 93, 95–100 all contain the phrase "יהוה מלך" or "Yahweh reigns."

> And the word of Yahweh came to Haggai, the prophet, saying:
> "Is now the time for you to dwell in your richly paneled houses,
> when my house lies wasting?" (Hag 1:3-4)
>
> And the word of Yahweh came to me saying: "The hands of Zerubbabel have started this house, and his hands will complete it. Then you will know that Supreme Commander Yahweh has sent me to you. Because who despises the day of small things? They will rejoice and see the plumb line in the hand of Zerubbabel." (Zech 4:8-10)

The prophets warn the people that they need to complete God's house, and, in an unusual moment in the biblical narrative, the people listen to the prophets of Yahweh, do what they say, and complete the job.

Inclusive vs. Exclusive Identity

Early in the psalms, the "nations" are most often understood as adversaries to the divine.

> You have rebuked the nation.
> You have destroyed the wicked.
> You have wiped out their name forever. . . .
> The nations have sunk in the pit they dug.
> They have captured their own foot in the net they hid (Ps 9:5, 15)
>
> Yahweh breaks the counsel of the nations,
> and hinders the thoughts of the peoples. (Ps 33:10)
>
> The nations roar and kingdoms shake.
> God speaks and the earth melts. (Ps 46:6)
>
> You are Yahweh.
> Commanding God of Israel,
> awaken to punish all the nations,
> do not show mercy to any who treacherously plot iniquity. (Ps 59:5)

The tone changes in the psalms in the second half of the Psalter:

> All the nations that you made will come
> and worship before you as Sovereign.
> They will honor your name! (Ps 86:9)

Recount God's glory among the nations!
And God's deeds among all the people! (Ps 96:3)

Say among the nations, "Yahweh reigns!"
The world is established and never shakes!
God will judge people with fairness. (Ps 96:10)

Yahweh has made deliverance known!
God has uncovered righteousness before the nations. (Ps 98:2)

The nations will fear the name of Yahweh,
and all the kings of the earth will fear your glory. (Ps 102:15)

This tension between a more nationalist/separatist perspective and the more global/universalist is seen in the other literature of the post-exile period as well. While the stories of Ruth and Jonah are set much earlier in the history of Israel, Ruth in the period of the Judges and Jonah in the eighth or ninth century BCE, the style and vocabulary of the Hebrew suggests they were not written down until after the exile, likely when the people needed reminding of their message.

Jonah is an Israelite prophet called to preach a word of judgment on the Assyrian city of Nineveh. In the postexilic community, anyone who heard "Nineveh" would immediately associate it with the worst of humanity. No one would object to the message Jonah was called to preach: "So Jonah began to come to into the city, a day's walk, and he called out and said, 'Forty days more, and Nineveh will be overthrown!'" (3:4). What no one could anticipate, however, was Nineveh acting in repentance in the hope God might relent from punishment. When that happens, Jonah speaks for everyone who ever has experienced grace given to someone they hated:

> But [God's failure to destroy Ninevah] seemed like a great injustice to Jonah, and he became angry. He prayed to Yahweh, and he said, "O please, Yahweh! Isn't this what I said would happen when I was in my land? On account of this, I hurried to flee to Tarshish because I knew that you are a God of grace and mercy—slow to anger with an abundance of committed love, someone who would relent from destruction. So now, Yahweh, take my life from me because it is better to die than to live." (4:1-3)

God's mercy and grace irritate Jonah not only because the Ninevites whom he hates receive God's unmerited favor but also because God's grace damages Jonah's reputation. Jonah proclaimed that Nineveh would be overthrown in forty days. When that doesn't happen, Jonah becomes a "false" prophet.[3] God makes clear that Jonah's reputation does not mean as much as the lives of the people of Nineveh. The book of Jonah, certainly not the person of Jonah, reinforces the message seen in the later psalms: God is concerned about the world.

The book of Ruth echoes this message by addressing a specific problem that occurred in the period of Israel's return: foreign wives. Ruth, a Moabite woman, marries into the tribe of Judah and becomes the great-grandmother of David. Fortunately, this event happened in the Judges period, because it would not have happened under the governorship of Nehemiah or the instruction of Ezra.

When the archetype for the new vocation of "scribe," Ezra, returned to the holy land and discovered that people had taken foreign wives for themselves, he wept and decreed, "Therefore, now let us make a covenant to our God to send out all the women and their offspring, from us. In keeping with counsel of my master and those who tremble at the commandments of our God. Let it be done as the Torah says" (Ezra 10:3).

The governor Nehemiah responded with even more anger invoking the sins of Solomon and saying,

> In those days, I saw the Jews who had married women from Ashdod, Ammon, and Moab. Half of their children spoke the language of Ashdod. And they could not recognize the language of Judah. But spoke the language of each of their people. So I contended with them, and I cursed them, and I beat some of them, and I pulled their hair. I made them swear an oath to God, "You shall not give your daughters to their sons or take from their daughters for your sons or for yourselves!" (Neh 13:23-25)

Ethnicity was associated with religion. The book of Ruth, however, reminds readers that ethnicity is not the problem, but faith. As already seen, foreign wives who worship Yahweh are welcome: Tamar (Gen 38) and Zipporah (Exod 18), among others.

---

3. Deuteronomy 17 says that prophets who proclaim something that doesn't happen are "false prophets."

Neither Ezra nor Nehemiah were prophets, and the Bible doesn't say that they made these decisions under the direction of God. But neither was willing to take on what would apparently be the herculean task of guaranteeing every foreign wife had converted to worship Yahweh and that their conversion was genuine. Instead, they each took the pragmatic solution to the problem and ordered the foreign wives to be sent away.

The tension of being a "light to the nations" versus a "holy priesthood" is seen in the postexilic literature, and the question is never finally answered. By the New Testament period, the tension still existed. The "holy priesthood" arguments are seen in the religious leadership's insistence on adherence to the holiness code by everyone to distinguish "us" over against "them." Non-Jewish participants of the Jewish faith, however, exist in the narrative: Gentile "God-fearers" in the text who would worship in the synagogue, like the Ethiopian eunuch, Cornelius in Acts, and the audience Paul preached to in Antioch in Pisidia, where he said, "My brothers, children of the family of Abraham, and also the ones who fear God with you, to us, this word of salvation has been sent" (Acts 13:26). The synagogue worship had a place for the descendants of Abraham and "others."

Conclusion

The biblical story begins in many places. It begins at creation. It begins with Abraham. It begins with the exodus. It begins with the settlement. The story also contains many endings, but those endings always carry with them a sense of expectation. The major "endings" of the text are always cliffhangers:

1. Genesis ends with the seventy children of Israel in Egypt. Only one aspect of God's promise to Abraham has been fulfilled. Abraham has a child, but the children of Israel aren't yet a "great nation" and are not settled in the land.

2. The Torah ends in Deut 33 with Moses dying. After he gives his "St. Crispin's Day" speech to encourage the people to take the land, the book ends.

3. The "former prophets" (Joshua, Judges, 1 and 2 Samuel, and 1 and 2 Kings) end in exile but see Jehoiachin released from prison and fed from the king of Babylon's table.

4. Jonah ends without telling the reader how the person of Jonah responds to God's speech.

5. The end of the writing prophets (and the last words in most English Bibles) is found in Malachi 4, where God promises to send the prophet Elijah to restore the hearts of the people to avoid punishment.

6. The end of the writings (the last word in the Hebrew Bible) is 2 Chronicles 36, where Cyrus the great promises an end of the exile and the rebuilding of the temple.

David Clines has said that one theme of the Torah is "partial fulfillment" and therefore partial unfulfillment.[4] Yahweh's relationship to Israel and the world is a journey with fulfilled promises and hope, unfulfilled promises and despair, and renewed hope for a future. The exile is another step in that journey, and one of the steps in that journey was telling the story, with its ups and downs, from Genesis to Malachi.

The book of Psalms walks alongside Israel on that journey. The stories and the questions and the answers from Genesis to Malachi found their way into the worship life of Israel. Their hymnbook, likely first compiled in exile and edited over the next several centuries, mirrored Israel's historical journey. The entire book of Psalms, however, also serves as a microcosm of a faith journey:[5] from the naïve stage of faith in Ps 1, where obedience promises to bring blessing; to the crisis of faith in Ps 73, where the success of the wicked causes the righteous to struggle; to the naïve praise of Ps 150, where God is praised for no reason other than being God.

In keeping with the tradition of open endings, the psalms do not resolve the problems of the psalmists living out that faith. Before the Hallelujah psalms act as a doxology from Pss 146–150, the psalmist, David, still needs rescuing: "Rescue and deliver me from the hand of foreigners whose mouths speak lies and whose right hand works lies" (144:11). The psalms' immediate response to David's need is Ps 145, another "psalm of David," where David praises God for help and deliverance. The five-psalm doxological conclusion follows, and each of them open with "Praise Yahweh!"

Perhaps the "endings" in the biblical narrative seem open because the reader is looking for some sort of resolution in the narrative, when the resolution is found in God.

---

4. David J. A. Clines, *The Theme of the Pentateuch* (Sheffield: Sheffield Academic, 1997), 30.

5. Walter Brueggemann, "Bounded by Obedience and Praise: The Psalms as Canon," in *The Psalms and the Life of Faith* (Minneapolis: Fortress, 1995).

1. The sojourn of the children of Jacob in Egypt is not about unfilled promise but rather God's provision.

2. The end of Deuteronomy is not about "taking the land" but rather God's presence with the people.

3. The end of the exile is not about Jehoiachin or the exile but about the mercy of God.

4. Jonah is not about Jonah but God's about measureless compassion.

5. Malachi is not about the coming "Day of the Lord" but God's about desire for families to be whole and healthy.

6. The reader does not need to read about the return of the exiles and rebuilding of the temple in Chronicles because the story is about God's committed love to Israel.

In the end, the psalms do not necessarily answer the specific complaints of the psalmists. However, the psalms do speak to their need. Much like the psalmist of Ps 73 and Job, in the presence of Yahweh, the questions are answered:

> Praise Yahweh!
> Praise God in the holy sanctuary.
> Praise God in the expanse of the firmament
> Praise God for divine might!
> Praise God for surpassing greatness!
> Praise God with the sound of the trumpet!
> Praise God with harp and lyre.
> Praise God with tambourine and dance!
> Praise God with strings and flute!
> Praise God with loud cymbals.
> Praise God with joyful cymbals!
> Let everything that breathes praise Yahweh.
> Praise Yahweh! (Ps 150)

In doing so, the psalms teach again, in the end, that the biblical narrative is not so much about stories and the poems, or the details of the narrative, but about God. It does not matter what part of the text one focuses on—creation, covenant, settlement, wisdom, even exile; each of these is a way to talk about the nature of the divine, who can be talked about in a number of ways and, as the psalms illustrate, sung about in a number of ways as well.

Questions for Further Discussion

1. The exile was Israel's "dark night of the soul," and they came out of it different. How do crises or struggles affect belief? Does it matter if the crises were the result of behavior (as with Israel) or came independent of any explanation?

2. How is the tension to be a "light to the nations" and a "holy priesthood" manifested in contemporary expressions of faith?

3. As shown in the ending of every major section of the Hebrew Bible, God seems to be more about the journey than the destination. What might that teach about how to live life well?

4. Rather than "I told you so," the prophets demonstrate empathy and encouragement from the moment of exile. What instruction might that offer when bringing pastoral care to someone in crisis (even as crisis of their own making)?

5. If the exile was not a "timeout," if it wasn't when Israel was placed in the "penalty box" but was simply a new place for the people to live out their calling, what does that mean for the person trying to live out the life of faith today? Is there any place, any time, or any age when one is expected *not* to live out their calling?

www.ingramcontent.com/pod-product-compliance
Lightning Source LLC
Chambersburg PA
CBHW062008220426
43662CB00010B/1269